Working with Resistance in Rational Emotive Behaviour Therapy

Productive therapeutic change is facilitated when the therapist and client have a good therapeutic relationship, share views on salient therapeutic matters, agree on goals to enhance client well-being, and understand what they each have to do to achieve the goals of therapy. In this book Windy Dryden and Michael Neenan address the difficulties that both client and therapist bring to rational emotive behaviour therapy (REBT) when either party is resistant to change.

Divided into two parts, 'Client resistance' and 'Therapist resistance', *Working with Resistance in Rational Emotive Behaviour Therapy* tackles the challenges experienced by both client and clinician when using REBT. Addressing issues of resistance enables both the client and practitioner to move beyond problems in the consulting room and build a more productive relationship, resulting in more effective sessions and assisting in the resolution of underlying problems for which the client has sought help.

Working with Resistance in Rational Emotive Behaviour Therapy is essential reading for any practitioner hoping to use REBT more effectively in their day-to-day practice.

Windy Dryden is Professor of Psychotherapeutic Studies at Goldsmiths, University of London.

Michael Neenan is Associate Director of the Centre for Stress Management, Kent, and an accredited cognitive behavioural therapist.

Working with Resistance in Rational Emotive Behaviour Therapy

A Practitioner's Guide

Windy Dryden and Michael Neenan

Routledge
Taylor & Francis Group

LONDON AND NEW YORK

First published 2012 by Routledge
27 Church Road, Hove, East Sussex BN3 2FA

Simultaneously published in the USA and Canada
by Routledge
711 Third Avenue, New York NY 10017

Routledge is an imprint of the Taylor & Francis Group, an Informa business

A previous edition of this book, *Dealing with Difficulties in Rational Emotive Behaviour Therapy* by Michael Neenan and Windy Dryden, was published by Whurr 1996.

British Library Cataloguing in Publication Data
A catalogue record for this book is available from the British Library

Library of Congress Cataloging in Publication Data
Dryden, Windy.
   Working with resistance in rational emotive behaviour therapy : a practitioner's guide / Windy Dryden and Michael Neenan.
       p. cm.
   Includes bibliographical references and index.
   ISBN 978-0-415-66479-0 (hardback) – ISBN 978-0-415-66750-0 (pbk)
1. Change (Psychology) 2. Rational emotive behavior therapy. I. Neenan, Michael. II. Title.
   BF637.C4D79 2011
   616.89'142–dc22
                                                              2011016302

ISBN: 978-0-415-66479-0 (hbk)
ISBN: 978-0-415-66750-0 (pbk)
ISBN: 978-0-203-55331-2 (ebk)

Typeset in Times by Garfield Morgan, Swansea, West Glamorgan
Paperback cover design by Andrew Ward
Printed by TJ International Ltd, Padstow, Cornwall

Contents

Preface

This book addresses the manifold difficulties that both client and therapist bring to rational emotive behaviour therapy (REBT). As usual, Albert Ellis (1985, 2002), the founder of REBT, led the way with his book originally titled *Overcoming Resistance: Rational Emotive Therapy with Difficult Clients*. Ellis stated that the psychotherapy literature on difficult and resistant clients is extensive but 'much less attention has been given to the difficult and resistant therapist' (Ellis 1985: 161). The most difficult client to deal with, Ellis suggests, is the therapist. In order not to present a lopsided view of who creates the most problems in therapy, we have divided the book into two equal parts: 'Client resistance' in Part I, followed by 'Therapist resistance' in Part II.

The idea of resistance in psychotherapy has traditionally pointed to the idea that while people seek psychotherapeutic help for their psychological pain and to develop their potential, in a myriad of different ways they 'resist' such help. At first sight this seems to place all the responsibility on the client for 'resisting' help that they have sought, but the concept of resistance is much broader than this. It encompasses the therapist and the therapist–client pairing. We use this broader use of the concept in this book.

We have deemed it useful to make reference throughout this book to the concept of the working alliance as a generic perspective on resistance in psychotherapy. This concept was introduced by Ed Bordin (1979) as a tripartite perspective on why psychotherapy works and why it stalls. Bordin (1979) argued that there are three domains of the alliance:

- *Bonds* – the interpersonal connectedness between therapist and client
- *Goals* – what both therapist and client are aiming to achieve in psychotherapy
- *Tasks* – what both therapist and client do to achieve their goals.

Later, one of us (WD) added a fourth domain – views – which points to the fact that both therapist and client have certain views about salient aspects of psychotherapy not covered by the three other domains (Dryden 2006, 2011).

From a working alliance perspective, productive therapeutic change is facilitated when therapist and client

- have a well-bonded therapeutic relationship
- share similar views on salient therapeutic matters (e.g. the conceptualisation of the client's problems and how best they can be addressed)
- agree on goals of therapy that will enhance the client's well-being
- understand what each has to do to achieve the goals of therapy and are able and prepared to undertake such tasks.

The working alliance perspective on resistance to change is that difficulties can occur in one or more domains of the alliance, but that these can be tackled by both parties if there is the will to do so.

While this is a book on resistance in REBT, we have drawn on working alliance theory in the way we have structured the book in that we hold that this more generic theory brings coherence to the way REBT therapists need to intervene to get the therapeutic wagon moving in the right (i.e. therapeutic) direction.

Given this more generic perspective, our aim in this book is to offer ways of tackling difficulties in REBT that will assist their resolution and thereby help to build a productive and less stressful working alliance. While we obviously cannot guarantee therapeutic success, we do impress upon our readers that the use of persistence, force, ingenuity, energy and persuasion is more likely to overcome blocks in therapy than stale, unimaginative or insipid approaches. This book obviously cannot focus on every problem or difficulty in REBT, so some readers may be disappointed not to see their particular problems dealt with. Therefore we suggest to those readers that they consult other REBT texts (such as Dryden 2011) as well as apply or develop their own problem-solving abilities.

One of the continual pleasures and challenges in REBT is in increasing our stock of techniques and strategies in order to remove roadblocks in therapy – there never seems to be a shortage of them! Such a process keeps us on our therapeutic toes and prevents psychotherapy from degenerating into an assembly line. We hope that we have communicated our enthusiasm for problem-solving to the readers of this book.

Windy Dryden
London and Eastbourne

Michael Neenan
Chelmsford

June 2011

Acknowledgement

We wish to thank *The Rational Emotive Behaviour Therapist* for permission to use material from the following article (in Chapter 1):

Dryden, W. (2010) 'What is Rational Emotive Behaviour Therapy (REBT)? Outlining the approach by considering the four elements of its name.' *The Rational Emotive Behaviour Therapist*, 13(1): 22–32.

Chapter 1

What is rational emotive behaviour therapy (REBT)?

Introduction

In order to get the most out of this book, you need to know the nature of rational emotive behaviour therapy: this introduction is based on the four elements that comprise the name of the therapy: rational, emotive, behaviour and therapy.

Rational

When Albert Ellis established the therapy in the 1950s, he called it 'Rational Therapy' (Ellis 1958). He did so because he wanted to stress that emotional problems are based on irrational thinking and that if we are to address these problems effectively, we need to change such thinking to its rational equivalent. It is interesting to note that while REBT has had two previous names, the term 'rational' is common to all three names. It is the constant feature that spans REBT's more than fifty year old history. So what do REBT therapists currently mean by the term 'rational'? We can best answer this question if we contrast it with the term 'irrational'.

The terms 'rational' and 'irrational' in current REBT theory are most commonly used as adjectives in front of the noun 'beliefs'. Such beliefs can also be thought of as attitudes in that they describe a person's stance or position towards something.

Let us consider the major characteristics of rational beliefs and contrast these with the major characteristics of irrational beliefs. In Table 1, we consider the rational belief in the left hand column and the irrational belief in the right hand column to facilitate the comparison.

Emotive

The term 'emotive' in REBT means that which is relevant to your emotions. Like every other approach to therapy, REBT is based on a model of

Table 1 Major characteristics of rational and irrational beliefs

A *rational belief is flexible or non-extreme*	An *irrational belief is rigid or extreme*
A rational belief is flexible Here is an example of a rational belief that is flexible: 'I want my colleague to like me, but she does not have to do so'	**An irrational belief is rigid** Here is an example of an irrational belief that is rigid: 'My colleague has to like me' To compare this belief with the flexible version in the left hand column, we need to state it in its full form: 'I want my colleague to like me, therefore she has to do so'
Imagine that you hold such a belief. As you do so you will see that this belief is flexible because while you assert what you want (i.e. 'I want my colleague to like me . . .'), you also acknowledge that you do not have to get what you want (i.e. '. . . but she does not have to do so').	Again imagine that you hold this belief. As you do so you will see that this belief is rigid because you not only assert what you want (i.e. 'I want my colleague to like me . . .'), but also demand that you have to get it (i.e. '. . . therefore she has to do so').
A rational belief is non-extreme Here is an example of a rational belief that is non-extreme: 'It is bad if my colleague does not like me, but not the end of the world'	**An irrational belief is extreme** Here is an example of an irrational belief that is extreme: 'It is the end of the world if my colleague does not like me' To compare it to the non-extreme version in the left hand column, we need to state it in its full form: 'It is bad if my colleague does not like me, and therefore it is the end of the world'
Again imagine that you hold this belief. As you do so you will see that this belief is non-extreme because while you assert that you find the event negative (i.e. 'It is bad if my colleague does not like me . . .'), you also acknowledge that such an evaluation is not extreme because it could always be worse (i.e. '. . . but not the end of the world').	Again imagine that you hold this belief. As you do so you will see that this belief is extreme because you not only assert that you find the event negative (i.e. 'It is bad if my colleague does not like me . . .'), but also claim that it could not be worse (i.e. '. . . and therefore it is the end of the world').
A rational belief is true Imagine that you hold the following rational belief that I introduced above: 'I want my colleague to like me, but she does not have to do so'. You will note that this belief is made up of two parts:	**An irrational belief is false** Now imagine that you hold the following irrational belief that I introduced above: 'My colleague has to like me'. Again this belief is made up of two parts:

(continues)

Table 1 (*continued*)

A rational belief is flexible or non-extreme	An irrational belief is rigid or extreme
• 'I want my colleague to like me . . .'	• 'I want my colleague to like me . . .'
• '. . . but she does not have to do so'	• '. . . and therefore she has to do so'

Let's take one part at a time. First, you can prove that you would like your colleague to like you; after all, this is your desire. Also, you can probably cite reasons why you want your colleague to like you (e.g. it makes for a good working relationship where you can help each other). So, the first part of your belief is true.	Let's take one part at a time. First, you can again prove that you would like the other person to like you for reasons discussed opposite. So, the first part of your belief is true.
Now let's look at the second part of the rational belief. You can also prove that the other person does not have to like you. To state otherwise would be to deny that person free choice.	Now let's look at the second part of the irrational belief. You cannot prove that your colleague has to like you. If that were true, she would have no choice but to like you. This demanding component of your irrational belief in effects robs your colleague of free choice, which she retains in the face of your demand. Thus, this second part is false.
So if both parts of this rational belief are true, we can say that the belief taken as a whole is true.	As both parts of a belief have to be true for the belief to be true, we can say that the irrational belief is false.
	Also, when we consider this irrational belief in its short form (i.e. 'My colleague has to like me'), it is clear that it is false since it again attempts to rob your colleague of the freedom not to like you which she does in reality have.
A rational belief is sensible Taking the rational belief, 'I want my colleague to like me, but she does not have to do so', we can ask the question: does this belief make sense? We can answer that it does since you are explicitly acknowledging that there is no connection between what you want and what you have to get.	**An irrational belief is not sensible** Taking the full form of your irrational belief, 'I want my colleague to like me, and therefore she has to do so' we can again ask the question: does this belief makes sense? Here our answer is that it does not because it asserts that there is a connection between what you want and what you have to get. The idea that because you want something you have to get it is, in fact, childish nonsense when coming from an adult.

(*continues overleaf*)

Table 1 (*continued*)

A rational belief is largely constructive	An irrational belief is largely unconstructive
When you hold a rational belief, the consequences of doing so will be largely constructive. For example, let's suppose that you hold the following rational belief, 'I want my colleague to like me, but she does not have to do so', and you bring this belief to a situation where your colleague snaps at you for no good reason. In this situation you will experience three different but related consequences, which we will now illustrate:	When you hold an irrational belief the consequences of doing so will be largely unconstructive. For example, let's suppose that you hold the following irrational belief, 'My colleague must like me', and you bring this belief to the situation where your colleague snaps at you for no good reason. In this situation you will experience three different, but related consequences, which we will now illustrate. As we do so, compare these consequences to those that stem from your belief if it were rational (see opposite):
• Emotional consequence: here you will tend to be concerned about your colleague's response, but not anxious about it. • Behavioural consequence: here you will be likely to enquire of your colleague in an open way if there is anything wrong. • Thinking consequence: here you will tend to think that your colleague is upset with someone or something which could be to do with you, but may well be nothing to do with you.	• Emotional consequence: here you will tend to be anxious, rather than concerned, about your colleague's response. • Behavioural consequence: here you will tend to avoid your colleague or try desperately to get her to like you. • Thinking consequence: here you will tend to think that your colleague is upset with you rather than with someone or something that had nothing to do with you.

emotions. Since REBT is a therapeutic approach, it is primarily concerned with relieving people's emotional disturbance. However, it also acknowledges that people are bound to have negative emotions when faced with negative life events (henceforth called adversities in this book). To accommodate these two positions REBT distinguishes between emotions that are negative in tone and have largely unconstructive consequences and emotions that are negative in tone and have largely constructive consequences. The former are known as unhealthy negative emotions (UNEs) and the latter as healthy negative emotions (UNEs).

The REBT model of emotions

The REBT model of emotion states that the emotions that we experience are based largely on the beliefs that we hold about ourselves, others and the world. More specifically it states that our unhealthy negative emotions about life's adversities are based largely on the irrational beliefs that we hold about these adversities and that if we want to experience healthy negative emotions about the adversities in question we need to change our irrational beliefs to rational beliefs.

This is shown in the following figure in which 'A' stands for adversity, 'B' for beliefs and 'C' for the consequences of these beliefs (in this case the emotional consequences). This is REBT's famous 'ABC' model, which is outlined in any REBT textbook (e.g. Dryden and Branch 2008).

A	B	C
Adversity	Irrational beliefs	Unhealthy negative emotions
Adversity	Rational beliefs	Healthy negative emotions

Let us illustrate this model by referring to the example that we introduced earlier in this chapter.

A	B	C
Adversity 'My colleague may not like me'	**Irrational belief** 'My colleague must like me'	**Unhealthy negative emotion** Anxiety
Adversity 'My colleague may not like me'	**Rational belief** 'I want my colleague to like me, but she does not have to do so'	**Healthy negative emotion** Concern

Because life's adversities are negative, it is not appropriate for someone to feel good about them or even neutral about them. It is healthy to experience negative emotions, but not problematic ones about such life events. These problematic emotions in REBT are known as unhealthy negative emotions (UNEs) and these are listed in Table 2 with their alternative healthy negative emotions.

We want to make two points here:

1   As detailed above, unhealthy negative emotions largely stem from irrational beliefs about life's adversities while healthy negative emotions stem largely from rational beliefs about these same adversities.

Table 2 The eight UNEs and HNE alternatives

Unhealthy negative emotions	Healthy negative emotions
Anxiety	Concern
Depression	Sadness
Guilt	Remorse
Shame	Disappointment
Hurt	Sorrow
Unhealthy anger	Healthy anger
Unhealthy jealousy	Healthy jealousy
Unhealthy envy	Healthy envy

2   We do not have commonly agreed words in the English language to describe healthy negative emotions. The terms that we have used in the right hand column of the above table are my [WD] own. Clients and therapists are free to use alternative terns that are more meaningful to them.

Intellectual vs. emotive understanding

The other major area where the term 'emotive' comes up in REBT is in distinguishing between two different types of understanding: intellectual understanding and emotive understanding (Ellis 1963). These are particularly important when a person is trying to change an irrational belief to its rational belief alternative.

Let us illustrate this distinction by using the above example where the person holds the irrational belief (i.e. 'My colleague must like me') and his colleague has snapped at him. Let's suppose that the person acknowledges that his irrational belief is irrational (meaning that it is rigid, false, not sensible and largely unconstructive – see Table 1). And let's assume, furthermore, that he acknowledges that his rational alternative belief (i.e. 'I want my colleague to like me, but she does not have to do so') is rational (meaning that it is flexible, true, sensible and largely constructive). When the person's understanding of these two points is intellectual in nature, he says things like 'Well, I can understand this in my head, but not in my heart' and 'I understand it, but I don't feel it'. Here, he will still feel anxious about the prospect of his colleague not liking him, he will act in ways that are consistent with his irrational belief (i.e. he will either avoid his colleague or desperately try to get her to like him) and he will tend to think in highly distorted ways about his colleague (e.g. 'She is definitely upset with me' and 'If I don't win her over immediately, she will never like me again'). In other words, while the person understands intellectually the reason why his irrational belief is irrational and why your rational belief is rational, this understanding has little or no impact on his emotions, behaviour and subsequent thinking. He will still think, act and feel in ways consistent with his irrational belief even though he knows it is irrational.

However, when the person's understanding of these points is emotive in nature, he not only grasps the points intellectually, but also feels, thinks and acts in ways that are consistent with the rational belief and that are inconsistent with the irrational belief. Thus, the person will feel concerned, but not anxious about the prospect of his colleague not liking him, he will act in ways that are consistent with his rational belief (i.e. he will check out with her why she snapped at him) and he will tend to think in realistic ways about his colleague (e.g. 'She may or may not be upset with me' and 'If she is upset with me, we can talk it though and resolve the issue'). In other words, the person understands the reason why his irrational belief is irrational and why his rational belief is rational and this understanding has a decidedly constructive impact on his emotions, behaviour and subsequent thinking. He thinks, acts and feels in ways consistent with his rational belief.

In REBT, therefore, we argue that intellectual understanding is a necessary, but insufficient ingredient for constructive psychological change to occur. For this to happen clients need to act on their intellectual insight until it becomes emotional insight.

Behaviour

The term 'behaviour' in REBT refers to both overt behaviour and to an urge to act that is not translated into overt behaviour. The latter is known as an action tendency. REBT's model of behaviour parallels its model of emotions in arguing that irrational beliefs tend to lead to behaviour that is largely unconstructive in effect and that rational beliefs lead to behaviour that is largely constructive in effect. The former is associated with unhealthy negative emotions and the latter with healthy negative emotions.

This is shown below, where 'A' stands for adversity, 'B' for beliefs and 'C' for the consequences of these beliefs (in this case the behavioural consequences).

A	B	C
Adversity	Irrational beliefs	Unconstructive behaviour
Adversity	Rational beliefs	Constructive behaviour

Let us illustrate this model by referring again to the example that we introduced earlier in this chapter.

A	B	C
Adversity 'My colleague may not like me'	**Irrational belief** 'My colleague must like me'	**Unconstructive behaviour** Avoidance of colleague Desperate attempts to get colleague to like me
Adversity 'My colleague may not like me'	**Rational belief** 'I want my colleague to like me, but she does not have to do so'	**Constructive behaviour** Asking colleague directly if there is anything wrong

In Table 3, we outline the major behaviours associated with the eight unhealthy and healthy negative emotions listed in Table 2.

The behaviours listed in Table 3 are what a person does or tends to do when their irrational or rational belief about an adversity has been fully activated. However, the impact of belief on behaviour can be seen in other ways.

Short-term self-protective behaviour

In the 'ABC' model that we have presented in this chapter, an adversity occurs or is deemed to occur at 'A', the person holds a belief about this adversity at 'B' and experiences emotional, behavioural and thinking consequences of holding this belief at 'C'. In this model, the person's belief (e.g. 'My colleague must like me') is specific to the specific adversity that she encounters.

However, beliefs can be held at a more general level (e.g. 'People with whom I work must like me') and when a belief is more general in nature, the person has a tendency to bring such a belief with them, as it were, to situations where a relevant adversity may occur. Thus, in our example, if a person holds a general irrational belief (e.g. 'People with whom I work must like me'), the person will be hypersensitive to the possibility of not being liked by a colleague and act to prevent this adversity actually occurring (e.g. by being extra nice to a person whom she thinks may, but has not yet shown her some disapproval). In this way the person is acting to protect herself in the short term, but the longer term effect of this behaviour is unconstructive in a number of ways:

- She does not get to test out her hunch that the person will disapprove of her.

Table 3 Major behaviours associated with UNEs and HNEs

UNE with associated unconstructive behaviours and action tendencies	HNE with associated constructive behaviours and action tendencies
Anxiety • Withdrawing from threat • Avoiding threat • Seeking reassurance even though not reassurable • Seeking safety from threat	*Concern* • Confronting threat • Seeking reassurance when reassurable
Depression • Prolonged withdrawal from enjoyable activities	*Sadness* • Engaging with enjoyable activities after a period of mourning or adjustment to the loss
Guilt • Begging for forgiveness	*Remorse* • Asking, not begging, for forgiveness
Shame • Withdrawing from others • Avoiding eye contact with others	*Disappointment* • Keeping in contact with others • Maintaining eye contact with others
Hurt • Sulking	*Sorrow* • Assertion and communicating with others
Unhealthy anger • Aggression (direct and indirect)	*Healthy anger* • Assertion
Unhealthy jealousy • Prolonged suspicious questioning of the other person • Checking on the other • Restricting the other	*Healthy jealousy* • Brief, open-minded questioning of the other person • Not checking on the other • Not restricting the other
Unhealthy envy • Spoiling the other's enjoyment of the desired possession	*Healthy envy* • Striving to gain a similar possession for oneself if it is truly what you want

- She does not get to deal constructively with such disapproval should it occur.
- She tends to maintain her irrational belief since she is acting in a way that is consistent with it.

Over-compensatory behaviour

When a person holds an irrational belief and particularly one that is general in nature, she may try to deal with actual or potential adversities by behaving in a manner that is over-compensatory. By using over-compensatory behaviour the person is trying to prove to herself the opposite of what she actually thinks is the truth about herself, the other person or the world. A common example of this occurs when a person privately considers that she would be weak if she can't deal with a challenge, but tries to prove to herself that she is strong by facing an even greater challenge.

Therapy

The word 'therapy' comes from the Greek *therapeia*, meaning 'a service, an attendance' which, in turn, is related to the Greek verb *therapeuo*, meaning 'I wait upon'. REBT therapists, therefore, can be seen to offer a 'service' to people who have problems in a number of areas: emotional problems, practical, dissatisfaction problems and personal development problems (Bard 1980; Grieger and Boyd 1980; Wessler and Wessler 1980). A distinctive feature of REBT is that it outlines a logical order for dealing with these problems.

Disturbance before dissatisfaction

REBT argues that unless there are good reasons to the contrary, it is best for us to address our emotional problems before our dissatisfaction problems (Dryden 2009a). The reasoning is as follows. If we try to deal with our dissatisfaction before we deal with our emotional disturbance, our disturbed feelings will get in the way of our efforts to change directly the adversities about which we are dissatisfied.

For example, let's take the example of Paul, who is dissatisfied about his wife's spending habits. However, he is also unhealthily angry about her behaviour and every time he talks to her about it he makes himself angry, raises his voice to his wife and makes pejorative remarks about her and her spending behaviour. Now what is the likely impact of Paul's expression of unhealthy anger on his wife? Does it encourage her to stand back and look objectively at her own behaviour? Of course, it doesn't. Paul's angry behaviour is more likely to lead his wife to become unhealthily angry herself and/or to become defensive. In Paul's case, his anger had, in fact, both effects on his wife. Now, let's suppose that Paul *first* addressed his unhealthy anger and then discussed his dissatisfaction with his wife. His annoyance at her behaviour, but his acceptance of her as a person, would help him to view her own behaviour perhaps as a sign of emotional disturbance and his compassion for her would have very different effects on her. She would probably be less defensive and because Paul would not be unhealthily angry, then his wife would also be less likely to be unhealthily angry. With anger out of the picture, the stage would be set for Paul to address the reasons for his dissatisfaction more effectively.

Disturbance before development

In the late 1960s and early 1970s, one of us (WD) used to go to a number of encounter groups. This was the era of personal growth or development. However, there were a number of casualties of these groups and when these occurred it was because attendees were preoccupied with issues of emotional disturbance and they were being pushed too hard to go into areas of development that warranted greater resilience.

In general then, it is very difficult for us to develop ourselves when we are emotionally disturbed. To focus on areas of development when someone is emotionally disturbed is akin to encourage that person to climb a very steep hill with very heavy weights attached to their ankles. First, help the person to remove their ankle weights (i.e. address their emotional disturbance) before discussing the best way of climbing the hill!

Dissatisfaction before development

Abraham Maslow (1968) is perhaps best known for his work on self-actualisation. The relevance of this concept for our present discussion is this. It is very difficult for humans to focus on higher order 'needs' when we are preoccupied with issues with respect to lower order needs. Thus, if individuals are faced with a general dissatisfying life experience which cannot be compartmentalised and also want to explore their writing ambitions, they should address the former first unless this life dissatisfaction will help them write a better book!

While we have outlined REBT's preferred order in dealing with problems, it also values flexibility. Thus, if people want to deal with their problems in a different order, they should do so and observe the results. If it works, that is fine. If not, REBT's preferred position may prove to yield better results. The proof of the pudding is in the eating.

Conclusion

While outlining REBT by considering the four elements that comprise its name is not comprehensive, it does introduce those who are relatively unfamiliar with REBT to some of its key elements.

Part I

Client resistance

Chapter 2

Dealing with client resistance in the bonds domain of the working alliance

Developing and maintaining a therapeutic relationship is one of the biggest challenges in psychotherapy. Bordin (1979) argued that the bond between therapist and client (which is what most people in the field mean by the therapeutic relationship) is one of three domains of the working alliance discussed briefly in the Preface (see p. vii).[1]

This chapter focuses on tackling those obstacles and difficulties primarily created by the client which block or impair the creation of a successful relationship.

When clients resist forming a therapeutic bond

An appropriately bonded therapeutic relationship will encourage each client to carry out his or her goal-directed tasks. Therefore, it is important for REBT therapists to pay attention to their clients' anticipations and preferences in this domain, e.g. one client desires a formal relationship based on the therapist's expertise and authority within her field, while another client seeks an informal 'chat' and a more relaxed approach to therapy.

However, some clients' preferred bonds will actually reinforce rather than help them to overcome their emotional problems. For example, a female client who one of us (MN) saw said that she could not stand much stress or pressure in her life, so 'could you be very gentle with me'. I did not speak for ten minutes and she enquired if I was going to ask her questions. I replied: 'I don't want to put you under any pressure'. She laughed, but the serious point was that if I wrapped her in cotton wool, she stood little chance of tackling her anxiety and social avoidance. This explanation of my clinical rationale for not 'tiptoeing' through therapy with her opened the way for her to develop greater resilience towards life's vicissitudes.

Clients who exhibit dire needs for love and approval (e.g. 'I must be approved and if I'm not I am worthless') often expect the therapist to meet

---

1 One of us (WD) later added a fourth domain known as 'views (Dryden 2006, 2011).

these needs. While REBT therapists offer clients unconditional acceptance as fallible human beings, they are cautious about giving clients excessive warmth for two major reasons (Dryden and Ellis 1997). First, clients may feel better in the short term if they think that their therapist greatly approves of them, but will not necessarily get better in the long term because their disturbance-creating beliefs remain largely unexamined and therefore intact. It is far better to teach such clients unconditional self-acceptance irrespective of what the therapist thinks about them, for example:

> 'When you're no longer anxious about whether or not I like you, it will probably be the time to end therapy. Then you'll be much stronger to deal constructively with the inevitable rejection or disapproval that occurs in life.'

Second, therapists may strengthen their clients' discomfort intolerance beliefs, (e.g. 'I can't face my problems on my own. It's too hard. I need lots of support from my therapist'). Thus, such clients avoid taking the primary responsibility for bringing about change in their lives and believe that they cannot be happy without the continual support of others. The therapist can repeatedly counter with the self-defeating nature of this outlook, for example:

> 'If I have to hold your hand throughout therapy, how will you learn to walk on your own? When I let go of your hand when therapy is finished, what happens to you if there is no one else to grasp it?'

Therefore REBT seeks 'to help them [clients] become independent, to think for themselves and acquire self-helping habits rather than to remain needy of therapeutic succouring' (Albert Ellis, quoted in Dryden 1991: 52). However, as REBT is opposed to dogmatism, therapists may decide to display undue warmth for limited periods if it is deemed to be clinically justified (e.g. with suicidal clients or with those recently bereaved).

In order to determine the type of bond which is clinically effective at any given time in therapy, Kwee and Lazarus (1986) advocate therapists adopting the stance of an authentic chameleon, that is 'the therapist mak[ing] use of the most helpful facets of his or her personality in order to establish rapport with a particular client' (Kwee and Lazarus 1986: 333). The role of an authentic chameleon should not lead to a lack of genuineness on the therapist's part (trying to be all things to the client but without any obvious sincerity or conviction). Properly applied, the therapist as authentic chameleon is a flexible device which allows the therapist to adapt herself to and blend in with the requirements of the bond domain whenever necessary.

Therapists can develop this role by, among other things, giving clients a Life History Inventory to complete (Lazarus and Lazarus 1991). Parts of this questionnaire ask clients to specify how therapists should ideally interact with their clients and what personal qualities they should possess. If clients have had previous therapy, they can be asked what they found helpful and unhelpful about it with particular emphasis on the kind of bond that facilitated therapeutic progress, e.g. 'He was firm with me. If he had been soft with me I would have run rings round him'. In a similar vein, clients can be encouraged to examine those individuals in their lives who have or had positive or adverse effects on their personal development. Such an examination 'may provide the therapist with important clues concerning which types of therapeutic bonds to promote actively with certain clients and which bonds to avoid developing with others' (Golden and Dryden 1986: 370). All the aforementioned methods can help therapists to forge a productive and enduring bond with clients.

When clients' interpersonal style promotes resistance in REBT

Other difficulties in the bond domain relate to clients' interpersonal styles. Such styles of interaction may include passivity, over-excitability, overly intellectual or dominant. Therapists who reinforce these interpersonal styles run the risk of failing to construct a working alliance which promotes client learning. For example, *passive* clients need to be encouraged to participate so that gradually their 'brains take more of the strain' of therapy (Dryden and Neenan 2006), e.g. 'You might be expecting me to do most of the work in therapy but, in fact, we can't make much progress unless you also lend a helping hand'. REBT therapists may need to 'tone down' their active-directive approach in order to draw increased activity from passive clients. Therapists who actually increase their active style in order to provoke or arouse clients into action may have the opposite effect of encouraging greater passivity on their part.

Over-excitable clients are not usually able to examine productively their problems if the therapeutic relationship or milieu is emotionally charged, e.g. through the use of cathartic or abreactive techniques. With these clients, therapists should employ more cognitive techniques such as looking at the short- and long-term consequences of their irrational ideas in the hope of encouraging a more contemplative approach to life. A 'quieter' interpersonal style can be adopted by therapists in order to reduce the level of emotional arousal in the sessions.

Clients who present with an *overly intellectual* style of interaction may provide seemingly plausible and 'rational' explanations of their problems and thereby avoid or bypass talking about their emotional reactions to these problems, e.g. 'My wife's infidelity was the natural consequence of our deteriorating relationship. Therefore it is totally absurd to suggest I was upset over this when it was bound to occur'. With such clients, Dryden and Yankura (1993: 239) suggest that 'counsellors should preferably endeavour to inject a productive level of affect into the therapeutic session and employ emotive techniques, self-disclosure and a good deal of humour' in order for clients to release their feelings.

Clients who like to *dominate* in or take charge of relationships need to be treated with caution by REBT therapists. Because of the vigorous, persuasive and active-directive approach of REBT, such clients may believe that their authority and sense of control is being threatened or undermined and therefore 'fight back' to re-establish their control. This can lead to a power struggle between the therapist and client resulting in an impasse in therapy. Therapists should be mindful to employ strategies that preserve such clients' sense of control and authority and thereby emphasise that they are in charge of their thoughts and beliefs and whether to change them, e.g. 'If you decide to change your belief of never showing any weakness, what idea would you choose to put in its place that you consider would be more helpful?'

The choice of which interpersonal style to employ should be based on clients' accounts of which factors produce the best learning environment for them. Dryden and Yankura (1993: 239) 'try to develop a learning profile for each of our clients and use this information to help us plan our therapeutic strategies and choose techniques designed to implement these strategies'.

Problems in client–therapist matching

This refers to bringing together a corresponding or suitably associated pair of individuals to create a working bond. Poor matching in REBT (e.g. the client thinks the therapist is too old, the wrong sex or too confrontational) can lead to obstacles in the client's progress as she becomes more pre-occupied with what she dislikes about the therapist rather than focusing on her problems. The therapist should ask the client what particular quality or characteristic of his blocks therapeutic progress. The client might reply: 'You're a man. How can you possibly know what it is to be raped? Therefore you can't help me'. The therapist can state (if he has worked with survivors of rape):

> 'It's perfectly true I've never been raped. I've counselled individuals, both male and female, who have been. What I do with these individuals is to help them tackle their ideas, among others, of worthlessness or self-blame and their feelings such as shame and guilt. Do you want to commit yourself to a few sessions and see if I can help you?'

If the client agrees but the poor matching continues, the therapist should respect the client's preferences and refer her to a female counsellor. Another tack that the therapist can use is to compensate for his client-perceived 'flaws' and adopt some of the client's recommendations (e.g. 'My therapist should relax more and let things unwind at a gentler pace') in order to form a good therapeutic relationship. Alternatively, the therapist may wish to maintain his hard-working stance (e.g. 'This really is the best and quickest way to overcome your problems') and through such sincerity the client may naturally overcome her dislike of or aversion to certain of his qualities as a therapist.

When clients believe that therapists can't help them unless they know what it's like to have their problem

Matching problems can occur when clients think that their therapist should have had the same problem and recovered from the problem with which they are struggling. This frequently occurs with substance misusers. One of us (MN) is frequently asked if I have had a drink or drugs problem. When I reply that I have not, clients usually respond: 'If you haven't been there yourself, then you won't know what it's all about. You haven't got a clue what heroin withdrawals feel like.' I point out that medication can be used to moderate the severity of the withdrawals, but therapy is not about endlessly discussing the drugs they have used and swapping lurid anecdotes with the former addict-turned-counsellor. Therapy is focused on looking at the emotional and behavioural problems clients are attempting to keep under control through drug use. As one of us (MN) is trained to deal with such problems, this will also produce a significant decrease in or eventual elimination of my clients' drug use. I have found that this kind of rationale has persuaded the vast majority of my clients to stay in therapy with a non-addict. For those few not convinced, I have given them the phone numbers of local self-help groups such as Narcotics Anonymous or Alcoholics Anonymous. Therapists who deal with clients who devoutly believe in the 'I've been there' school of psychotherapy require convincing arguments to maintain credibility in their clients' eyes, e.g. 'Do you expect your doctor to have experienced your problems before they can help you?'

When the therapeutic relationship becomes too cosy

Different kinds of problems may emerge if the client and counsellor have an enjoyable relationship and avoid the hard work and discomfort usually associated with therapeutic change. If the client does eventually tackle their problems, this may well lead to a deterioration in the 'feel good' atmosphere of the relationship and therefore there is a tacit agreement to prevent this happening. Dryden and Yankura (1993: 238) suggest that this 'problem can be largely overcome if counsellors first help themselves and then their clients to overcome the philosophy of low frustration tolerance implicit in this collusive short-range hedonism'.

When clients have doubts about the therapist's credibility and/or trustworthiness

Resistance in REBT can occur if the client has doubts about the therapist's credibility as a helper or about the therapist's trustworthiness.

Doubts about the therapist's credibility

The main goal of REBT therapists is to help clients to surrender their irrational philosophies of living and replace them with rational ones. Such an ambitious aim may engender doubts in some clients as to whether the therapist has the clinical competence or expertness to help them achieve such a goal, particularly if the problems are of a long-standing nature. For example, a client might say: 'Have you dealt with these kind of problems before? Have you helped others to get rid of these problems? I'm not sure anyone can help me'. In order to convey credibility, therapists can present clinical examples of past successes, training qualifications, accreditation to a professional body, articles and/or books written and so on.

Grieger and Boyd (1980) suggest that once therapy gets under way the therapist's behaviour can quickly confirm or contradict the impression of expertness that she has been trying to create. Confirmation is much more likely

> by getting right to work [in the first session], the client is sensitively yet firmly led into a productive diagnostic exploration of the problem(s) . . . there is no fumbling around, prolonged and unnecessary chit-chat, or sparring back-and-forth in terms of the relationship.
>
> (Grieger and Boyd 1980: 54)

Through the therapist's manner and actions he or she is implying to the client: 'I know how to help you overcome your problems, so let's get going'. If some clients are still sceptical about the therapist's ability to help them, the therapist can suggest some trial psychotherapy sessions as a means of establishing her credentials.

Doubts about the therapist's trustworthiness

Trust in the therapist enables clients to disclose often intimate problems secure in the knowledge that they will not be humiliated or ridiculed, their problems trivialised or the therapist will make any personal gains from their disclosures. However, not all clients will automatically trust their therapist and therefore therapists need to create a milieu in which it can develop. Clients can be congratulated whenever they make a disclosure and assured that it is safe to do so (the information is not going to leak out of the psychotherapy room). Therapists can make use of their own clinically relevant self-disclosure as an example of 'how to open up' or offer encouragement to the client to make initial or further disclosures. If the client is slow to respond to these techniques, it is important that therapists do not display an attitude of discomfort intolerance (e.g. 'For Christ's sake, when are we going to get started!') or put the client under pressure through their unvarying active-directive style. Walen et al. (1992: 44) point out that it is important to 'take some time to get to know the client and get a feel for his or her thinking. The patient is more likely to discuss personal problems if he or she believes that the therapist is truly interested in listening'.

REBT therapists also need to be alert to the dysfunctional aspects of some clients' difficulties in developing trust with them, e.g. 'Because I've been hurt badly in the past, I absolutely must be sure that you won't let me down. I couldn't stand it if this happened again'. Therapists need to probe for examples where their clients believe their trust has been betrayed in order to understand their current wariness, e.g. do they place absolute trust in others and therefore demand unimpeachable behaviour from them? Have they been too quick to trust others and thereby feel easily hurt when things go wrong? If they are let down again, why do they see this as the final straw? As well as tackling some of these ideas, therapists can suggest that they be granted a small measure of provisional trust as a means of testing them out while acknowledging the uncertainty involved.

Other forms of relationship-focused client resistance

When shame prevents self-disclosure

Fear of personal disclosure resulting in feelings of shame may lead clients to be reluctant to talk about the full extent of their concerns Thus, a client who thinks, for example, that he can't admit to the therapist that he has sexual feelings towards his sister as it is disgusting, and therefore he is disgusting, will withhold disclosure for fear of being shamed by the therapist.

By offering clients a general stance of unconditional acceptance as fallible human beings, therapists can encourage them to reveal their 'shameful' thoughts and feelings and engage in the disputing of their associated self-defeating ideas (e.g. having sexual feelings towards siblings does not mean that you are going to have sex with them or that such feelings mean you are a bad person). Through such methods clients can learn to be more open in therapy and get 'at the source of some of the things they find most bothersome' (Ellis 1985: 12).

Dealing with transference and non-transference issues

Resistance to creating a productive relationship can occur through the process of transference, i.e. clients displace on to therapists the feelings and attitudes they have towards significant others in their lives. For example, a person who believes she must defer to authority figures in her life tells the therapist: 'I will work hard in therapy because you know what's best for me'. The client in this case will probably make good progress but for non-therapeutic reasons. The therapist can applaud her determination to work hard but question her obeisance, e.g. 'It's more important that you independently decide what's best for you from a position of self-acceptance rather than automatically accepting wisdom from on high'. The client might agree with this viewpoint but again for the wrong reason – because the therapist told her. To overcome this problem, the therapist needs to leave most of the decisions involving therapeutic progress to the client without confirmation from him that she is making the right ones. By developing independent thinking, she can challenge her 'worshipful' attitudes towards others in her life.

Clients may develop non-transference feelings for the therapist whereby, for example, a female client falls in love with her therapist because he embodies certain qualities she finds highly desirable in a man, and not because he represents a father figure to her. Thus resistance can develop as the client impedes her own progress in order to stay in therapy as long as possible. The therapist needs to tackle this problem sensitively but firmly: first, by revealing and disputing the irrational ideas underlying her strong feelings, e.g. 'As I've fallen in love with my therapist, I must stay in therapy indefinitely. I couldn't bear not to see him again'; second, while pointing out to the client that he is flattered by her feelings for him, the purpose of therapy is working hard to tackle her presenting problems and not to foster a romantic relationship. Such a 'cold water' approach may have the desired effect of dampening her romantic ardour and refocusing her attention on why she originally came to therapy. However, if her feelings are unabated, a referral to another counsellor is indicated.

When clients are wilfully resistant

Ellis (1985, 2002) described clients who deliberately and obstinately fight against therapy and frequently attempt to initiate and win power struggles with the therapist as wilfully resistant. In an effort to make the therapeutic relationship more productive and less obstructive, the therapist can point out to such clients how self-defeating their behaviour actually is:

Therapist: It seems that everything I say about your depression and this theme of failure in your life is immediately shot down in flames by you. Wouldn't it be better if you actually considered some of the points I'm making? Some of them might even help you.

Client: Nothing you've said has been remotely helpful. In fact, I don't think you're going to be any help at all. You head shrinkers are all the same – bloody useless!

Therapist: How many 'head shrinkers', as you call them, have you seen in the last year?

Client: About six.

Therapist: You don't stay long in therapy then?

Client: What's the point if no one's helping me?

Therapist: What sort of help are you looking for?

Client: I don't know. You lot are supposed to be the experts. That's a joke.

Therapist: Well, I don't know what those other therapists did with you, but I will help you to locate some attitudes that you have which contribute to your depression and we'll work together to get rid of those attitudes and replace them with more constructive ones. This therapy will require a lot of work from you, particularly outside of sessions.

Client: I'm supposed to do your work for you then? I thought I was the client. You're supposed to tell me what's wrong and get me better.

Therapist: I don't have a magic wand to make you better. If you don't do any work then therapy will be a waste of time for you, like your previous encounters in therapy.

Client: And for you. If you fail with me you won't be able to tell everyone how wonderful you are. Oh dear.

Therapist: Let's get something crystal clear in your mind: I have no personal interest whatsoever in whether your problems are sorted out, but I will do my professional best to help you if you commit yourself to change. The decision is yours.

Client: What are you trying to do – scare me? You're just trying to be tough. If I tell you you're 'crap' and walk out right now, it'll be a different story then. I wonder how you handle failure?

Therapist: I would assume better than you do as I don't get depressed over it. I don't put my ego on the line in that I have to get you better in order not to feel worthless or useless. Whether we make a lot of progress or, what you

	seem to want, to emerge victorious from therapy having beaten me down is irrelevant to me personally. If you remain miserable and depressed, which is highly likely, it certainly won't stop me enjoying my life. So if you want to waste time or leave, please go ahead. You will lose out, not me.
Client:	All right, keep your hair on. No need to be like that. You might be able to help me after all. I just wasn't sure about you, that's all. Okay, so how are you going to get me over my depression?
Therapist:	As I said earlier, we *(emphasises word)* are going to do it, not just me. I think one of your major problems is what is called in REBT 'discomfort intolerance'. This means that you don't do any sustained hard work to overcome your problems because you believe it is too difficult or uncomfortable. Instead, you just waste time in therapy playing games, sabotaging progress, that sort of thing. This time you could behave differently if you choose to.
Client:	*(reluctantly)* All right, I'll give it a go, but I'm not promising anything.
Therapist:	Okay, let's see how we get on then.

By not engaging in a power struggle with the client or desperately trying to persuade him to stay in therapy, the therapist shows that she has kept her ego out of the psychotherapy room and therefore will not be crestfallen if no progress is made, the client abruptly terminates or he continues to act in an obnoxious manner. The therapist's forthright approach starkly illustrates to the client the likely consequences of his recalcitrant behaviour – he will remain emotionally disturbed. The therapist hypothesises that this disturbance is partly maintained by the client's discomfort intolerance ideas which lead him to fritter away valuable therapy time rather than confront his problems. By persistently and forcefully maintaining a clinical focus and thereby not getting 'sucked into' the client's attempts to undermine therapy, she eventually secures his tentative agreement to participate constructively in it.

When clients are involuntary

Involuntary clients are those who reluctantly come to therapy at the insistence of others (e.g. parents, partners, courts, employers) and claim that they have no emotional or behavioural problems. The following techniques can be employed with such clients. First, agreeing with clients that others are probably wrong about them but examining their claims anyway, e.g. 'I'm sure your wife does exaggerate how much you drink, but as we have this hour together, shall we try and see why she's upset about it?' Second, agreeing with clients that others have probably 'got it in for them' but that still does not solve their problems, e.g. 'It must be very bad living at home with your parents on your case all the time, but your own behaviour in response to theirs is making life more difficult for you than it has to be'. Third, agreeing with clients that therapy is probably a waste of time and even though they have to be here, they still retain the upper hand, e.g. 'I know being here is part of the probation order but you still have the choice whether to cooperate. In that sense, you have more power than the courts or myself. So why not use that power in a way that might actually help you?'

Such methods may turn involuntary clients into voluntary ones and thereby entice them into the orbit of therapy.

When clients have hidden agendas: The importance of accepting clients unconditionally

Hidden agendas are the covert but real reasons why some clients enter therapy rather than the ostensible ones they disclose to the therapist. For example, a drug addict enters therapy 'to get off drugs for good' but actually seeks to sabotage it in order to prove he is a 'hopeless addict' and thereby continue his drug use; a woman attends couple psychotherapy to save her relationship although in reality she wants to end it, but guilt prevents her from doing so.

By giving all clients unconditional acceptance as fallible human beings, Ellis (1985, 2002) suggested that REBT can provide a therapeutic milieu which encourages the development of an honest and open alliance that makes it more likely that clients will reveal their hidden agendas. Thereafter, disputing of their associated irrational beliefs can be undertaken. In the above examples, the therapist tackles the drug addict's hopelessness, 'I'll always be a junkie. I was born one', and the woman's self-damnation, 'I would make him so miserable if I left him. I would be such a terrible person for doing that to him'. It is important that therapists remain alert for clues that might be offered by clients as to their real motives for being in therapy, e.g. the woman's frequently stated worries about her partner's inability to cope on his own if she left him rather than focusing on how she can help to save the relationship.

When clients want to argue

Some clients may turn the therapy room into a place for an argument. Whatever the therapist says, they will argue with it. They hold that therapy will not be able to help them, that they will never change or that the therapist does not understand 'real life' problems. They argue with every response the therapist makes to them. Here it is important that therapists do not engage in arguing with clients over such issues because it may help to create a power struggle which results in an impasse in therapy. Dryden and Neenan (1995) suggest the following possible resolution to this problem:

> If you win the argument you also lose it because you will remain emotionally disturbed. If I win the argument you will also win because I can help you to overcome your emotional disturbance. Now whom do you want to win the argument?
>
> (Dryden and Neenan 1995: 7)

Clients usually suggest the therapist and then therapy can constructively proceed. If some clients state that they want to win, they are likely to find they have secured a Pyrrhic victory, i.e. won at considerable emotional cost to themselves (see the section of this chapter on dealing with wilfully resistant clients, above).

Certain clients may wish to engage in a prolonged discussion of or argument over the use of the terms 'rational' and 'irrational'. As these terms are widely used in REBT, the impression might be created that the therapist has a superior understanding of or greater insight into these concepts:

Client: Who can say what is irrational or rational? It's all subjective anyway. Isn't it rather arrogant of you to claim that you have a monopoly on these terms?

Therapist: Well, it would be if we claimed such a thing, but we don't. In REBT, the terms 'rational' and 'irrational' have commonplace meanings of, respectively, 'self-helping' and 'self-defeating'. In other words, whatever helps or blocks the clients from achieving their goals in life. These terms are used in a relative sense and not an absolute one.

Client: Relative to what?

Therapist: To the client's subjective view of reality. We stand behind the client, so to speak, so we can try to understand his or her view of reality and those aspects of it which are causing trouble.

Client: But if people are disturbed they are obviously not conforming to some fixed and external objective reality. So getting better means agreeing with that reality if they want to be happy.

Therapist: Clients certainly don't have to conform to anything in REBT. As I've said, we look at reality from their viewpoint, not ours. Obviously empirical reality acts as some form of objective standard clients can test their beliefs against. But we don't have, as you seem to think, some objective reality kit that clients can take home, assemble and then follow the instructions for a happier life.

Client: But someone's view of reality is true to them and yet you're trying to get them to see it differently.

Therapist: If someone is depressed because he believes he is utterly worthless, do we agree with him and let his suffering continue?

Client: No, I suppose not even though he truly believes that he is worthless.

Therapist: He sees his beliefs as facts while we see them as hypotheses. By seeking evidence for and against his beliefs we hope that the evidence will prove to him that he is not worthless and thereby moderate or remove his depression. Remember, clients come to see us asking for help because there are things in their lives that they want to change.

Client: I can certainly agree with that but I think our 'nature of reality' debate is still clouded by certain issues.

Therapist: Well, I think more discussion will be counterproductive as it will drain away therapy time and, I think, prove largely ineffective.

Client: Obviously that's your hypothesis and not, therefore, a fact. Further discussion could help me to be more receptive to REBT and give me greater insight into my problems. I believe, as a general rule, that every important issue has to be discussed thoroughly.

Therapist: My hypothesis, which is based on previous encounters with clients who wanted prolonged debates of a similar nature, is that we will get distracted from the real purpose of therapy which is tackling your guilt and procrastination. What is really needed to overcome these problems is concerted action and not more philosophical discussion. Philosophical indecision might be one of the reasons for your procrastination.

Client: So now you are imposing your views on me. You're telling me what is best for me. My view of things no longer counts. My problems are unique and not to be brushed aside so flippantly.

> *Therapist:*   I assure you that I am neither imposing my views on you nor brushing aside your problems. Your problems are unique in the sense that they belong to you and no one else. However, the reasons for your problems and the solutions to them are usually anything but unique.
>
> *Client:*   I'm not persuaded that we can reach a compromise yet when we are still clashing on the question 'what is reality?' How can we know that what we believe can ever be objectively validated or that you're right in what you say? Can my problems be so readily understood?
>
> *Therapist:*   Well, I think that I have sufficiently explained the REBT position on these issues and that the clinical way forward is to start assessing your presenting problems so that we can devise some strategies for change.
>
> *Client:*   And if I disagree, what then?
>
> *Therapist:*   Then you might wish to find another type of psychotherapy approach which suits your philosophical outlook. I can certainly make a referral for you.
>
> *Client:*   And if I decide to stay?
>
> *Therapist:*   At the start of the next session, as this one is now drawing to a close, we will focus on those irrational or self-defeating ideas underlying your procrastination and guilt. Then we will look at ways of challenging those ideas through a variety of homework tasks. The choice is yours.
>
> *Client:*   Well, obviously I want help with these problems otherwise I wouldn't be here, but I'm still very concerned that you have prematurely shut off debate on what I consider to be important issues.
>
> *Therapist:*   Okay, let me make a suggestion. As we are working through your problems and certain philosophical issues naturally arise from our problem-solving approach, then we can set some time aside to discuss these issues without holding up our work schedule. Is that agreeable?
>
> *Client:*   I can live with that. So we get down to business, as you would say, at the next session.
>
> *Therapist:*   We've already started.

Important points to note in this extract from therapy are the following:

1   The therapist explains the terms 'irrational', 'rational', 'the nature of reality', etc. only from the REBT viewpoint and does not launch into a more general discussion of these issues as she considers this would be

clinically inappropriate. Therapy provides a platform for change through direct action and not a forum for abstract arguments.

2 Even while the therapist is discussing these issues with the client, she is forming hypotheses about his presenting problems and suggests that his desire for prolonged philosophical debate might be linked to his procrastination.

3 The client's reluctance to be drawn into an early problem-solving focus gives the therapist the opportunity to push the client to make a decision about whether to stay in REBT. If he chooses to remain, his expected role is described for him.

4 In order to develop a therapeutic alliance with the client, the therapist suggests a compromise that provides for some philosophical inquiry within the overall strategy of 'more work and less waffle'. The therapist's final comment demonstrates that REBT therapists are always looking for ways to introduce efficiency into therapy.

When clients want their therapist as a friend

Sometimes clients can make the mistake of viewing the therapist as another (or the only) friend in their life and therefore expect the therapist to 'indulge' them, e.g. meet them outside of sessions, turn up for therapy only when they feel like it, lend them money, be a taxi service for them, allow them to bring alcohol to the session. Clients can become indignant, hurt or rejected when the therapist turns down their requests, e.g. 'I thought you're supposed to be on my side'. As Walen et al. (1992: 44) point out: 'the basis for the therapeutic relationship is not friendship but professional competence, credibility, respect, and commitment to help the client change'. Therefore the therapist in his or her role as a concerned professional can respond:

> 'If I behave like your friend, how much real progress do you think you are going to make? The business of therapy is lots of hard work to overcome your problems. So let's sort out what our respective roles are.'

The earlier this is done in therapy, the less misunderstanding will occur.

The foregoing account of clients' difficulties in forming a productive relationship with the therapist is not meant to be exhaustive; also these and other problems can occur at any time during therapy rather than all appear in its early stages. Therefore the therapist should be prepared to monitor continually the bond domain of the working alliance. The strength of the bond will be tested, often severely so, as the therapist introduces the client to the 'ABC' model of self-created disturbance, which is discussed in Chapter 3.

Dealing with client resistance in the views domain of the working alliance

Effective REBT, in our opinion, is based on a number of agreed understandings between therapist and client. If both disagree on any aspect of the process, a potential obstacle to the client's progress exists and needs to be identified, explored and resolved. Such disagreements that therapists may have about therapy are often based on different views that they respectively hold about this activity.

As this is a book on working with resistance in REBT, we concentrate on client resistance in the views domain on the alliance with special reference to how REBT conceptualises client problems and their amelioration. We note that client resistance in the views domain may occur in more generic areas. Thus, clients and therapists may disagree on the practicalities of therapy (i.e. fees, how long therapy should last, how long sessions should last and how often they should meet) and on the issue of confidentiality and its limits (for a discussion on these more general points, see Dryden 2011).

Whatever the issue is concerning possible discrepant views on therapy held by therapist and client, we argue that therapists need to be explicit with clients about the views that they hold about different aspects of therapy and need to encourage their clients to be explicit about their views as well. We further recommend that therapists engage their clients in an honest and open discussion of their respective views when these are at variance with one another. If these differing views cannot be reconciled and this fact makes therapy non-viable, at least this decision has been made on the explicit exchange of information and the therapist may effect a suitable referral.

When clients hold views about therapy that are very different from those inherent in REBT

Clients may come to psychotherapy expecting to be the passive recipients of the therapist's insights into their problems and through this osmotic process (absorption of the therapist's wisdom) leave therapy 'cured'. As rational emotive behaviour therapy (REBT) is a collaborative endeavour in emotional and practical problem-solving, clients are quickly disabused of their ideas of inaction or minimal effort by frequent use of the words 'us' and 'we', e.g. 'Let us put our heads together and see what we can do to overcome your problems'. This theme of a hard-working partnership often needs to be repeated throughout the course of therapy.

Some clients may protest that this places too much responsibility on them, e.g. 'You're supposed to be helping me, not the other way round!' In order to make some headway with their problems, clients need to develop a philosophy of effort ('There's no gain without pain'). The client's expected role in therapy can be outlined, e.g. an early problem-solving focus, learning a particular model of largely self-induced emotional disturbance, carrying out homework tasks, in order to emphasise the work the client will have to do. If the client still insists on the gain without the pain, the likely results of this attitude can be spelled out: 'If you put nothing into therapy, it's hardly surprising if you get nothing out of it. Therefore you're going to remain emotionally disturbed'. Frequent encouragement from the therapist that hard work pays off, supported by case examples of clients who had similar problems and eventually overcame them, can motivate such clients to adopt a problem-solving role.

When clients think that therapy is about ventilation of feelings or open-ended exploration of problems

Some clients think that in therapy they need to express their feelings and talk about their problems at interminable length. Such clients believe that therapy is the arena in which they are allowed to 'get it all out'. Any infringement on their right to do this might impair the development of a productive alliance. However, as REBT advocates an early problem-solving focus, client (or therapist) long-windedness will usually interfere with therapeutic efficiency.

Many REBT therapists argue that it is important to socialise clients into REBT at the outset. Here is how one of us (WD) approaches this task (see Dryden 2011).

Well, now, there are a number of approaches to counselling and it is important that you understand something of the one that I practise, which is known as rational emotive behaviour therapy (REBT). REBT is based on an old idea attributed to Epictetus, a Roman philosopher, who said that 'Men are disturbed not by things, but by their views of things.' In REBT, we have modified this and say that 'People are disturbed not by things, but by their rigid and extreme views of things.' Once they have disturbed themselves they then try to get rid of their disturbed feelings in ways that ultimately serve to maintain their problems.

As an REBT therapist I will help you to identify, examine and change the rigid and extreme beliefs that we argue underpin your emotional problems and to develop alternative flexible and non-extreme beliefs. I will also help you to examine the ways in which you have tried to help yourself that haven't worked and encourage you to develop and practise more effective, longer-lasting strategies. At the beginning of counselling, we will consider your problems one at a time and I will teach you a framework which will help you to break down your problems into their constituent parts. I will also teach you a variety of methods for examining and changing your rigid and extreme beliefs and a variety of methods to help you to consolidate and strengthen your alternative flexible and non-extreme beliefs. As therapy proceeds, I will help you to take increasing responsibility for using these methods and my ultimate aim is to help you to become your own therapist. As this happens, we will meet less frequently until you feel you can cope on your own.

As will be reiterated in Chapter 8, a socialising statement such as the one in the box is presented and discussed piece by piece. Presenting a block of material without giving your clients an opportunity to share their under-standing of it and a chance to discuss it is likely to engender client resistance, rather than dilute it.

It may also be necessary to make a compromise between the client's view concerning ventilation of feelings and the therapist's view on the import-ance of being explicit about the nature of REBT. Wessler and Wessler (1980) suggest that before introducing such clients to the 'ABC' model of emotional disturbance (a framework where clients' problems are con-ceptualised in REBT terms – see below), let them 'complain, whine, emote, and generally say what concerns them . . . [but] we would not ordinarily devote more than a half session to such expression of feelings' (Wessler and Wessler 1980: 69). As the socialising statement makes clear, REBT ther-apists are not interested in feelings per se but the irrational ideas lurking behind them and this should be made clear to clients at the outset. By quickly identifying, challenging and changing these ideas, clients' emotional problems can be ameliorated as rapidly as possible.

Another way to staunch clients' long-windedness without necessarily upsetting the burgeoning relationship is to ask permission to interrupt them, e.g. 'If you are giving me more information than is necessary to gain an understanding of your problems, can I have your permission to step in and stop you?' In this manner, therapists can communicate to clients that action is required from them rather than more talk. Interrupting without permission can create the impression of therapist rudeness or insensitivity.

Some clients may want immediate help with practical problems rather than following the REBT approach of tackling emotional problems first and then their practical aspects next. For example, a client wants to discuss a career move because she has to give an answer to her boss within 24 hours of the first therapy session. The client may not realise or admit how anxious she is about making a decision. The therapist can discuss the pros and cons of such a move, her vocational expectations, etc., in order to help her make up her mind. In this way, the therapist addresses both her immediate needs as well as developing hypotheses about her anxiety which he can present in subsequent sessions. Some REBT therapists might declare 'We don't do it that way!' with this about-face in the order of problem-solving. These therapists should address their own intransigence so they realise that clients' requirements take precedence in therapy over their own rigid adherence to REBT protocol.

When clients have difficulties accepting the 'ABC' model

The 'ABC' model of emotional disturbance is the cornerstone of REBT theory and practice (Dryden 2009a). It is also known as the 'ABC's of REBT. This model sets out a primarily cognitively orientated theory of emotions. 'A' stands for adversities, which are negative activating events (including interpretations and inferences) that are mediated by beliefs ('B'), which, in turn, largely determine the emotional, behavioural and consequences one will experience at 'C'. Clients are taught that 'B' not 'A' lies at the core of their emotional reactions to events, e.g. 'It's not being rejected that makes you depressed but rather the beliefs that you hold about being rejected that are mainly responsible for your current state'. For many clients, the 'B'–'C' connection represents a paradigmatic or radical shift in their understanding of emotional causation, e.g. 'You mean to tell me that I upset myself over my neighbour's obnoxious behaviour and he doesn't have much to do with it?' Hence the many difficulties, sometimes sheer incredulity, clients experience in accepting the 'ABC' model and which we will now examine.

When clients think that 'A' causes 'C'

'A'–'C' thinking refers to clients' statements which place primary responsibility for their emotional problems ('C') on others, external events, or the world ('A'), e.g. 'My boss makes me angry'; 'The weather makes me depressed'; 'Life makes me feel ashamed of myself'. There is no inkling in these statements of any sense of personal involvement in helping to create these emotional reactions. Such clients are dubbed in REBT as 'A'–'C' thinkers. Probably the majority of clients who enter therapy will subscribe to this type of thinking, which will have been reinforced by family, peer and cultural teaching, e.g. 'My parents always told me that without a good job you're nothing in life'; advertising which equates a 'beautiful body' with being happy and worthwhile. Because the 'A' and 'C' components are usually so inextricably linked in the client's mind, the therapist has to prise them apart in order for clients to see the presence and importance of their belief system ('B'). This is necessary in order to teach clients the principles of general and specific emotional responsibility (Dryden and Branch 2008). This usually involves a two-stage process whereby clients are taught how their thoughts influence their feelings before focusing on the disturbance-producing properties of rigid musts and shoulds. Understanding the thought–feeling link is a vital part of clients' induction into REBT and often more time is spent on establishing this general connection, thereby 'opening the way' for them to grasp the specific role of dogmatic thinking in their emotional disturbance.

When clients have difficulties with the concept of general emotional responsibility

The concept of general emotional responsibility states that you feel as you think and therefore clients' individual thought patterns are elicited in order to show them how they largely disturb themselves over adverse or unpleasant events in their lives. As some clients might be clamouring to tell their 'He/she/it makes me miserable' stories, therapists can, if it seems clinically relevant, get their point of view across first as in the following:

Therapist:	Just before we come to your problems, you seem very anxious. Is that because you got here ten minutes' late?
Client:	Yes, that's right. I rushed all the way here. I was desperate not to be late.
Therapist:	What were you anxious about in getting here late?
Client:	That you would think very badly of me. I want your help but I can't get here on time. That would make me more inadequate than I already am.
Therapist:	Let me ask you this: is it simply getting here late that makes you anxious or your belief that it would reveal more of your inadequacy?
Client:	Both?
Therapist:	Well, if you got here late and you didn't really care at all, would you be anxious?
Client:	I suppose I wouldn't have been. I just didn't want to appear more screwed up than I already am.
Therapist:	Can you see what point I'm trying to make?
Client:	Well, I suppose if I didn't have that idea, I wouldn't have been anxious.
Therapist:	Good. That our ideas and thoughts largely create our emotional problems is a point I will keep on coming back to. Okay, what would you like to talk about?

In this example, the therapist immediately orientates the client towards 'B'–'C' thinking and thereby establishes a reference point he can repeatedly bring her back to in order to help attenuate her 'A'–'C' thinking. Throughout therapy, therapists need to be mindful of only employing 'B'–'C' language to reinforce the 'ABC' model they are teaching and 'wean' their clients off 'A'–'C' language:

> *Client:*   My husband treats me like a doormat.
> *Therapist:* Why do you let him treat you like that?

Clients frequently protest that 'I didn't say that!' Therapists need to keep on explaining why they are restructuring clients' statements in this way. However, therapists should be wary of restructuring too much or too often as this can be easily interpreted by the client as arrogance, insensitivity, rudeness, not listening or attempts at brainwashing. Such zealousness can impede the development of or eventually destroy the working alliance as each side 'digs in' to defend their view of emotional causation.

Some clients might agree that lateness per se (or being early) is not the cause of their anxiety, but the meaning they attach to their lateness is the real culprit. However, even though they acknowledge the instrumental role of their thinking in this example, they are not persuaded it has any relevance to the real problems they want to discuss in therapy – problems where, in their view, 'A' really does cause 'C'. For example, clients may state that losing their job made them very depressed. Here therapists can use a technique known as contrasts (Wessler and Wessler 1980) to demonstrate that clients' thinking still plays a primary role in their emotional problems:

> *Therapist:* Would fifty people, all at the same position and salary as you, all be depressed about losing their jobs?
> *Client:*   Well, they wouldn't be happy about it.
> *Therapist:* Probably not, but would they all be depressed?
> *Client:*   I expect a few of them wouldn't be too upset. Their job might not mean everything to them like it does to me.
> *Therapist:* And that's the point – different ideas about the same situation lead to different emotional reactions to it. Was there a time in your life when you lost a job but didn't become depressed about it?
> *Client:*   Yeah, when I was a lot younger. But it wasn't important to me unlike this job.
> *Therapist:* Then it didn't matter so much, now it's everything to you.

> *Client:*   That's true. I wasn't so wound up about it then.
> *Therapist:*   With this present job, have you always believed that it
>   means everything to you?
> *Client:*   I've always considered it to be very important to me, but
>   I suppose I became totally wrapped up in it after the
>   divorce and my social life began to disappear.
> *Therapist:*   If you had lost your job before the divorce, would you
>   have been so depressed?
> *Client:*   I would have been really irritable and miserable for a
>   while but nothing like I am now.

In this illustration, the therapist employs three different ways to demonstrate to the client that 'B', not 'A', is mainly responsible for his 'C' reactions to losing his job:

1   By asking the client if a large number of people (fifty in this example) would all react in exactly the same way to the same event. The client grudgingly concedes that a few might not. It is advisable at this stage of therapy not to push for a higher number who would have reacted differently; it is enough that he has made the concession. The client then unwittingly provides the answer to why these few would not become depressed – 'their job might not mean everything to them like it does to me'; in other words, it is the reason for his existence.

2   By seeking evidence from earlier in his life when he did not become depressed about losing his job. This evidence contradicts his 'A'–'C' statements because his attitude then towards his job was more relaxed as opposed to his current all-or-nothing thinking.

3   By showing him that even in his present job, his attitude to it has not remained constant and therefore produced different emotional reactions pre- and post-divorce.

It is important when teaching the 'B'–'C' connection not to create the impression or state as a fact that thinking totally produces feeling and that unpleasant life events are of no significance in the development of emotional disturbance. As well as being contrary to REBT theory and practice, the potentially destructive effects upon the working alliance hardly need spelling out. Therefore, therapists are strongly reminded not to minimise the impact of clients' adversities upon their feelings. For example, 'Your girlfriend running off with your best friend must seem like the ultimate betrayal, but isn't your view of yourself as now completely worthless because of this betrayal actually the most devastating act of all?' Here the therapist is trying to be strongly empathic yet challenging at the same time. Obviously some clients will insist that 'A' does cause 'C' and rest their case with the horror of the Nazi concentration camps, an example that clients frequently use in order to demolish the therapist's arguments. This issue will be considered later in the chapter.

Another means of conveying 'B'–'C' thinking to sceptical clients is to teach them that they feel as they think (Burns 1980):

Therapist:	How would you feel if you believed your life was empty, boring and friendless?
Client:	I expect I'd feel pretty bad.
Therapist:	If you were to be more precise, which emotion in particular would 'pretty bad' refer to?
Client:	I'm not sure what you mean.
Therapist:	Well, would you feel depressed, angry, hurt, for example?
Client:	Oh, I see what you mean. Er, depressed. Yeah, that's it, depressed.
Therapist:	Okay, how would you feel if you were going to a job interview and believed that all the other applicants would perform better than you?
Client:	I'd feel bloody anxious. Who wants to be judged as inferior?
Therapist:	You've just reinforced my point. One last example. How would you feel if you believed that you had acted like a drunken fool at a party and made an unwanted pass at a friend's wife?
Client:	If I did behave like that, I would feel very ashamed and avoid both of them for a while. But surely not everyone would feel like that? I know someone who definitely would not have felt like that.
Therapist:	Because he would have told himself . . .?
Client:	Probably because he couldn't care less and that parties are for enjoying yourself.
Therapist:	And that's why he would have felt very differently about it.

In this therapy excerpt, the therapist is teaching the client to note how his thoughts precede and influence his feelings. Important points to consider are the following:

1   In response to the therapist's first question, the client says he would feel 'pretty bad'. REBT practice requires that the client specify an unhealthy negative emotion (e.g. anxiety, guilt, depression) in order to make explicit the cognitive content of that particular emotion. By

accepting 'pretty bad' as an emotion, both therapist and client would remain stranded at a level of vagueness and uncertainty – which emotion(s) is the client actually referring to? – which would diminish both the educational and therapeutic aspects of REBT.

2   The client has provided more grist for the cognitive mill by emphasising the anxiety-provoking nature of being seen as inferior in others' eyes.

3   While the client says he would feel ashamed of his drunken behaviour, it occurs to him that not everyone would feel the same way and thereby implies a challenge to the therapist's thesis. However, he actually strengthens the therapist's arguments because his friend would think very differently about the same situation and therefore not become emotionally disturbed about it.

Therapy provides many examples where clients can be repeatedly shown that they feel as they think (e.g. strong emotion or signs of physical tension in the session) in order for them to identify and challenge their disturbance-producing ideas.

When clients believe that others make them upset

In the mind of many clients, other people are undoubtedly the source of their emotional problems and this is reflected in their use of language, e.g. 'You make me angry by asking all these questions'; 'My wife makes me feel guilty because I forgot her birthday'. Such statements imply that clients have no control over their feelings and therefore cannot be held responsible for them. Other people not only cause these problems but also usually have the solution to them, e.g. 'If my wife would stop going on about how much her birthday means to her then I wouldn't feel so guilty'. The therapist's task is to teach clients that they largely disturb themselves over others' behaviour. This will be revealed by examining their internal statements or self-talk; so with regard to the first example, the therapist might say to the client, 'Let's see what you're saying to yourself that really gets you angry about these questions I'm asking you'. The idea that clients disturb themselves and thereby need to restructure their statements accordingly is often met with incredulity, and sometimes downright hostility:

> *Client:*   What do you mean that I upset myself? You're making me angry by saying that.
> *Therapist:*   How am I doing that?
> *Client:*   By talking bloody crap!
> *Therapist:*   I am not expecting you to agree with me, but why do you get angry about me expressing a point of view?

Client:	Because you shouldn't talk such crap. No one goes around saying 'I upset myself'. If they do, they must be a complete nutter.
Therapist:	Let me ask you this: if you were sitting there thinking he is talking crap but I couldn't care less what he says, would you get so steamed up about it?
Client:	Well, if I couldn't give a toss what you say, then I'd just probably laugh at you.
Therapist:	And am I responsible for making you laugh as well?
Client:	Yeah, because you're still talking crap.
Therapist:	Okay, so I have this tremendous power over you to make you angry, happy, sing and dance, whatever. So are you just a puppet manipulated by others?
Client:	No one controls me.
Therapist:	I apparently do.
Client:	No, you certainly don't!
Therapist:	Well, you can't have it both ways. So who controls your thinking and decides how to respond to things?
Client:	I do.
Therapist:	Therefore who makes you angry?
Client:	I suppose the answer is me, but I'm still not convinced.

In this excerpt, the client is still very doubtful about the therapist's arguments but at least the client has made small inroads into the therapist's thinking, which the client can now seek to widen and deepen. Other clients may see lack of emotional control as a way of life because they believe others have deprived them of it:

Client:	I've felt depressed on and off for about fifteen years. My husband has made me like this.
Therapist:	How has he been able to do that?
Client:	Getting at me all the time. Putting me down, telling me I'm useless at everything. That sort of thing.
Therapist:	Do you agree with him?
Client:	It's not that I agree with him. He makes me feel like that. It's been going on for so long.
Therapist:	How did you see yourself before you met him?
Client:	I didn't have much confidence in myself, low self-esteem, that sort of thing. I was grateful that he married me and took me off the shelf.
Therapist:	I understand how difficult it must be living with all that verbal abuse, but don't you really agree with his put

> | | |
> |---|---|
> | | downs because these ideas are already in your head? Do you know who put them there? |
> | *Client:* | He did. |
> | *Therapist:* | No, you did. You've already told me how you saw yourself before you met him. Because you have a self-depreciating philosophy, you easily agree with and apply to yourself what your husband says about you. |
> | *Client:* | It's hard to believe what you say. I've been thinking it's him all these years and you say it's mostly my fault. If it's true what you say, then I must be really pathetic for making myself so unhappy for all these years and not seeing it. |
> | *Therapist:* | I certainly would not agree that you are pathetic and we'll come to that in a moment, but if we don't agree with or believe what others say about us, then they can't really affect us. |
> | *Client:* | Okay, if I accept what you say, how do I learn to turn him off after all these years? |
> | *Therapist:* | By examining your ideas rather than his. |

Clients are ultimately responsible for their ideas and beliefs; others cannot put ideas into their heads unless they are allowed to in some way, e.g. a man who complains that his girlfriend's unkind comments make him feel worthless as a lover is shown that her comments are only adding to his considerable self-doubt about his sexual prowess. Other clients may say they are not responsible for the way they think as they have been 'brainwashed' by others or society, e.g. 'The reason I'm always on a diet is because everywhere you look you see pictures of thin women. You can't feel good about yourself if you're not thin'. Rather than being brainwashed, clients are shown that they are insufficiently critical of the messages delivered by others, media, advertising, society, etc. Therapy can become the forum where clients restore their critical faculties by subjecting their 'brainwashed beliefs' to scrutiny.

Another problem that clients have with accepting emotional responsibility is that they confuse responsibility with blame and proceed to condemn themselves as in the following therapy excerpt:

> | | |
> |---|---|
> | *Client:* | I've been thinking it's him all these years and you say it's mostly my fault *[the therapist never used the word 'fault']*. If it's true what you say, then I must be really pathetic for making myself so unhappy for all these years and not seeing it. |

So it is easy to understand clients' reluctance or refusal to acknowledge their self-induced emotional disturbance. The therapist's skill is to encourage clients to accept responsibility but without blaming themselves for this disturbance:

Therapist: Let's be really clear on the important differences between responsibility and blame. Because you feel as you think, you are mainly responsible for the negative ideas that keep your depression going. Of course, your husband has greatly reinforced what you already think. Now, if you accept responsibility for your emotional states, you can also decide not to condemn yourself for creating them.

Client: What do I do if I don't put myself down?

Therapist: You can learn to accept yourself with these problems and I'll teach you ways of fighting back so you can gain greater control of your emotions. Now can you put all that back to me in your own words?

Client: Let me see if I've got this straight. I've mainly been messing myself up all these years. I don't have to put the boot in any more – I'll leave that to my husband. I can be responsible for my feelings and still remain nice to myself. And you're going to teach me how to get rid of these bad feelings. Sounds too good to be true.

Therapist: Very well summarised. Now let's get to grips with your problems.

When clients believe that they can't escape their past

Many clients often state that past events dictate or shape their present feelings and behaviour and therefore they are prisoners of the past, e.g. 'He took all the money from our joint account and ran off with someone else. I was devastated. It still makes me very bitter after all these years and I'll never be free of it'. The client assumes that past, albeit grim, events have an iron grip on her present and future life. REBT therapists seek to show clients that it is not past events which cause present problems, but rather the attitudes they have constructed from these events and continue to reindoctrinate themselves with in the present. However, many clients want to explore their past, often at interminable length, in order to get at the roots of the problem. While acknowledging that a client's irrational beliefs have a developmental history 'the crucial thing is for him or her to give up these currently held ideas so that tomorrow's existence can be better than yesterday's' (Grieger and Boyd 1980: 76–7). The following excerpt will clarify some of these points:

Client:	My parents dumped me in a children's home when I was 10 years old. Unwanted, unloved, abandoned.
Therapist:	And how do you feel today about being dumped in a children's home twenty years ago?
Client:	That's a stupid question! How do you expect me to feel – happy? I'm still angry and depressed of course. My parents made me feel worthless by what they did to me.
Therapist:	Even if that was their intention then, why do you still believe you are worthless today?
Client:	Because of what happened when I was 10. What do you expect me to say to them as they hand me over to a children's home: 'It's okay, I forgive you?' If I could understand why they did it to me I might feel a bit better about myself.
Therapist:	Let's say they did it because they couldn't cope financially with your upbringing. Would you feel happier?
Client:	No. Other parents managed it.
Therapist:	I understand how very difficult it must have been to see it any other way when you're 10, but when did you start to think for yourself – 16, 18, 21?
Client:	18, I suppose.
Therapist:	Okay, you've had twelve years to challenge this idea that you're worthless. Have you made any progress?
Client:	How can I make progress? It's their idea, not mine.
Therapist:	Well, let's say you got the idea from your parents, but you have been carrying it in your head ever since. *(tapping his forehead)* You still choose to believe it. That's the point.
Client:	I never thought of it like that. Is it really possible to see it any differently after all these years?
Therapist:	Yes it is, and it certainly won't take twenty years to change and they will probably be much happier than the last twenty.
Client:	I'd like to try it then.

The concept of free will can also be used to encourage clients to accept emotional responsibility. If they believe they have some freedom of choice in how they respond to past and present events in their lives, this can be contrasted with their 'chained to the past' arguments, e.g. 'We've already discussed how you chose not to be ground down by certain unpleasant past events, so why with this particular event, losing your job two years ago, do you believe you can't recover from it?' In this case, the client is not exercising his free will, for whatever reason, and the therapist needs to discover why.

Responding to the 'concentration camp exception' argument

Many clients may grudgingly accept that their thinking, rather than events, does play a significant part in creating their emotional problems, but then counter with an argument that they believe will knock the wind out of the therapist's sails: 'It might be true in my case but there's absolutely no way that argument can be used with those who suffered in the Nazi concentration camps. Their suffering was totally caused by others'. While agreeing with the client's last point, the therapist can point out that those not selected for immediate extermination were put to work in the camps under the most appalling conditions and that their attitude to survival was crucial in determining how they coped with this barbarous treatment. Thus, some individuals were sustained by their religious faith which meant that God was with them even (or particularly) in the camps; some Jews willed themselves to survive in order to bear witness to Nazi atrocities in the post-war reckoning. Others, like Viktor Frankl (the founder of logotherapy and a survivor of Auschwitz), showed themselves that only they, not the Nazis, could deprive themselves of their humanity. Whatever the foundation of their belief, it gave individuals the determination to stay alive and fight back in their own way. Similar stories of incredible fortitude are described in Alexander Solzhenitsyn's *The Gulag Archipelago*, an account of the hardships and brutality of the Soviet prison camp system.

When clients say: 'I don't think anything'

Some clients protest that nothing passes through their mind when they experience, for example, anxiety or anger, e.g. 'One minute I'm fine, the next minute I'm a quivering jelly. It just came out of the blue'. Therefore, they claim, the 'ABC' model does not apply to them. Beck (1976) points out that many of our thoughts and ideas are automatic and therefore it is not always immediately apparent to us what we are thinking. However, it is relatively easy to gain access to our automatic thoughts and ideas as they usually lie just outside of our awareness:

Therapist:	Just before you turned to jelly, did anything happen that you can remember?
Client:	Only that the phone rang. My sister answered it. It was only my girlfriend saying she'd be round later. So it was good news.
Therapist:	Were you expecting bad news?
Client:	Well, I was a bit worried.
Therapist:	What about?

Client:	To be honest, we've been having trouble, rowing and stuff. I know this other bloke has been sniffing around. I think she likes him. She was seen talking to him the other day.
Therapist:	How much do you care about her?
Client:	I'm nuts about her. I'd be devastated if she dumped me.
Therapist:	So you were looking forward to her phone call but at the same time you were thinking . . .?
Client:	She'd given me the elbow and run off with him. I'm feeling a bit jelly-like again. Oh God!
Therapist:	Do you still believe that your anxiety came out of the blue?
Client:	No, but that doesn't make it any easier to deal with.
Therapist:	We'll come to that.

In this illustration, the 'way in' that the therapist was looking for to tease out the client's thinking was his remark that the telephone call 'was good news'. This enabled the therapist to test out the hypothesis that the client was expecting the opposite. This revealed a string of anxious thoughts culminating in feelings of devastation at the prospect of being rejected. Corroboration was given by the client that the therapist was on the right track by the return of his 'jelly-like' symptoms.

Some clients can be very insistent that there is no 'B' between the 'A' and 'C'; therapists should not be discouraged by this and persevere (but not dogmatically) in order to reveal it to them. As Hauck (1980: 237) says: 'Don't lose faith in your theory'.

When clients want to explore their feelings, not their thinking

Many clients assume that lengthy explorations of their disturbed feelings will somehow help to remove them. Such an approach to therapy may have been strengthened by their previous experiences with psychodynamic therapy. Therefore they want to focus only on feelings and not get side-tracked into discussing the ideas that might be linked to their problems, e.g. 'I'm not interested in my thoughts. Feelings are what it's all about. What's down here, not up there' (pats her stomach, then taps her head). What is often implied in such statements is that thinking and feeling are totally separate processes. Ellis (1994) has consistently argued since he founded REBT in the mid-1950s that sustained feeling is usually accompanied by or the direct result of sustained thinking; in many respects, thinking and feeling are the same thing. REBT therapists therefore seek emotional change by scrutinising clients' disturbance-producing ideas:

Therapist:	If you change your thinking, you'll be able to change your feelings. They are so closely tied together.
Client:	I thought they were miles apart.
Therapist:	Well, let's try an experiment. You talk about a feeling and as soon as an idea emerges I'll stop you. Is that okay?
Client:	Yeah, I'm willing to try that. Well, I get angry a lot in my life. I explode more than I care to admit. People seem to get in my way all the time and . . .
Therapist:	Please stop. An angry idea seems to be that people are blocking and frustrating you in some way. I'm not saying it's the main one, but an idea did rear its ugly head very quickly.
Client:	I thought I was still talking about my feelings.
Therapist:	Well, you are – through your ideas. Can we try another experiment?
Client:	Okay, I hope this one will make things clearer.
Therapist:	Let's stay with it for a bit longer and it should do. Describe a recent event where you felt upset, but don't identify the emotion. Leave that to me.
Client:	Well, my husband keeps promising to take me away for the weekend, and a few weeks ago we were ready to go and he cancelled it at the last minute due to business problems. I felt so let down, even betrayed by his behaviour. I was so looking forward to going.
Therapist:	Okay, was the feeling hurt?
Client:	Yes it was. How did you know that?
Therapist:	By listening for the ideas underlying the feeling. Did you sulk?
Client:	For the whole weekend. How did you know I sulked?
Therapist:	Because particular behaviours are associated with certain emotions and I'm able to work out both by . . .
Client:	Would it be my ideas?
Therapist:	Go to the top of the class. Do you want to try this therapy as a way of changing some of the unpleasant feelings you've described?
Client:	I'll try it, but I'll keep an open mind at the same time.

Clients need to be reminded frequently of the distinction between thinking and feeling and how the former significantly influences the latter, so they can understand within the 'ABC' model the origins and maintenance of their emotional problems. As we have pointed out, because this is a crucial task for the therapist to perform, establishing general emotional responsibility in the early stages of therapy is usually considered to be more important than focusing on the particularities of its specific REBT form (though not all REBT therapists would agree with this double-barrelled approach to self-created disturbance and therefore some teach only its specific form).

When clients have difficulties with the concept of specific emotional responsibility

REBT's conception of emotional disturbance is that it stems mainly from individuals' rigid and absolute beliefs in the form of musts, shoulds, have to's, got to's and oughts, e.g. 'I must have your love and I am worthless without it'; 'You have to make things easy for me and if you don't, I can't stand it'. Emotional health in REBT is seen as underpinned largely by non-dogmatic desires and preferences, e.g. 'I would greatly prefer your love but I don't need it. If I don't receive it, it would be hard to accept, but I can still accept myself'; 'I hope you make things easier for me but you don't have to do so. If you don't, it would be hard, but I can stand the struggle involved'. Clients are taught to detect and discriminate between their demands and needs (irrational or self-defeating) versus their desires and wants (rational or self-helping).

Dealing with clients' use of the word 'should'

At first glance, the word 'should' may seem innocuous, yet its potentially pathological character can appear when clients transmute preferential shoulds into absolute ones, e.g. the annoyance-inducing 'You (preferably) shouldn't talk to me like that' versus the anger-producing 'You (absolutely) shouldn't talk to me like that!' In the following extract, the therapist shows the client how his self-created disturbance primarily arises from his emphasis on the rigid use of 'should' rather than directly caused by his girlfriend's non-compliance:

> *Client:*   My girlfriend makes me angry. She never listens to my point of view.
> *Therapist:* How does she make you angry?
> *Client:*   I've just told you – she should bloody well listen to what I'm saying! She does my head in.
> *Therapist:* I want to put it the other way round: you make yourself angry by continually demanding how she should be behaving.

Client:	Well, she should listen. I listen to her.
Therapist:	You listen to her, so she should *(stresses word)* listen to you.
Client:	Exactly. Wouldn't you get angry if I didn't listen to you?
Therapist:	No, because there's no reason why you absolutely should *(stresses word again)* listen to me, but it would be desirable if you did because I'm here to help you. Look, every time you use the word 'should' in an absolute sense you're setting yourself up as a dictator and demanding how your girlfriend should behave. You're also firing up your own boiler and ready to explode when she doesn't do what you demand. So you do your head in, not your girlfriend.
Client:	Okay, you might have a point there, but it would be nice if she did listen to me. You're not going to disagree with that, are you?
Therapist:	No, that's fine if you keep to that desire. Now, how would you feel if you believed that 'it would be very nice if she listened to me but there is no reason why she absolutely should listen to me'?
Client:	I'd be pissed off, but not angry. My boiler wouldn't be at danger level.
Therapist:	Do you enjoy exploding in front of her?
Client:	No, I don't! I feel like a right prat.
Therapist:	So how can you stop behaving like a 'right prat' as you call yourself?
Client:	Stop making myself angry.
Therapist:	And how can you accomplish that?
Client:	Not using the word 'should'.
Therapist:	Only in its absolute form. There's nothing wrong with using it as a preference, but when you cross that dividing line . . .
Client:	I'll start exploding again.
Therapist:	Right. I'll show you how to keep on the non-exploding side of that divide.

Points to note in this exchange from therapy are the following:

1   The therapist ties the client's absolute 'should' to his anger and contrasts it with the preferential statement 'it would be nice if . . .' in order to produce a different emotional outcome.
2   The therapist is modelling specific emotional responsibility by saying she would not disturb herself because she is not insisting that the client

listens to her; however, she does point out that she still adheres to her non-disturbed desire for his attention.

3   By focusing on what the client does not like about his angry behaviour, the therapist hastens his acceptance of specific emotional responsibility, but makes sure he puts it in his own words so that they both agree on the cognitive roots of his anger.

4   The therapist emphasises that it is only absolute shoulds the client should steer clear of and not the preferable form that has just been used in this sentence.

Responding to the 'It's only a word' criticism

Horney (1950) spoke of the 'tyranny of the shoulds' that people live by. 'Musturbatory' (musts) thinking plays a similarly totalitarian role in people's lives. Clients are usually unaware of the absolutist philosophies that lie behind their unconditional musts and which lead them to inflict emotional harm upon themselves. When the therapist helps the client to identify their rigid belief in the form of a 'must', for example, they may say that as must is only a word, it can't have so much power. In the interchange below, the therapist helps the client see that it is not the word 'must' that has the power to disturb her, but the meaning that she invests in the word:

Client:	I'm really anxious about the exam.
Therapist:	What are you anxious about?
Client:	Failing, of course.
Therapist:	And if you did fail, what then?
Client:	If I fail the exam, I'll be completely useless.
Therapist:	Are your friends as anxious as you are?
Client:	Well, no one wants to fail, but some of my friends are pretty okay about the exam.
Therapist:	And that's why it's not the exam itself that's making you anxious; it's the way you think about the exam that is the real problem.
Client:	What, my thinking?
Therapist:	Something like 'I must pass this exam in order not to see myself as completely useless'. Does this sound familiar?
Client:	Yeah, I can hear myself saying that. But how can that make me anxious?
Therapist:	Your use of the word 'must' puts you under tremendous pressure and drives your anxiety. It does not allow you any room to manoeuvre if things go wrong.
Client:	It's only a word. Aren't you going over the top?

Therapist:	It's a word that contains a self-defeating outlook and packs an emotional wallop. What kind of outlook do you think your friends hold – the ones who are not stressed out about the exam?
Client:	That's easy: they say they're going to do their very best, but it's not the end of the world if they fail. They certainly wouldn't see themselves as I would. They can always take it again.
Therapist:	What do you notice between their attitude and yours?
Client:	They are not driving themselves round the bend like I am.
Therapist:	Are they studying any less than you are?
Client:	I don't think so. As we're talking about this, I realise I get so anxious that my brain freezes and I can't take anything in.
Therapist:	Right. That won't help your studying. Do you now see how you make yourself anxious?
Client:	Yes.
Therapist:	How?
Client:	By saying to myself that 'I must succeed at all costs'. I'm not allowing myself the possibility of failing. It's beginning to sink in, so how do I get rid of this horrible word?
Therapist:	Well, it's not the word itself you want to get rid of but the self-defeating ideas that lurk behind it. We could start by looking at the healthy and flexible attitudes some of your friends seem to have. Maybe you could learn to adopt and act upon some of these attitudes if you find them helpful.
Client:	I hope so.

Once clients have accepted emotional responsibility at both the general and specific levels (though, as we have said, not all REBT therapists agree with this double-headed approach to teaching self-induced disturbance), they are now ready to formulate their goals for change.

Chapter 4

Dealing with client resistance in the goals domain of the working alliance

Goals for change are what usually bring clients to the therapist's office. Bordin (1979) suggests that agreement between the therapist and client on the latter's goals for change is one of the key components in the development of a successful working alliance. However, what may seem like a relatively straightforward process is often filled with misunderstandings and pitfalls as both sides strive to reach an agreement on therapeutic change. REBT therapists like to establish treatment goals that are specific, clear and measurable, so that progress or the lack of it can be determined. This chapter looks at some of the difficulties that clients experience in following or accepting such criteria for goal-setting.

When clients want to change 'C' by changing 'A' rather than by changing 'B'

Clients frequently state that their goal in therapy is to get others (e.g. partner, in-law, boss, neighbour) to change before they can or that simply through others changing, they will automatically feel better, e.g. 'If my husband pays more attention to me then I won't be so angry; so what can I do to get him to change?' This is what in REBT we refer to as changing the 'A'. Such clients need to be socialised to REBT goal-setting methods in order for them to profit from this approach. REBT's position on this is that it is important for the client to target his disturbed feelings for change before trying to influence others to change. He does this of course by changing 'B'. So how can REBT therapists respond when clients want to change their disturbed feelings at 'C' by changing adversities at 'A'? Here is an example:

> *Therapist:* In REBT, the focus of change is squarely on the client. You are the one seeking therapy, not your husband.
>
> *Client:* But he's the one making me angry, so the focus should be on him. He should damn well pay more attention to me!

Therapist:	REBT is first and foremost about helping clients to overcome their largely self-created emotional upsets – in your case, anger – and then deciding what practical steps can be taken to make life more pleasurable for or acceptable to them.
Client:	How can I agree to that when I'm not the problem?
Therapist:	You are the one that's angry, not your husband. If I did agree with your goal, how am I supposed to change him when he isn't here, and, by what you say, wouldn't be seen dead in therapy?
Client:	Well, I thought you would be able to tell me how to change him.
Therapist:	I don't have such magical powers, but later in therapy we can look at ways in which you might be able to exert some influence on his behaviour.
Client:	Why can't we do that now?
Therapist:	Because it's highly unlikely that you will positively influence him while you're angry.
Client:	How can you be so sure?
Therapist:	Because it hasn't worked so far.
Client:	Okay, (*wearily*) you win. What do we do then?
Therapist:	I'll show you how to stop making yourself angry about his behaviour and then . . .
Client:	Am I just supposed to put up with it then? Not care any more?
Therapist:	No, you can express strong annoyance or disapproval of his behaviour while at the same time trying to get him to change.
Client:	What if that doesn't work?
Therapist:	Then you can decide not to go back to making yourself angry and consider other options.
Client:	Such as . . .?
Therapist:	How long you're prepared to continue to put up with it.
Client:	You mean leave him?
Therapist:	That could be a longer-term option if his behaviour doesn't change.
Client:	I couldn't do that.

In this illustration, the following are important points to note:

1   The therapist repeatedly puts the locus of change within the client and does not let the therapeutic focus switch to her husband's behaviour.

This is necessary if the client is to accept emotional responsibility for her anger.

2   If the therapist did focus on her husband, this would not only be a highly unrealistic goal to agree to, but also smack of therapist arrogance (he can change people's behaviour without them coming to therapy). However, he does say there might be ways of influencing her husband's behaviour as part of her goals after she has undisturbed herself. Therefore he is linking the work she has to do on herself with future potential benefits.

3   The client believes if she gives up her anger, the only alternative is not to care any longer. The therapist shows her that she can display healthy negative emotions which express her disappointment while at the same time seeking constructive ways of attempting to change her husband's behaviour.

4   If the client's attempts fail, she has the choice whether to make herself angry again or decide on another course of action. When she says, 'I couldn't do that [leave him]', the therapist can make a mental note that she may be harbouring other disturbance-producing beliefs that require therapeutic attention, e.g. 'I couldn't bear living on my own that's why he has to change'; 'Despite his behaviour, I need him in order to be happy'.

Clients who blame external events or circumstances (e.g. stuck in a boring job, noisy neighbours) for their emotional problems might understandably state that their goal is to get out of or away from these adverse 'A's (activating events) as quickly as possible. This is a practical goal rather than an emotional one. However, if therapists accede to this goal, they will be helping clients to change the 'A' rather than stay put and undisturb themselves in the face of these 'A's. The therapist is not advocating that clients should 'just put up with it' but the danger in the practical solution is that their disturbance-creating beliefs will remain intact, e.g. 'I can't stand a job that isn't always interesting'; 'I'm moving away because I'm ashamed of myself for not being able to confront them about the noise'. If similar circumstances or events occur again, this will probably reactivate the clients' irrational or self-defeating ideas. Once clients remove their emotional disturbances (putting up with his job so 'I can learn to stand it'; accepting herself for her perceived weakness and learning assertive techniques) they can then decide what productive course of action to pursue.

Helping clients translate behavioural goals into emotional ones

Clients may present in therapy complaining of, for example, lack of confidence, procrastination or social avoidance, e.g. 'I'm fed up with always putting off writing this article. What I need from you is a good kick up the backside to get going'. While it might be tempting to offer the client a collection of behavioural techniques in an attempt to overcome his procrastination, the real challenge for the therapist is to reveal to the client the emotional blocks behind it:

Client:	If I could get going on this article, I'd be really happy.
Therapist:	Okay, vividly imagine that you're sitting down at your desk ready to start your article. Now how do you feel?
Client:	I feel uncomfortable, a bit edgy. Not relaxed at all.
Therapist:	But what emotion are you experiencing?
Client:	I'd say anxiety.
Therapist:	What is anxiety-provoking in your mind as you sit there ready to start?
Client:	I'm not sure if it's going to be good enough.
Therapist:	And let's assume it won't be. Then what?
Client:	The publishers might reject it *(client appears very tense)*.
Therapist:	Let's say that they do. Picture yourself reading the rejection slip in mounting disbelief. Then what?
Client:	That's it. The rejection slip means I'm a miserable and worthless failure. A despicable fraud.
Therapist:	So what you're most anxious about is having your article rejected by the publisher which, if it happened, your belief would be that this would prove that you are a failure and a fraud. Is that right?
Client:	*(sighs deeply)* Yeah, that's the squalid truth. I keep on trying to deceive myself that I'm a lazy bastard. It doesn't hurt as much.
Therapist:	Okay, if I can help you feel concerned about the possibility of failure and teach you self-acceptance whatever happens, will that help you to tackle your procrastination?
Client:	It sounds all right in theory.
Therapist:	Well, you put all your energy into writing a good article rather than wasting it on fear of failure. If it gets turned down, you can ask for constructive feedback and resubmit it. If you don't submit it, you definitely will fail in your bid to become a writer.
Client:	Yeah, I know. That's the real goal – coping with failure.
Therapist:	If you're prepared not to let yourself be intimidated by it, you'll stand much more chance of becoming a professional writer through sustained and persistent effort.

> *Client:*   Okay, I'll give it a shot. I hope I don't have to put in too
> much effort.

In the above extract from therapy, important points to consider are the following:

1   Procrastination is usually underpinned by anxiety and the therapist demonstrates how to 'release' it by encouraging the client to imagine carrying out the avoided activity. Another way of identifying the underlying emotion would be a homework task for the client of actually sitting and starting to write the article.
2   That the client's presenting problem as defined, avoiding writing an article, looks very different when assessed through inference chaining – fear of failure and subsequent self-damnation.
3   The initial goal was for a 'good kick up the backside to get me going', which probably meant a stiff talking to from the therapist. The goal that emerged from the assessment was much more ambitious: overcoming the client's anxiety and replacing it with concern while learning to accept himself in the face of possible rejection from the publishers. If the client does not strive for such goals he will probably bring about what he fears – seeing himself as a failure.
4   The client's parting comment 'I hope I don't have to put in too much effort' may indicate the presence of discomfort intolerance ideas. Wessler and Wessler (1980: 104) state that discomfort intolerance is almost always involved in procrastination as the 'short-term discomfort of engaging in a task is avoided in spite of the potential long-term benefits of completing the task'.
5   Though it did not emerge in the therapy extract, less commonly found in procrastination is a kind of narcissistic anger that some individuals have about putting forward for judgement themselves or their work when their superiority or talent should be self-evident. The client had this problem as well and one of us (MN) negotiated with him the following goal: to see himself as a fallible and equal rather than superior human being, but he might be a superior writer and the only way to find out was to submit his work.

When clients want to set indifference as a goal

REBT therapists prefer clients to select healthy negative emotions and their associated constructive behaviours as therapeutic goals. However, clients often believe that indifference, passivity or resignation is the best way to deal with emotional distress, e.g. 'This is the third girlfriend to dump me in as many months. I feel really down-in-the-dumps about it. I want to feel

completely indifferent about it all then I'll be able to handle it'. The trouble
with indifference as a goal is it implies that clients are trying to suppress
their rational desires for unpleasant events not to have occurred; indifference does not help clients to pursue appropriate courses of action to prevent
a bad situation from becoming worse. Also indifference to unpleasant
events often means living a life of pretence and usually leads to inner
conflicts. These points will be illustrated in the following discussion:

Therapist:	If I teach you how to feel indifferent, how will that help you?
Client:	I won't give a damn about being dumped and my depression will go.
Therapist:	Will you ask more women out?
Client:	No, I'll give that a rest for a while.
Therapist:	Is that what you want?
Client:	Not really. Not at all actually.
Therapist:	Look, the big problem with indifference is that it really gets you nowhere. You will still be miserable but desperately trying to pretend otherwise, you'll avoid the opportunity of changing some aspects of yourself which might be turning women off and may lead to more successful relationships. And you can learn how to feel sad about being rejected without becoming depressed and withdrawn. How does that sound?
Client:	Well, they all said how possessive I was and it turned them right off. I don't want to be like that. I want to be more relaxed with women.
Therapist:	And be able to handle rejection?
Client:	Yeah, that too.
Therapist:	So how will pretending to be indifferent help you?
Client:	It won't. I'll be even more screwed up.
Therapist:	Okay, what are your new goals then?
Client:	Stop pretending that rejection doesn't hurt, make some changes and go out with more women. It sounds good as I say it.

Clients often assume that if they surrender their demands (musts and
shoulds), the only alternative that is being offered by the therapist is to feel
passive in the face of negative life events, e.g. 'He is always insulting me.
What am I now supposed to do with that obnoxious bastard – roll over and
play dead!' This problem may have been partly created by the therapist in
not building up quickly enough the rational (self-helping) alternative to
anger, namely, annoyance or irritation. Clients can be shown that there is a

middle way between demands and passivity – a philosophy of desires and preferences expressed in mild, moderate, strong or intense terms. Particularly with angry clients, it is usually important for them to feel strong or intense healthy negative emotions if they are to eliminate their anger. In the above example, the client can confront his detractor with a quote from Voltaire, the eighteenth-century French philosopher: 'Sir, I dislike intensely what you say but will defend to the death your right to say it'.

When clients want to feel happy in the face of adversity

Instead of seeking indifference to adverse events, some clients believe that meeting them head on will nullify them, e.g. 'I've been turned down yet again for another job. Let's go out and party and drink to failure – screw success. That's how I want to feel'. However, as a goal this has a hollow ring to it and will probably become more apparent if the job rejections continue. Clients must have had some constructive purpose in seeking employment which the therapist needs to tease out and contrast with their celebratory attitude to failure. A healthy negative emotion such as sadness or disappointment, underpinned by rational beliefs, will help to keep clients focused on job hunting while acknowledging without despair the unpleasantness of repeated rejection. If clients want to celebrate something, they can toast the indomitability of their spirit enshrined in their new outlook.

When clients want to feel a less intense version of a disturbed emotion

This goal implies that clients only want to diminish the strength of their unhealthy negative emotion(s) rather than remove them. Therefore they will still be holding on to lingering irrational beliefs, e.g. 'I still must have his love but I don't want to feel so uptight about it'. Albert Ellis has suggested 'there is an emotional variable of intensity which goes with the must' (quoted in Dryden 1991: 20) which means that the client below wants to express her 'must' in less dogmatic ways to reduce her anxiety. However, this still makes her highly vulnerable to emotional disturbance:

Therapist: How does your anxiety interfere with the relationship?
Client: Well, I'm always worried if he still loves me, dread him going off with someone else, and would get very depressed if he left me because without him my life would be nothing, I would be worthless. Those are the things I get very anxious about. I want to feel less anxious.

Therapist: Doesn't sound as if your anxiety helps you to enjoy the relationship.

Client: Not much.

Therapist: So will reducing your anxiety rather than getting rid of it make much improvement?

Client: It will probably help a bit.

Therapist: But will you be substantially happier?

Client: In all honesty, probably not. It's been going on for so long.

Therapist: The real problem, as I see it, is you hanging on to that 'must' – 'I must have his love because without him my life would be nothing, I would be worthless'. That statement keeps your anxiety going very powerfully.

Client: Well, what else can I do or say? That's what I believe.

Therapist: Just imagine that a few months from now your anxiety has gone because you have successfully disputed your anxiety-provoking ideas. You've become a new woman: enjoying life rather than dreading it, savouring love rather than being a slave to it. How would you now feel in the relationship?

Client: Like a great burden has been lifted off my shoulders. It would be wonderful.

Therapist: And how much would you now enjoy the relationship?

Client: A tremendous amount . . . but it's all a pipe dream, isn't it?

Therapist: It doesn't have to be if you can learn to dump your 'must' and only feel apprehensive or concerned about losing his love. At least it won't leave you tied up in emotional knots: never really enjoying what you believe you desperately need.

Client: What you say is very true but changing after all these years does seem very scary. However, I'm willing to give it a go.

Therapist: So are we agreed that we're going to remove your anxiety rather than just reduce it if you want a real change in the way you see the relationship and yourself within it?

Client: Yes, I really do know that I need more than a Band-Aid to sort this problem out. I want my self-respect back.

Therapist: And it will probably come back when you've freed yourself from the ball-and-chain you call love. Or what has been called 'love slobbism'.

Client: It sounds hideous, like some disease. Is there an antidote?

Therapist: I will show you how to inoculate yourself against it.

Points to consider in this extract are the following:

1   The therapist is reluctant to help perpetuate the client's emotional disturbance and shows her the negligible practical benefits to the relationship if she only reduces her anxiety. The therapist points out the crucial role of her 'musturbatory' thinking in maintaining her anxiety about the 'dreadful' prospect of losing her husband's love.
2   The client is stumped as to how to overcome her anxiety but the therapist uses tantalising imagery as a means of encouraging her to commit herself to the possibilities of real change.
3   The therapist offers the client different ways of feeling in the relationship that will help her to avoid the usual emotional havoc she experiences: highly anxious about losing her husband's love; the prospect of deep depression if her fear is realised.
4   The therapist renegotiates the new goals with the client in order to confirm she has understood and accepted his clinical rationale for change – 'Yes, I really do know that I need more than a Band-Aid'.
5   The therapist points out that the client's self-respect is more likely to come back through developing a healthier form of love and abandoning her 'love slobbism'. This will be achieved by maintaining her strong desires for love while removing her dire necessities for it and by proving to herself that she can still survive and be happy even without love.

When clients state that they never want to be unhappy again

Some clients state as a goal for therapy that they never want to be unhappy again. However, as well as flying in the face of human experience, such a goal may contain the seeds of future disturbance when the client experiences again unpleasant events in her life. Even though REBT therapists encourage clients to strive for happier and longer lives and, if possible, achieve self-actualisation (realising one's potential), they are also aware that the human capacity for self-disturbance can be only minimised, not eradicated. Therefore the therapist should declare that the goal is unobtainable and probe for the client's reasons for choosing it, e.g. 'I've had five years of hell with this depression and I never want to go through it again. I deserve every area of my life to be happy from now on'.

The therapist can point out he would be a very poor therapist if he agreed to such a goal and 'set out with you on the road to eternal happiness' because he would be colluding with the client's delusion that such a goal is obtainable. Also there is no inherent 'deservingness' in the universe of permanent happiness, but hard work and determination are likely to bring more rather than less happiness. If the client is afraid of becoming depressed again, she can learn to develop an 'early warning system' based on cognitive, emotive and behavioural cues to fight back and limit its impact. The client may have an implicit demand in her goal that needs to be isolated and challenged: 'I must never become depressed again'.

Similar unrealistic goals are advanced by clients who want a particular problem not to reappear rather than seeking pervasive happiness in their lives, e.g. 'I hope that this therapy will get rid of my panic attacks for good'. As with all treatment goals, it is important to explain that change is a non-linear process and therefore clients can expect setbacks and relapses. Also progress is usually measured along three dimensions:

1   *Frequency* – are the panic attacks less frequent than before?
2   *Intensity* – are the panic attacks less intense than before?
3   *Duration* – do the panic attacks last as long this time?

REBT therapy has built-in relapse prevention methods if clients are prepared to forcefully and consistently dispute their disturbance-creating ideas for the rest of their lives.

When clients set vague goals

When asked about what they want to achieve from therapy, many clients respond with goals that are quite vague (e.g. 'I want everything to be okay in my life' or 'I want to find out who I really am'). If this vagueness in goal-setting is not dealt with 'both therapist and client are likely to end up frustrated when they look back to determine the utility of the therapy experience' (Walen et al. 1992: 52). Therefore the above statements need to be refined in order to produce goal-setting clarity:

Therapist: What isn't okay in your life at the moment?
Client: Everything.
Therapist: Such as . . .?
Client: Well, my job is deadly dull, my relationship is going nowhere, I seem to be falling out with my friends, arguing with my parents all the time. Do you get the picture?
Therapist: So it's one big mess then.
Client: Right. Give the man a coconut.
Therapist: Well, let's start clearing up the mess. Each problem area we can link to a clear and specific goal.
Client: I don't follow.
Therapist: What would you like to achieve with your relationship difficulties for example?

Client:	I want to leave my girlfriend, but I really don't like living on my own.
Therapist:	Because . . .?
Client:	I'm no good at entertaining myself. I need company all the time.
Therapist:	Do you get depressed on your own?
Client:	Yeah, I do.
Therapist:	If I could help you overcome your depression, what effect would that have on your relationship?
Client:	I would definitely leave her and learn to stand on my own feet without rushing from one usually lousy relationship to another.
Therapist:	Is that out of desperation to avoid loneliness?
Client:	Yes, I'm ashamed to say.
Therapist:	But you will probably start picking more suitable partners from a position of strength, not desperation.
Client:	I certainly hope so.
Therapist:	Right, so we can apply this process to each of your problems, one manageable piece at a time. How does that sound?
Client:	Sounds good. Things are already much clearer.
Therapist:	That's because your initial goal of wanting everything to be okay was very vague. What we needed to find out was, what wasn't okay in your life? Pinpoint the specific problem areas we need to work on and then develop clear goals for change like overcoming your depression. That's how we moved from vagueness to clarity.

The therapist can liken her goal-setting role to looking through a camera viewfinder: if the picture is fuzzy, then bring it into focus. The other client statement, 'I want to find out who I really am', might suggest that the client sees therapy as a metaphysical journey of self-exploration while the REBT therapist expects to have a relatively clear idea of the destination before she sets out. In this way, therapy remains structured and problem orientated rather than letting the client ramble on in a disorganised fashion. Problem-solving training for this client begins with such questions as 'What prevents you now from knowing who you really are?' or 'How will you clearly know when you've found your true self?'

When clients fail to see the difference between short-term and long-term goals

REBT offers clients two forms of change: elegant and inelegant (Ellis 1980). Elegant change involves clients removing their goal-blocking musturbatory (irrational) thinking and replacing it with a goal-attaining rational philosophy of living. Elegant or profound philosophical change in REBT can occur in specific events or towards life in general, but both forms aim at a significant reduction in self-created disturbance. Inelegant change is usually concerned with symptom-removal but without concomitant philosophical change, e.g. a client is relieved that his wife is not going to leave him after all but avoids looking at his underlying belief that 'she must not leave me because my life would be over'. Therefore the client might feel better for superficial and palliative reasons but it is unlikely he would get better because his disturbance-producing ideas remain intact and ready for reactivation when the next marital problem arises. Therapists would do a disservice to their clients if they did not specify the important differences between quick fixes and lasting changes:

> *Client:*   What I want from coming here is to learn relaxation and a bit of positive thinking to get me through these talks. I get so anxious about doing them.
>
> *Therapist:*   Are they a regular feature of your job?
>
> *Client:*   Yes, I do a lot of in-house presentations to colleagues.
>
> *Therapist:*   What do you think you are anxious about?
>
> *Client:*   Making mistakes, looking like a fool, having my colleagues think badly of me. Those sorts of things.
>
> *Therapist:*   Out of that list, which one are you most worried about?
>
> *Client:*   My colleagues thinking badly of me. I couldn't bear that. But what's that got to do with learning relaxation?
>
> *Therapist:*   Well, if you're really worried about losing your colleagues' approval, relaxation won't make much impact upon that.
>
> *Client:*   But it will help me to calm down.
>
> *Therapist:*   It might help you to some extent but your need for their approval will continue to fuel your anxiety and . . . does it get in the way of giving a really polished performance?
>
> *Client:*   Yeah, it could be better.
>
> *Therapist:*   What I want to offer you then is the choice between tinkering with your problem and overhauling it.
>
> *Client:*   An overhaul sounds pretty drastic.
>
> *Therapist:*   Well, do you want the quick fix of a relaxation tape or to develop natural confidence, poise and polish in the long term?
>
> *Client:*   Put like that – the overhaul.
>
> *Therapist:*   *(chuckling)* Well, step this way, sir, for an overhaul.

In the above extract, the client accepted the therapist's persuasive rationale for fundamental change within a specific problem area. The therapist did not attempt to impose her view on the client – the client does not have to embrace the elegant solution to his problem(s). As it turned out, the need for approval underlay all his workplace interactions and also affected his social life. Eventually, he chose to pursue a profound philosophical change throughout his life.

Some clients turn up for therapy wanting 'to kick around a few ideas'. This usually refers to their belief that they have some understanding of the causes of their problems but hope therapy will clarify their thinking on these issues, e.g. 'I've always felt that I haven't done as much with my life as I'd like to because I lack confidence. If you could help me to see it more clearly why I'm like this, I know I can make more progress'. What they are seeking is insight into their problems. Once this is gained they believe their problems will spontaneously resolve themselves.

Ellis (1963) distinguished between intellectual and emotional insight: the former is self-helping ideas lightly and intermittently held while the latter refers to those same ideas deeply and consistently held. In order to move from intellectual to emotional insight, clients usually need to undertake a lot of hard work to effect an amelioration in their problems. However, many clients believe that intellectual insight alone is sufficient to bring about such change and therefore want to terminate therapy when they believe such insight has been gained. The therapist needs to point out the short-term nature of this option – seeing clearly the reasons for one's problems is not the same as doing something about them. Unless the client, as in the above example, challenges and changes his confidence-draining beliefs in a variety of situations, he will remain marooned at the level of intellectual insight and will not achieve significant change in the long term.

When clients have conflicting goals

Sometimes a client will present in therapy with a list of goals that conflict, but she remains unaware of their inherent contradictions. This may occur, among other reasons, because the goals reflect her disturbance or she has not considered sufficiently her longer-term aims. While the therapist does not want to dismantle her goals in a brusque manner for fear of damaging the working alliance, the therapist does need to demonstrate their essential incompatibility:

Therapist: If I've understood you correctly, you want to learn to be more self-accepting and at the same time make people like you.

Client: Yes, that's right. I won't be so hard on myself and have lots of friends.

Therapist:	Why are you so hard on yourself?
Client:	Well, I get depressed because I don't have any friends . . . well, one or two, but not close friends.
Therapist:	You appear to want self-esteem, not self-acceptance.
Client:	Aren't they the same thing?
Therapist:	In REBT, we see self-acceptance as just that irrespective of whether or not you have friends. Of course having friends is very nice – we wouldn't argue with that. Self-esteem depends on things going right in your life, like having friends, and when things go wrong it's usually down you go. *(drops his pen to the floor)* So self-acceptance and making people like you are totally contradictory and therefore won't work.
Client:	But you said I could be self-accepting and have friends. Now you're contradicting yourself.
Therapist:	You can have both as long as you have a healthy desire for friendship, but as soon as you convert that desire into a desperate need for friendship you destroy your base of self-acceptance. Your goals are continually fighting each other.
Client:	I understand what you say but self-acceptance without friends is a lonely existence.
Therapist:	I'm sure it is but I didn't say that. You can learn to stop putting yourself down while at the same time changing those aspects of yourself which might be turning people off. Can you think of anything?
Client:	Well, I have been told – quite often, actually – that I pour out my problems within a few minutes of meeting someone.
Therapist:	Right, so you can learn to develop self-acceptance and start building up a circle of friends. Now your goals will be compatible.
Client:	What happens if I don't make any friends? Am I still supposed to accept myself?
Therapist:	Yes, and persist in uncovering the blocks to friendship. But, let's take it one step at a time.

In this illustration, the therapist is teaching the client the following:

1   Self-esteem is conditional on having friends while self-acceptance is not; however, the therapist is careful to support the client's desire, but not her dire needs, for friendship.

2   Self-acceptance does not mean splendid isolation but the starting point for a non-damning examination of those attributes which may be keeping potential friends at bay.
3   The client's goals for change are now complementary rather than contradictory. Her last comments indicate that she has a lot of hard work ahead if she wants to internalise the principle of self-acceptance as she is still making it conditional on having friends rather than unconditional.

When clients have hidden agendas: offering constructive alternatives

Clients who bring hidden agendas into therapy construct two sets of goals: the therapist works on the ostensible goal advanced by the client while the client pursues the real one (see Chapter 1). Needless to say, this involves a lot of wasted time and effort on the therapist's part. However, it is important that therapists do not display any anger when they discover their clients' real motives for coming to therapy and, instead, try to encourage a constructive course of action:

> *Therapist:*   So all that stuff about staying off drugs forever and becoming a model citizen wasn't true. You're really here because you want a court report from me which you hope will keep you out of prison. Is that right?
>
> *Client:*   Yeah. I don't want to go prison.
>
> *Therapist:*   There's no guarantee that a court report from me will keep you out of prison.
>
> *Client:*   Every little bit helps though.
>
> *Therapist:*   I'm not going to write one for you because you're here for opportunistic reasons and have not shown any real evidence that you are committed to therapy. I don't turn out court reports like an assembly line.
>
> *Client:*   There's no point in staying then.
>
> *Therapist:*   Look, let's say you don't go to prison, what then?
>
> *Client:*   Don't know.
>
> *Therapist:*   Come on, I know your track record. Back to drugs, crime and the occasional overdose. How long before you're back in court yet again? I know you've been in prison before.
>
> *Client:*   It might be different this time. *(irritated)* Well, what else is there for me? Everything's messed up in my life.

Therapist:	I can arrange admission to a drug rehab. Is might be the answer. You've shown many times that you can't stay off drugs on your own.
Client:	Yeah, I know, but rehab, it's just like a prison.
Therapist:	I wouldn't agree. You'll have to work much harder in a rehab. You can leave any time you want which therefore requires a lot of motivation to stay there. Will you at least consider it?
Client:	Yeah, I'll think about it, but I'd rather have a court report.
Therapist:	As I'm not going to write one, does this mean this will be our last session?
Client:	More than likely.
Therapist:	Okay, let's spend the rest of the session then looking at the advantages for you, one by one, if you go to a rehab. Agreed?
Client:	Yeah, all right, it won't hurt.

In this extract, the therapist has revealed the client's hidden and real agenda, but without agreeing to it. After explaining her reasons for not writing a court report, she attempts to interest the client in a longer-term goal which may actually help him to become and remain drug free. The client's response suggests he is only interested in things that serve his immediate interests and therefore will probably not remain in therapy. However, the therapist does not resign herself to the client's likely termination and seeks to keep him in therapy by itemising the longer-term benefits of a drug rehabilitation centre.

Dealing with other problems in goal-setting

Some clients may be so emotionally disturbed that they are unable to discuss with the therapist any constructive goals for change, e.g. 'My life is a complete and utter shambles. I can't see it any other way'. At this point in therapy, it would be unwise for the therapist to persist in her attempts to focus the client's vision beyond his present problems when he is 'myopic'. The therapist should tackle first the client's immediate disturbances (e.g. depression and anger) and help him to create order out of chaos; then from a non-disturbed viewpoint, the client can decide what longer-term therapeutic goals to pursue (his vision has now been restored, so to speak).

Switching from an unhealthy to a healthy negative emotion may 'seem unattainable to clients because they cannot conceptualize the new emotion and may not agree that it is adaptive and more functional' (Walen et al. 1992: 53). For example, a man who beat up his wife said the only way to prevent him from doing it again was to feel guilty – 'I need to keep on reminding myself what a bad person I really am'. Initial attempts to encourage him to feel remorse for his actions but avoid self-condemnation proved fruitless as he believed this would 'let me off the hook'. However, seeing himself as a bad person led to heavy drinking and further assaults upon his wife. After admitting the self-defeating nature of his guilt, he agreed to the new emotional goal of remorse. This would enable him to examine the reasons for his violent behaviour (which he was much less likely to do while feeling guilty) and learn non-violent methods of dealing with his frustrations. Also he was encouraged to examine frequently the effects of his violence upon his wife so that he would not minimise her suffering through self-absorption in analysing 'my dysfunctional behaviour'.

Other clients are caught in a cleft stick over emotional change: while acknowledging that their present feelings do engender personal distress, they still consider that these are the right feelings to retain rather than relinquish:

Client: I know I'm going to burst a blood vessel or have a heart attack if I don't stop all this anger, but I know I'm right over this issue. I must be right because otherwise I wouldn't be angry, would I? So how can I give up my anger? That will mean defeat.

Therapist: Well, being angry doesn't automatically mean that you're right. On the other hand, you can be right without being angry. Have your displays of anger actually produced any tangible benefits?

Client: He knows I'm angry.

Therapist: But has he stopped parking in your reserved space?

Client: No, he bloody well hasn't!

Therapist: Do you think he gets pleasure from seeing you so angry?

Client: Probably. I often see him smirking.

Therapist: You say you don't want to be defeated yet you're the one losing your cool and parking elsewhere. Is that how you define winning?

Client: What else can I do? At least I haven't lost my anger and turned into a wimp. That would be the ultimate humiliation.

Therapist: Look, you've tried it your way for several months and he hasn't budged. How about cooling down for a while and calmly considering a range of options that you probably haven't seen because of that red mist in front of your eyes?

Client: Will it work?

> *Therapist:*   I don't know yet but your way certainly hasn't. If my
> approach doesn't work you can always go back to your
> anger and putting your heart and arteries under tremen-
> dous stress. Do we have a deal?
> *Client:*   Okay, I'm willing to give it a whirl.

The therapist shows the client that even if he has right on his side, his anger has not produced any practical returns and therefore he has 'lost' the struggle so far. By surrendering his anger the client can channel his energy into a hoped-for constructive resolution of this problem. As a further means of encouraging therapeutic movement, the therapist is careful to retain the anger option for future use if the planned strategy does not work. Also the therapist reminds the client of the adverse physical effects of prolonged anger. The idea of a 'deal' allows the client to sheathe his sword of anger while retaining his dignity.

Once clients have identified and agreed upon their outcome goals and thereby committed themselves to the process of change, the next stage is for them to execute the necessary tasks that will realise these goals. For between the desire and reality of change falls the long shadow of hard work which we examine in Chapter 5.

Dealing with client resistance in the tasks domain of the working alliance

In Chapter 3, we discussed the principle of emotional responsibility whereby clients accept that they largely disturb themselves with irrational beliefs about adverse events in their lives. This principle allows them to gain insight into their problems. Therapeutic responsibility encourages clients to take action in order to tackle their problems. This aspect of therapy requires clients to have a highly active role which is clearly spelt out to them by the therapist, for example:

> 'I can teach you how to play chess but I can't play the game for you. Similarly with your problems, I can teach you what accounts for and maintains them but you have to undertake the hard work in order to overcome them.'

This chapter examines the difficulties that clients experience when they attempt to translate REBT theory into everyday practice by undertaking various tasks.

When clients say 'I've tried disputing, but . . .'

Clients are expected to dispute their disturbance-creating beliefs in a variety of contexts if they wish to effect significant reductions in their emotional problems. This is one of their major tasks in REBT. Ellis (1979) pointed out that clients need to employ considerable force and energy in attacking their irrational ideas if they wish to uproot them. Also disputing should be undertaken in a sustained manner so that clients are chipping away continually at these ideas rather than in a sporadic or haphazard way. However, clients frequently engage in disputing in a tepid, intermittent or lacklustre fashion which results in little or no relief from their emotional distress:

> *Client:* This disputing business doesn't work.
> *Therapist:* In what way?

Client:	Well, I tried disputing a couple of times and nothing happened.
Therapist:	What was supposed to have happened?
Client:	My anxiety was supposed to go, wasn't it?
Therapist:	I don't believe I ever said you would be cured in a few weeks. What belief were you challenging?
Client:	I think it was something about I must not show any weaknesses to friends.
Therapist:	Because if you do that would mean . . .?
Client:	How pathetic and useless I am.
Therapist:	Now you're supposed to have a clear idea of the belief you're attacking. Maybe you need to write it down and keep it with you. You told me last week that you've had this belief for about fifteen years. Now how deeply do you believe it?
Client:	As deep as you can go. Probably need dynamite to shift it.
Therapist:	Okay, we'll try that as a last resort. So fifteen years of the old belief versus two weeks of the new rational belief, which was . . .?
Client:	Oh, something like preferring not to show any weaknesses and not having to put myself down if I do show them.
Therapist:	Well, you missed out '. . . but there's no reason why I must not show any weaknesses . . .'. That statement cuts the heart out of your irrational idea. You'll also need to write down that belief in order for it to sink in. Now fifteen years versus two weeks. What were you expecting to happen?
Client:	A lot. It sounds silly now you put it in perspective. I know it's going to be harder than I thought.
Therapist:	How much effort did you put into your challenges?
Client:	Not much – I was watching television at the same time. Doesn't matter, does it?
Therapist:	Unless you inject a great deal of passion, energy, force, power and persuasion into your disputing, you are hardly likely to root out your anxious thinking. So dispute, dispute, dispute. And not in front of the television but where it really counts – in the company of your friends. These methods are more likely to produce progress.
Client:	Yeah, I know what you say is true and I suppose I'll just have to try harder.

In this excerpt from therapy, the therapist is teaching the client the following important points:

1   Real change does not occur after a few stabs at disputing. The client's misunderstanding regarding the process of change is compounded by his vagueness about his targeted belief for disputing.
2   Contrasting the client's fifteen years of habituation to irrationality with his first tentative steps at challenging is designed to show him the hard work that lies ahead.
3   Unless he has a clear understanding of his newly acquired rational belief and expressed in its full preferential form (the therapist fills in the gap), it is unlikely to have much therapeutic impact upon him.
4   Disputing should be carried out persistently with force and energy in those situations where the client experiences his anxiety – just anywhere will not do!
5   The client's last comment 'I suppose I'll just have to try harder' may indicate that he has not yet grasped what is expected of him or he has discomfort intolerance beliefs, e.g. 'I want to change but it must be easier and I won't do anything if it is going to be too hard'. The therapist would seek evidence to support or discredit one of her alternative hypotheses.

When clients want to try, rather than do

It is important that clients commit to undertaking an activity in contrast to only attempting it. When clients agree to carry out homework assignments, they frequently say 'I'll try to do them' rather than 'I'll do them'. The former attitude implies a good chance of failure or at best only half-hearted attempts, while the latter attitude suggests that the tasks will be carried out with the probability of making faster progress and deeper change. Therefore, it is important that therapists elicit a commitment to 'doing' rather than to 'trying'. These points are illustrated in the following excerpt:

Therapist: Now, we've negotiated this homework task of you asserting yourself with a work colleague. Will you carry out this task?
Client: Yeah, I'll try to.
Therapist: Let me ask you this: will you try to leave the session when it's finished? Will you try and drive your car home? Will you try and eat this evening? In other words, you're going to do these things. So will you try to carry out your homework task or will you do it?
Client: These other things are easy to do, that's why I do them. Now this other business of asserting myself, that's different.

Therapist:	Did you try to learn to drive and cook for yourself? Were they easy to do when you first started?
Client:	I know what you're getting at – I did them and they weren't easy at first.
Therapist:	And how much progress did you make by actually doing these things rather than trying to do them?
Client:	I made quick progress. Okay, I'll do *(emphasises word)* the homework task. Satisfied?
Therapist:	You are not doing the task for me: it's for your benefit. You've identified unassertiveness as a problem you wish to overcome.
Client:	You don't give up, do you? I'll do the task because it's going to help me.
Therapist:	Good.

When clients have issues about the place of homework in therapy

Some clients believe that just talking to their therapist will produce constructive change within them. This viewpoint may have been strengthened by their previous experiences with therapeutic approaches that did not emphasise the importance of homework tasks or did not assign any. Pondering on therapeutic ideas between sessions might bring greater understanding of their problems but an armchair philosophy to problem-solving remains just that – clients can glimpse the exciting possibilities of change but do not realise them because they fail to act on their emerging rational ideas. Such clients need to realise that what happens outside of therapy is usually considered in REBT as more important than what happens inside it as clients learn to develop both confidence and competence in facing their problems. Therefore an hour-long weekly session is the starting point for change with the other 167 hours outside of therapy providing its driving force. Such increasing independence as a problem-solver reduces the potential for dependence upon the therapist, e.g. clients carry out their homework tasks only in order to gain approval from the therapist rather than seeing the tasks as a means of standing on their own feet. Such arguments can help clients to see that homework is essential if they wish to effect deep and enduring change in their lives.

When clients think that they have to go slowly with homework tasks

When some clients agree reluctantly to undertake their homework tasks, they then insist that these tasks have to be done slowly or in a piecemeal fashion, e.g. 'I have to take it one tiny step at a time doing this exposure work. Any quicker and I'm going to feel terrible. I can't stand feeling like that'. Ellis (1983a) criticised gradualism in therapy for creating the impression that change can be brought about only in a slow and painless way and thereby actually reinforcing clients' discomfort intolerance beliefs (that they cannot bear much or any discomfort in facing their problems). Gradualism can, from this perspective, increase the degree of difficulty clients will experience in tackling their problems. Ellis encouraged clients to use implosive (flooding) methods to confront immediately and fully their fears in order to achieve rapid amelioration of them and significantly increase their tolerance level for discomfort. However, many clients will be unlikely to favour this method of change. As a therapeutic compromise between implosion and gradualism, Dryden (1985) suggests challenging, but not overwhelming tasks. These points will be clarified in the following dialogue:

Therapist:	If you take tiny steps in overcoming your agoraphobia, how long before you can, for example, walk to and go into a supermarket on your own?
Client:	I don't know, but certainly many months, even a year or more.
Therapist:	Would you like to make faster progress?
Client:	I suppose I would but I feel dreadful when I go outside. I get so panicky. It's so bad I can't stand it. That's the real problem.
Therapist:	That statement 'I can't stand it' is so common among people with anxiety problems. The 'it' usually refers to the tremendous discomfort they experience in facing their fears.
Client:	I know how they feel – it's the same for me.
Therapist:	Do you believe that you can overcome your problems without any discomfort?
Client:	I know that is impossible but it's got to be kept at an absolute minimum.
Therapist:	What would be the effect on your progress if every time you carry out a homework task you say to yourself, 'I can't stand it! I can't stand it'?
Client:	I'll have a ball-and-chain around my ankle. Probably stop doing the tasks or find endless excuses not to do them.
Therapist:	There is a very dramatic and rapid way to overcome what we in REBT call 'discomfort anxiety' and which is what you suffer from.
Client:	I don't think I'm going to like this . . .

Therapist: This involves jumping in at the deep end, so to speak. This means walking to and staying in the supermarket and putting up with the tremendous discomfort you will experience. So you stay in the situation until the discomfort passes. In this way, you make rapid progress and learn that you can stand it but without liking it one bit.

Client: You're either joking or you're mad!

Therapist: Neither. I'm serious. I would teach you a variety of techniques that will help you to stay in the situation. Some clients are amazed with their progress when they do it this way.

Client: Look, I'm not going to do it, so you'd better change the record.

Therapist: Okay, there is a middle way between tiny steps and jumping in at the deep end and it's called 'challenging, but not overwhelming'.

Client: This sounds ominous . . .

Therapist: Well, the task would be harder than you like, such as walking to the end of your road rather than the front gate, but would fall short of the terror you're imagining if you went to the supermarket straightaway. So you would learn to tolerate the discomfort quite quickly without being paralysed by it.

Client: That might be something I'm prepared to try but I want more discussion about it first.

Therapist: Certainly. Where shall we begin?

When clients fail to carry out homework tasks

Some clients may be eager to carry out their homework tasks, yet come back to therapy the following week feeling despondent over their inability to execute them, e.g. 'I'm completely useless. I felt so confident and nothing happened'. As well as accepting themselves for not undertaking their tasks, clients can learn the 'win-win' formula of homework assignments: that if they did the assignment they would have won, and if they failed to do the assignment they also would have won because they learn which factors blocked or interfered with task execution. If they haven't done the assignment, client and therapist renegotiate the assignment, with the client committing to take the remedial steps that are required. This formula emphasises that clients are always on a learning curve in terms of tackling their problems.

When clients do not carry out the task as agreed

REBT homework assignments require clients to face unpleasant activating events ('A's) in order for them to challenge and change their disturbance-producing ideas. This is seen as the most efficient and enduring method of constructive change. However, clients may apparently agree to such a homework approach in therapy, yet at the next session declare success but for different reasons:

> *Client:* Homework went very well. I feel much more relaxed now in queues.
>
> *Therapist:* What was the irrational belief you were challenging?
>
> *Client:* 'I must not have my time wasted by being stuck in queues because I can't stand it.' God, I used to get so angry about bloody queues.
>
> *Therapist:* It seems you've had a great success. What happened?
>
> *Client:* Well, I was in this queue, listening to music, and I got to the checkout as calm as could be.
>
> *Therapist:* When you say 'listening to music', were you wearing headphones?
>
> *Client:* Yeah, I was.
>
> *Therapist:* What was the homework we agreed last week?
>
> *Client:* Stand in queues and vigorously challenge my irrational ideas.
>
> *Therapist:* Can you see how you've changed, perhaps in a subtle way, your homework?
>
> *Client:* Oh, the headphones. I thought they would help me.
>
> *Therapist:* They are a good idea if you're looking for a short-term solution. However, in REBT we encourage clients to look for longer-term ones and this involves facing unpleasant activating events; in your case, challenging and changing your anger-provoking beliefs when in queues. So all you've done is really to distract yourself from your anger.
>
> *Client:* I see what you mean, but aren't you going over the top on this issue?
>
> *Therapist:* Well, imagine distraction with music is the only technique you use, then one day you're in a long queue and your cassette player batteries are dead. Then what?
>
> *Client:* I hadn't thought of that. I suppose if I'm honest, I'll get angry over the batteries being dead because I can't block out with music my anger about being stuck in bloody queues!

> *Therapist:* Will you do the homework task we originally agreed then: to experience your anger and practise your new rational belief?
>
> *Client:* Yes I will. No distractions this time.
>
> *Therapist:* Good. Once you've overcome your anger, then you can choose from a non-disturbed viewpoint if you wish to wear headphones.

In this extract, important points to consider are the following:

1 The therapist elicits from the client details of the homework task to determine if she has carried out what was agreed at the previous session.
2 Feedback from the client shows she has altered the homework assignment by distracting herself from the 'A' (activating event) rather than facing it.
3 Wearing headphones is a practical solution to her problems rather than an emotional one favoured by REBT therapists, i.e. her anger-creating beliefs are being held at bay by the music rather than removed through disputing.
4 The therapist encourages the client to point out the limitations of the practical solution through the dead batteries example. This convinces the client to do the original homework task. The therapist, who does not want to appear a killjoy, suggests a possible return to the headphones once the client's anger has gone.

When clients say 'I'll do it tomorrow'

Clients can employ many excuses and delaying tactics in order to avoid carrying out their homework tasks. Underpinning the 'I'll do it tomorrow' syndrome is usually a philosophy of discomfort intolerance, e.g. 'These tasks involve too much hard work. I shouldn't have to work this hard to sort my problems out. There must be an easier way?' For some clients, this syndrome becomes a way of life as they search for the easy solution to their problems, which proves to be continually elusive. With homework avoiders, REBT therapists can point out that if they put nothing into therapy, they will get nothing out of it and thereby remain emotionally disturbed. Estimates can be made of the time clients are likely to spend in therapy (and money paid if they are private clients) as an inducement for them to start carrying out their homework tasks, for example:

> 'You've successfully avoided your assignments so far. At this rate, you'll be in therapy for the next couple of years instead of doing what

you really want to – going out with a woman. You'll be as lonely then as you are now and all because you won't push yourself.'

Confronting such clients needs to be done on a regular basis so they are not 'let off the hook', but confrontation in REBT means being assertive, not aggressive or abrasive. One method that can be used is but-rebuttal (Burns 1980):

Client:	Yes, you're right – I don't want to be in therapy for years but I'm not ready yet to ask someone out.
Therapist:	You haven't been ready yet for several months and I doubt you ever will be if you keep on defining rejection as an awful experience, the end of your world.
Client:	Yes, I know it sounds so silly, but I'll feel devastated if it happens.
Therapist:	As I've been explaining to you, your feelings are based on your ideas, so feeling devastated is not caused by rejection but by how you evaluate rejection. So rejection itself doesn't bring your world crashing down, your 'awfulising' about it does that. Now if you can learn to see rejection as unpleasant but not awful . . .
Client:	Yes, I know believing that would probably help me but, on the other hand, I don't think it will really work for me.
Therapist:	How can you know that when you haven't asked anyone out yet?
Client:	Yes, I haven't tried it, but when will I know it's the right time to start?
Therapist:	There's no perfect time to start. We've done a lot of preliminary work: rehearsal through imagery and behaviour, expressing forceful rational coping statements, learning assertiveness techniques, and so on. Now would be a good time to leave the laboratory and try these things out in the real world.
Client:	Yes, I suppose it is but you never know, she might say 'Yes' rather than 'No'.
Therapist:	That might be nice for you but it wouldn't help you. Do you know why?
Client:	I'm not sure really but it would make me feel a whole lot better.
Therapist:	Only in the short term because you'd be continually anxious about being dumped and how would you feel if you were?

> *Client:*   Devastated. Utterly depressed.
> *Therapist:*   Back to square one. So you need a number of rejections
>   first in order to cope constructively with them and then
>   you'll enjoy your first 'Yes' much more. Now will you
>   agree to face your first rejection?
> *Client:*   There's a woman I really fancy, but she wouldn't give me
>   the time of day. I'll try to ask her.
> *Therapist:*   Now we've been over this trying versus doing several
>   times . . .
> *Client:*   I meant I'll do it. I've got to do it if I want to stop living
>   my life as if I'm afraid of the dark.

The therapist wears down the client's 'Yes, but' statements until the client commits himself to carry out the homework task. The therapist's rebuttals underscore rational principles in an attempt to motivate the client. Even when the client becomes hopeful that the first woman he asks says 'Yes' rather than 'No', the therapist does not shrink from pointing out the self-defeating nature of his optimism. REBT therapists prefer to negotiate homework tasks that will bring about enduring rather than superficial change in clients' lives, so they are alert to the short-termism effect implicit in the assignments that many clients suggest. As pointed out earlier in this chapter, there is an important distinction between trying and doing which the client is reminded of. The but-rebuttal technique can be learnt by clients to deal with their own doubts or ambivalence about change.

When clients wonder about the relevance of tasks to their goals

Some clients become confused or are unsure about how some of the tasks they are expected to carry out relate to their goals, e.g. 'How the hell has making a fool of myself in public got anything to do with helping me to speak up in meetings?' Such perplexity on the client's part may have been partly engendered by the therapist not making explicit the link between task and goal. Whatever the cause, the therapist can help the client to make the connection between shame-attacking exercises (Ellis 1994) and her inability to express her opinions at meetings:

> *Therapist:*   Now let's go over this again: what are you most anxious
>   about at these meetings and thereby prevent yourself
>   from speaking up?
> *Client:*   I'm afraid of saying something stupid and looking a fool
>   in the eyes of others as well as my own.

Therapist:	What is it that you lack that I keep on hammering away at all the time?
Client:	Self-acceptance. I won't allow myself to look like a fool in the eyes of others.
Therapist:	Well, you're assuming you can control the way they see you. But what do you think you look like by staying silent at meetings?
Client:	I know that doesn't look good either.
Therapist:	So you've trapped yourself. Now what is the point of a shame-attacking exercise?
Client:	To learn to accept myself for saying or doing something foolish in public.
Therapist:	To accept yourself in the face of what . . .?
Client:	Others' criticism, laughter, disapproval, ridicule, whatever.
Therapist:	So how will these exercises help you at meetings?
Client:	Well, if I really accept myself then I'll be able to speak up instead of being struck dumb by my anxiety.
Therapist:	So you will be able to contribute to the meeting now more than just silence.
Client:	*(laughs)* I certainly hope so!
Therapist:	Do you now see the link between the task and your goal?
Client:	Yes, walking backwards down the road will help to set me free from my self-imposed restraints.
Therapist:	Watch out for lamp posts. Seriously, you'll probably find in time that these exercises will also liberate you in other areas of your life.
Client:	You're right. It's not just at meetings that I have problems in speaking up.

As well as clarifying the task–goal link, the therapist needs to ensure that the homework assignment logically or naturally follows on from the work done in the session, e.g. 'stay-in-there' activities (Grieger and Boyd 1980) would be typical tasks to negotiate if the session discussion focused on the client's discomfort intolerance beliefs which led him to avoid emotionally fraught situations. When clients agree to carry out a task, it does not automatically mean that they have sufficient skills to accomplish it; therefore therapists need to ascertain if their clients have any task-relevant skills deficits or if they have a skill in their repertoire, but subjectively believe that they are unable to use this skill in a particular setting. For example, a client may say he has no idea of how to start a conversation with a woman he is attracted to or that he knows how to do it with other women but lacks the confidence with this woman. The therapist can employ behavioural and imaginal rehearsal to teach the client the necessary task skills as well as elicit and challenge any assignment-blocking beliefs. Such preliminary work increases clients' confidence in their ability to carry out successfully their homework tasks.

Once the above considerations have been dealt with, the therapist needs to pin down clients to when, where and how often they will undertake their tasks rather than a vague assurance that 'I really will do it in the coming week'. The therapist can applaud the client's determination and add that specificity with homework tasks will help to concentrate the client's mind even more on the work ahead. Both therapist and client can keep a written record of the homework task to reduce or eliminate ambiguity or disagreement when it is reviewed at the next session. Being clear and specific during homework negotiation enables the therapist to whittle down clients' excuses for not carrying out their assignments.

Troubleshooting in advance obstacles to clients undertaking homework tasks

Therapists need to help clients to identify and remove the potential or actual obstacles that might prevent them from undertaking their agreed assignments, e.g. 'Is there anything you can think of that might interfere with or block you from completing this task?' Clients' responses may include the following: there is a possible obstacle, e.g. 'I don't think I'm going to have enough time'; 'Nothing springs to mind' but actually they foresee one or two obstacles but reveal them only at the next session as a reason for not doing their tasks, e.g. 'My friend suddenly turned up and stayed the week'; they genuinely do not see any obstacles to homework completion. Therapists can offer their own hypotheses in order to jog clients' awareness of potential difficulties or suggest additional ones they have overlooked:

> *Therapist:* You say you can't think of anything, but you haven't actually done the homework task yet as it always seems to slip off your agenda for the coming week.
>
> *Client:* Well, I always mean to do it but after a hard day at the office, I look forward to relaxing in the evening.
>
> *Therapist:* Well, you could relax for part of the evening and then start writing that report. If you keep on relaxing but don't do the report, what will happen at work?
>
> *Client:* The you-know-what will hit the fan if it's not finished by the end of the month.
>
> *Therapist:* Three weeks to go then. It seems to me that the belief getting in the way is something like: 'As I've worked hard all day, I deserve to relax in the evening and I can't

	stand it if I can't indulge myself when I feel like it'. Can you hear yourself saying something like that?
Client:	Yeah, that sounds familiar. I can't seem to shift that idea at the moment. I've got to get that report done though.
Therapist:	Okay, what would be a good strong statement to get you going and challenge that motivation-draining idea?
Client:	What I found useful in the past when I've been shirking is to imagine being back in the army and the sergeant yelling at me: 'Get bloody moving or you'll get my boot up your backside!'
Therapist:	Use that image and let's throw in some rewards and penalties. Now what do you enjoy doing?
Client:	Relaxing.
Therapist:	No relaxing until after you've worked on the report. How long do you need to work on it for each night?
Client:	About two hours.
Therapist:	Two hours' work first and then relax. What don't you like doing apart from the report?
Client:	I hate doing DIY. There are shelves waiting to go up around the house and my wife keeps on at me to put them up.
Therapist:	If you don't work on the report, no relaxing. Two hours of DIY instead.
Client:	Anything but that.
Therapist:	Do you agree to carry out the homework task using rewards and penalties?
Client:	Yes I do.
Therapist:	Okay, let's write that all down in a homework contract and hope you will apply the penalties if you don't keep to it.
Client:	I've no excuse now for letting the report slip off my agenda.

The use of rewards and penalties (not punishments), also known as operant conditioning or contingency management, helps clients to shape new goal-directed behaviours (writing an important report) and reduce or extinguish goal-blocking ones (procrastination underpinned by low frustration tolerance beliefs). Operant conditioning methods can teach clients the pitfalls of short-term hedonism or instant gratification because avoiding hard work and discomfort takes them further away from their goals rather than closer to them. Grieger and Boyd (1980: 145) suggest that rewards and penalties provide 'the extra incentive that makes the difference between avoiding or completing it [homework]'. Ellis (quoted in Dryden 1991) added that if clients fail to administer their own rewards and penalties, they can ask a friend, relative or partner to act as a monitor and help them to adhere to their contingency management programme; in the above example, the client can ask for his wife's assistance if he breaks his home-work agreement.

When clients don't know what homework tasks will help them

REBT therapists offer clients a wide range of homework assignments to help them tackle their emotional problems. These assignments can be placed within four main categories:

- *cognitive* – e.g. reading REBT self-help books
- *imagery* – e.g. rehearsing in the mind's eye carrying out a particular task
- *behavioural* – e.g. staying in an unpleasant situation until habituation occurs
- *emotive* – e.g. shame-attacking exercises which flood the individual with disturbed emotions in order to change them.

Some clients claim that none of the above modalities appeal to or will be able to help them and are unable to offer any alternative tasks they might be able to accomplish:

Therapist:	Now you say you want to develop more confidence particularly at work and with women. Right?
Client:	Yes, that's right.
Therapist:	And would you agree that the two of us just talking about your problems every week is not going to bring about much change in your life?
Client:	It hasn't done so far.
Therapist:	So what else needs to be done besides talking?
Client:	Got to get myself moving in some way.
Therapist:	Good. Now you said you're not interested in reading anything . . .
Client:	I can barely get through the newspaper. I only really read the sports section.
Therapist:	And the idea of imagining yourself as being more assertive at work won't help either.
Client:	My mind just goes blank. I've never been any good at visualising things.
Therapist:	The shame-attacking exercises would help to teach you self-acceptance which would then form the base from which to develop greater confidence in your life.

Client:	I don't fancy making a fool of myself. I can definitely do without that task. Next.
Therapist:	What about a relatively straightforward behavioural assignment like asking for the money back you lent to a friend in your office?
Client:	I couldn't do that; he might think I'm a scrooge.
Therapist:	What task do you want to do that you think will help you? You know yourself best.
Client:	I can't think of anything. It seems we're both stuck.
Therapist:	Well, let me suggest that your first homework task is to think of one.
Client:	What if I can't?
Therapist:	Then at the next session we'll look at how you blocked yourself from coming up with one. This will provide more information on the nature of your problems. So we will both learn from it. I haven't been able, so far, to interest you in anything. Maybe you'll do a better job.
Client:	I'll see what I can do. I'm not making any promises though.
Therapist:	Okay. At the end of each session it is important that you have a homework task to carry out. My task is to make sure that you have some. So we both have to work hard in therapy, and you outside of it as well, if you're to make progress.

In the above extract, it is obvious that the client's homework avoidance is linked to his presenting problems, but the therapist defers to the client's superior self-knowledge as a means of trying to tease out a task. When this proves fruitless and the client believes he has outmanoeuvred the therapist, she suggests that the first homework task 'is to think of one'. Even if he cannot think of a task, this will provide important cognitive data which will be examined at the next session. Therefore the client will not be returning to therapy empty-handed in the way he might be imagining. The therapist points out that both of them have tasks to perform if the client is to make progress, and emphasises the 'hard work' theme to alert the client to what lies ahead for him in and out of therapy.

When clients are apprehensive about being their own therapist once therapy ends

The ultimate aim of REBT therapy is for the therapist to become redundant and for clients to develop into their own self-therapist. When clients have shown proficiency in using the 'ABCDE' model to conceptualise and tackle their problems, therapy moves towards termination. Formal therapy may be over, but self-therapy requires lifelong practice in order to maintain therapeutic gains and deal effectively with future problems. Clients may be apprehensive that they will falter in or not be able to carry out self-therapy once they leave the protective umbrella of REBT:

Client:	I really like the idea of being my own therapist but I'm not sure if I will be totally successful on my own.
Therapist:	Being a self-therapist is not about achieving total success but managing your problems in a way that will greatly reduce your own level of disturbability.
Client:	I know that's more realistic but I'm not sure if now is the right time to leave therapy.
Therapist:	How can we put that to the test?
Client:	I knew you would ask me that. Leave therapy and find out, I suppose.
Therapist:	That will provide you with the best information to answer your question. Whenever you start upsetting yourself over problems in your life or start slipping back, what do you need to do?
Client:	Put the problem within the ABC framework in order to find out what I'm telling myself.
Therapist:	When you've located your irrational belief, then what?
Client:	Dispute it by asking myself is this belief logical, realistic and helpful?
Therapist:	And if the evidence is to the contrary . . .?
Client:	Set myself a number of tasks to think, feel and act against the irrational beliefs and thereby strengthen my rational ones. That's the theory, anyway.
Therapist:	And the practice. You have been doing it throughout the course of therapy. Why should you behave differently when you leave therapy?
Client:	Well, I suppose it's because you are not there any longer.
Therapist:	I'm only there one hour a week. Who actually did the hard work of change? Was I with you when you faced your panic in the supermarkets?
Client:	I did those tasks all on my own. In fact, you were the last thing on my mind when I was panic-stricken!
Therapist:	That's my point – you did them, not me. You are the agent of your own change. I was just acting as your consultant or adviser.
Client:	Okay, I accept that. I remember you saying that self-therapy is a lifelong task, but surely there will come a

	time when things will take care of themselves and I can put my feet up, so to speak?
Therapist:	With lots of practice, getting rid of your disturbance-creating ideas will become much easier, but you can never stop being a mental health mechanic otherwise you might find those ideas creeping back. Would your physical well-being look after itself if you stopped having baths or brushing your teeth?
Client:	Obviously not. So looking after your physical and mental health are equally important.
Therapist:	Exactly. Now if you really do get stuck on your own, you can come back to therapy and I'll be your adviser again for a brief period.
Client:	Thanks. That's good to know.

In the above therapy excerpt, important points to note are the following:

1   The client's doubts about becoming 'totally successful' as a self-therapist may reflect implicit irrational ideas, e.g. 'I must never be upset again'; 'I must be rational at all times'. The therapist will need to probe for and deal with these ideas if they are present before therapy is terminated.

2   The therapist maintains a problem-solving focus to the end of therapy by suggesting that the client's question will be answered only through leaving therapy.

3   The therapist encourages the client to go through again the 'ABCDE' model of emotional disturbance and its remediation to keep on reminding herself of what needs to be done when she is emotionally upset. Repeating the 'ABC's of REBT aids the process of constructive change.

4   When the client assumes that the therapist's absence in her life will adversely affect her progress, he points out that he was always absent during the real test of therapy – when she faced her problems on her own – and this did not undermine her progress. He advised her on problem-solving but she actually did all of the work.

5   The client wonders if lifelong self-therapy is really necessary as she believes her mind will eventually become self-regulating. The therapist makes an analogy with physical hygiene to show her that lifelong maintenance of her REBT skills is required if she wants to keep them.

6   If she develops serious difficulties as a self-therapist, she can return to therapy for further problem-solving. The therapist uses the word 'brief' to indicate that 'fine-tuning' of her new role is probably required rather than a wholesale reappraisal of it. The latter strategy may lead to the client feeling both discouraged about and deskilled in her new role.

Dealing with clients' other task-related difficulties

A crucial task for clients is to be receptive to and eventually accept the principles of general and specific emotional responsibility. Little, if anything, can be accomplished in therapy if clients continually blame others or events for their emotional problems. For an extensive discussion of encouraging emotional responsibility, see Chapter 2.

Setting an agenda in REBT allows each session to be focused on a specific set of items and thereby the most is made of therapy time. Agenda setting keeps both therapist and client on track in order to realise the latter's goals for change. However, some clients may object to what they perceive as a therapy straitjacket and an infringement of their right to talk about whatever comes to mind, e.g. 'Who are you to say what should be discussed?' The therapist needs to point out that each session agenda is negotiated and not imposed but it must have clinical relevance to the client's presenting problems. This means that idle chit-chat, endless pleasantries, meandering conversations, etc. are banished from the agenda in the drive for therapeutic efficiency, e.g. 'We are not here to discuss the weather or television programmes but to help you overcome your guilt feelings as quickly as possible. The session agenda makes sure that we never lose sight of that goal'. Clients can be assured that agenda setting is a flexible procedure and can be suspended if a crisis or other significant event supervenes, e.g. the client becomes suicidal.

For some clients, the word 'homework' is reminiscent of their schooldays and may have negative or unpleasant connotations for them, e.g. detention for not doing it, parental pressure to 'do your homework otherwise you'll end up bottom of the class'. Some clients may also assume that the therapist is being patronising towards them. Such reasons might lead to homework avoidance or rebellion against it. To forestall these problems occurring, a different term can be agreed upon, e.g. self-help tasks or outside therapy activities, which is more acceptable to and beneficial for the client.

The first four chapters of Part I looked at client difficulties in each of the four domains of the working alliance: bonds, views, goals and tasks. The final chapter in Part I explores client resistance in the various stages of the therapeutic process.

Chapter 6

A process-orientated view of client resistance

The REBT therapy process can be divided into beginning, middle and ending phases with their own distinctive features and client resistances. Though these phases may seem artificially contrived they can provide yardsticks of a client's progress; for example, in the middle phase, clients preferably should have greater confidence in tackling their emotional problems and identifying core irrational beliefs. This chapter deals with client problems typically experienced within these phases.

Dealing with client resistance in the beginning phase

In this phase, therapist and client develop a therapeutic alliance, an early problem-solving focus is established, the client is taught the 'ABC's of REBT and homework tasks are negotiated. Client resistances arising from these activities have been dealt with in earlier chapters.

Other problems that clients experience include what Grieger and Boyd (1980: 79) call 'the "cathartic cure" myth'. Because suppressed emotions (e.g. anger) have finally been released, clients can understandably feel a tremendous sense of relief and happiness at the end of the first session and thereby conclude that therapy is finished. From the REBT perspective, talking about one's disturbed emotions is, on its own, seen as a superficial remedy as clients have not yet identified, challenged and changed the irrational ideas that largely create disturbed emotions. In the above example, if clients leave therapy prematurely, they are likely to find that their relief is short-lived as their underlying ideas will stir up further anger. Such a rationale will help to disabuse clients of their 'I thought airing my feelings would get rid of them' notions and encourage them to stay longer in therapy to seek enduring methods of change.

When clients want it all sorted out today

Some clients come to therapy with the expectation that a couple of sessions will solve all their problems and when this obviously does not occur, rapid demoralisation can take place. Such clients need to be inducted into the realities of REBT and its goal-setting procedures:

Therapist: Where did you get the idea that I had a magic wand?

Client: I thought you therapists knew the answers to everything. You're supposed to be able to sort me out.

Therapist: Well, I hope I can sort you out but only with your considerable help. I certainly don't have the answers to everything, but I certainly do have an explanation of and solution to your emotional problems. I can't produce a magic wand; instead, I can offer you two very different words – hard work.

Client: (sarcastically) Great, that's really cheered me up. I thought I was coming here for help and I feel even more depressed now.

Therapist: Because . . .

Client: Because now it seems I'll never get over this depression. You're not going to be of any help.

Therapist: That's because you're placing all the responsibility for change on my shoulders. Look, if I had a formula for an instant cure I'd be a millionaire by now. The instant cure formula is totally unrealistic. It seems to me that part of your depression stems from a sense of helplessness and that's why you look to others to pull you out of it.

Client: Well, I certainly can't do it. I'm a failure.

Therapist: You haven't had much success so far but I do have a tried and tested formula for tackling depression that brings results.

Client: What is it?

Therapist: That your depression is created by certain ideas you hold and if you attack these ideas both inside and outside of therapy you'll probably be surprised how quickly you improve.

Client: Sounds like a lot of hard work.

Therapist: Yes, those two words again. Are you willing to take a risk and forget all about magic wands and instant cures?

Client: Reluctantly, but I'll have a go.

Therapist: Good. Now let's find out what you are making yourself depressed about in the first place and start sorting it out.

The client's reply, 'reluctantly', indicates that she is still hoping for an instant solution to her problems. As well as self-depreciation beliefs ('I'm a failure') regarding her inability to pull herself out of her depression, the client is probably also holding discomfort intolerance beliefs, e.g. 'I can't tolerate the hard work and struggle involved in facing my problems. There's got to be a quick and easy solution somewhere'. The solution offered by the therapist (though the client is not keen to hear it) is that hard work based on shared responsibility for change is the most effective way to lift her depression.

The therapist encourages the client to take up the offer of a 'tried and tested' formula by suggesting the likelihood of an early improvement in her mental state. Once the client is superficially persuaded by this rationale, the therapist then switches her to a problem-solving focus to discover her primary depression-inducing ideas. With this type of client, the therapist will need to keep on emphasising the self-defeating nature of the instant cure versus the self-helping one of hard work in order to deepen the client's commitment to constructive change.

When clients have misconceptions about REBT

Some clients' wariness about committing themselves to REBT stems from misconceptions they hold about its theory and practice. These misconceptions may have derived from, among other sources, critics of REBT (often those who have seen Albert Ellis work with the eponymous client in the film *Gloria*), former clients who have had negative experiences or outcomes with this approach and have laid the blame entirely at REBT's door, or some REBT therapists themselves who provide poor role models for the rational belief system they purportedly teach. Whatever their source, the therapist's task is to elicit clients' views, doubts or worries about REBT and discriminate them from genuine misunderstandings about its practice, e.g. 'Will I be in therapy for a long time?' and 'I'm afraid you're going to brainwash me' respectively (Dryden 2001). The following list includes three of the major misconceptions that clients have about REBT and provides answers to them.

REBT is a form of brainwashing

Leaving aside clients' assumptions that they have no control over their thinking, the brainwashing fear is that REBT therapists will 'implant' their point of view in their clients' mind and they will leave therapy as an REBT clone. What therapists actually seek to do is encourage clients to think for themselves by subjecting their self-defeating beliefs (e.g. 'I'm worthless and miserable without a partner in my life') to logical, realistic and functional examination as well as their rational alternatives (e.g. 'I would prefer a partner in my life but I don't need one and can be happy and self-accepting without one'). Clients are also urged to scrutinise REBT in a similar fashion. Albert Ellis (1983b), the founder of REBT, long argued that scepticism towards all things in life is an important feature of mental health. Therefore therapists work towards clients emerging from therapy as independent thinkers and not REBT robots.

A final point is that some clients confuse the force and energy employed by therapists to challenge their views with indoctrination. Such vigorous disputing has been found to be both effective and rapid in removing disturbance-creating ideas, but clients might feel initially overwhelmed by this approach, hence their suspicions about 'being brainwashed'. Such suspicions can be allayed by the therapist explaining the rationale for such methods.

REBT cares nothing for people's feelings

One criticism of REBT contends that it advocates a purely cognitive approach to understanding oneself and the world and therefore is devoid of emotion. Negative connotations associated with the word 'rational' conjure up images of cold, logical individuals who view others with icy detachment. However, this a caricature of REBT and not its actual practice. Though REBT is a primarily cognitively orientated approach to understanding emotional disturbance, it does use other senses to effect constructive change in an individual's life. In fact, thinking, feeling and behaving are given equal prominence in the name of this therapy though, to be accurate, thinking would be seen as first among equals because the other two modalities are used in the service of cognitive change.

Clients' emotions are almost always at the centre of the therapist's attention as therapists seek the most efficient way to replace their clients' unhealthy negative emotions (e.g. depression) with healthy negative ones (e.g. sadness, the self-helping alternative to depression). The most efficient way, as far as REBT is concerned, is for clients to identify, challenge and change through a variety of multimodal methods the irrational ideas underpinning their unhealthy emotions in order to create a rational and emotionally stable outlook. The word 'rational' has no sinister meaning, nor does it imply lack of emotion, but simply refers to whatever constructive means will help clients to attain their therapeutic goals and live happier and longer lives.

REBT teaches people to be selfish

Selfish individuals pursue their own pleasures and goals in life at the expense of others; their preoccupation with their own well-being makes them oblivious of or indifferent to the effects of their actions upon others. While REBT does urge clients to give priority to achieving their goals – after all, who else is going to do it for them? – it advocates a policy of enlightened self-interest and not selfishness. This policy reminds clients when planning their goals to take into account the concerns and wishes of others and thereby avoid acting in socially irresponsible or harmful ways; not to do so may rebound upon them and undermine their own goals, e.g. someone who wants a wide circle of friends but believes he should exploit them when necessary eventually finds himself rejected, alone and despised. REBT contends that if individuals choose goals that are both personally and socially responsible they are more likely to realise them as well as help to produce a more equitable and congenial society in which to live.

Another source of some clients' hesitancy in committing themselves to therapy is because they confuse REBT with the therapist's interactional style and therefore it is 'important for therapists to make enquiries which will help them to determine whether client objections are focused on issues pertaining to the therapy or the therapist' (Dryden and Yankura 1993: 197). If the therapist's style is the issue, e.g. 'You are asking too many questions' or 'You'll have to go more slowly if I'm to understand what you're saying', the therapist will need to modify it in order for therapy to proceed.

When clients won't be honest about negative reactions about therapy

Eliciting feedback from the client on each session is part of agenda setting. REBT therapists seek both positive and negative comments in order to help them tailor therapy to the individual client's requirements. While many clients might be ready to offer both types of feedback, some clients in the initial stages of therapy will need to be encouraged to provide critical comments while others will avoid doing so altogether. For this last group, such avoidance is often reflected in their presenting problems:

Therapist:	This is our third session of therapy. Was there anything I did today that was unhelpful, rude or insensitive?
Client:	No, you were wonderful as always. You are helping me so much.
Therapist:	Well, thank you for those comments, but you haven't voiced any criticisms yet about our three sessions.
Client:	They've all been excellent.
Therapist:	Did you notice what I did halfway through today's session?
Client:	Do you mean when you read the newspaper for a few minutes?
Therapist:	Yes. What did you think about me doing that?
Client:	Well, you're the expert. I'm sure you had a good reason for doing it.

Therapist:	I think the vast majority of clients would see that as downright rudeness. In what way did you see it differently?
Client:	I don't think you're rude. I think you are a very nice person.
Therapist:	Let me suggest something to you: if you make negative comments about me, you're afraid I'll reject or won't like you. This links in with your anxiety about losing the approval of significant others in your life.
Client:	*(hesitantly)* Well, I am a bit afraid of you not liking me if I say something that might not be nice. I'm always afraid of being rejected by everyone.
Therapist:	Well, we've shed some more light on your problems now. From my point of view, I will not reject you no matter what you say in therapy. But more importantly, I can teach you how to develop self-acceptance irrespective of whether people like you or not including myself.
Client:	If only I could be like that . . .
Therapist:	I assure you that such a goal is possible.

The therapist's hunch about the client's dire need for the therapist's approval militating against the client providing negative feedback was confirmed by the newspaper reading exercise. This was linked to a wider pattern of approval seeking in the client's life. The goal of achieving self-acceptance was offered to the client as the most effective way of overcoming these problems.

Dealing with client resistance in the middle phase

During this phase, the therapeutic focus is on strengthening clients' rational beliefs and weakening or removing their irrational ones. This is achieved by clients using multimodal methods of disputing (D) in a variety of problematic situations in order to internalise a new and effective (E) philosophy of living. This phase is often referred to as rational emotive behavioural working through and 'constitutes the heart of RE[B]T' (Grieger and Boyd 1980: 122). Client resistances encountered in this stage are now described.

When clients lack a criterion for coping

Some clients may want to discuss in each session what bothered them most in the preceding week rather than continue to work on a problem they wish to overcome. Such a lack of continuity from session to session may result in the fragmentation of therapy as both therapist and client lose their clinical focus and no real progress is made. Therefore it is important for the therapist to underscore the need for a coping criterion for each problem, i.e. a method of assessing when clients have reached the stage of managing a problem but not always smoothly or easily. The coping criterion can be used to determine the right time to switch from one client problem to another.

However, if circumstances warrant it, the therapist should be flexible and switch to another problem before coping criterion is attained on the previous one, e.g. a crisis in the client's life; another issue on the client's problem list is deemed to be of greater clinical importance than the one initially selected. Once the switch has been made, a coping criterion should be reached on the new problem before moving to another one. If the therapist believes the client is 'hopping' between problems, the therapist can explore with the client the cognitive dynamics involved in problem avoidance and the self-defeating nature of such behaviour.

When clients fear losing their identity if they change

Clients frequently complain of feeling 'strange' or 'unnatural' as they work towards attenuating their deeply held irrational beliefs and internalising a newly emerging rational outlook. This state is often called cognitive-emotive dissonance. Such a clash between old and new ways of thinking and feeling often leads to inner conflict or turmoil as 'they [clients] see a better way, but cannot yet actualize it, so they conclude that they cannot possibly overcome their disturbance' (Grieger and Boyd 1980: 161). The 'alien' and uncomfortable feelings that clients encounter in this stage of change often prompts them to leave therapy in order to feel 'natural' again. An example of cognitive–emotive dissonance is the 'I won't be me' syndrome:

> *Client:*   I don't want to be the submissive partner in my relationship any longer. I'm completely fed up with seeing myself as unworthy and grateful for anyone taking an interest in me.
>
> *Therapist:* So is striving for self-acceptance and being assertive helping to change this view of yourself?
>
> *Client:*   It's really helping a lot but it's such a weird feeling – it's as if I'm in someone else's body. This can't be me doing these things, it just isn't me. Sometimes the feeling is so uncomfortable I just want to give up therapy.
>
> *Therapist:* I assure you that these feelings belong to you and no one else. This feeling of a stranger inhabiting your body is

very common when individuals are sloughing off one self-image and acquiring another. Moving through this transitional phase requires a lot of persistence tolerating these feelings until the strangeness fades. When it does eventually fade, will you still believe that you are a stranger to yourself?

Client: I expect I'll feel much more relaxed and comfortable with my new image.

Therapist: A year from now or less, you may well see your old ideas and feelings as alien to you.

Client: I sincerely hope so.

Therapist: Have you ever been through a similar experience?

Client: I was a heavy smoker once and couldn't function without a cigarette. I just couldn't imagine myself without one.

Therapist: And when you stopped?

Client: A lot like now: quite frightening, uncomfortable, felt like I'd lost my identity, silly as it seems.

Therapist: So why did you persist?

Client: Because of the health benefits I wanted.

Therapist: And can you apply those same lessons today?

Client: Yes, I think I can. I do want very different things for myself now. So the quicker I cope with this strange period in my life and see it as a natural part of change, the quicker I will come out of it.

Therapist: Exactly.

In the above therapy extract, important points to consider are the following:

1 The therapist explains that cognitive–emotive dissonance is a phenomenon common to clients undergoing therapeutic change in order to put into perspective the client's disturbing feelings of unreality and depersonalisation.

2 To get through this 'transitional phase', persistence or tackling the client's discomfort disturbance is required to tolerate the above feelings.

3 The therapist encourages the client to look beyond this phase to the expected successful integration of the client's new thoughts and feelings; the old self-defeating ways will be then probably experienced as alien.

4 The therapist locates a previous episode of cognitive–emotive dissonance that the client overcame in order to apply the same lessons to the present one.

5   Though not mentioned in the above dialogue, clients can be warned about the 'I won't be me' syndrome in order to undermine its potentially adverse effects.

When clients don't see the differences between philosophical and non-philosophical change

During the middle phase of therapy, REBT therapists seek to determine the nature of clients' progress in tackling their emotional problems. The therapist's preferred solution (but not always the client's one) is the philosophical approach whereby clients' eradicate their 'musturbatory' thinking and replace it with rational preferences and desires. Non-philosophical solutions involve changing distorted inferences but not the underlying irrational ideas from where they derive, effecting behaviourally based change, or changing unpleasant activating events ('A's) rather than confronting them.

Some clients want the enduring benefits of a profound philosophical change yet employ non-philosophical methods in an attempt to achieve it. For example, someone who decides his inferences were wrong about his work colleagues' dislike of him fails to focus on the implicit irrational belief that 'They must like me in order for me to accept myself'. The danger here is that the disturbance-producing idea has been left intact and the client has not learnt any coping strategies if his inferences eventually turn out to be accurate. Also inferentially based change, like the other two non-philosophical solutions, has limited generalisability to the client's other problems as it does not usually provide the ideological context in which to understand which key ideas link his manifold problems, e.g. in the above example, the need for others' approval. Revealing and disputing these underlying ideas provides the most efficient means of tackling clients' problems rather than proceeding ponderously on a case-by-case basis.

This discrepancy between desiring philosophical change but using non-philosophical methods to achieve it may arise because clients, among other reasons, repeat parrot-fashion rational ideas or mechanically dispute irrational ones without realising what consistent and forceful action is really required of them or want lasting change with little effort. To deal with these difficulties, the therapist can clearly outline the considerable steps involved in philosophical change and contrast these with the clients' lack of commensurate effort in attaining it.

When clients don't realise that change would be so hard

Dryden and Neenan (2004b) argue that it is during the middle stage of REBT that clients show most resistance to change. Clients may have had an initial surge of progress or optimism in tackling their problems but now

have experienced setbacks, faltering progress or the sheer grind of overcoming a long-standing problem. Such obstacles can lead to disillusionment
or despair over the realities of change usually underpinned by discomfort
intolerance beliefs, e.g. 'If I had known how hard it was going to be, I
wouldn't have bothered in the first place'; 'I expected change to be difficult
but not this bloody hard!' Therapists need to make explicit clients' discomfort intolerance beliefs and encourage them to dispute vigorously these
ideas, e.g. 'Change should be hard not easy, so stop wasting valuable time
and energy moaning about it'; 'I'm going to stop whingeing and whining
and see this through to the bitter end'. Such determination will enable
clients to acquire a philosophy of discomfort tolerance and thereby help
them to realise their therapeutic goals.

When clients feel overwhelmed with their many problems

As clients move in to the middle phase of therapy, they may begin to realise
how many problems they have and may become discouraged. While
struggling to identify, challenge and change the irrational beliefs associated
with each of their problems, clients may fail to notice the emergence of a
particular theme which links these beliefs and coalesces into a core irrational belief because they feel overwhelmed by the number of problems
piling up. Core beliefs lie at the deepest level of cognitive awareness and
therefore are the most difficult to reveal, but once tapped into, allow clients
the opportunity for a profound philosophical change in their lives. Helping
clients to identify and work with these core beliefs often re-energises them
because they realise that awareness of such beliefs brings order into chaos:

Therapist:	We've unearthed quite a few dogmatic 'shoulds' in your various problems. With your boss . . .
Client:	He shouldn't overload me with work.
Therapist:	Stuck in queues, traffic jams, et cetera . . .
Client:	I shouldn't have to put up with the inconvenience of these things.
Therapist:	When things start going wrong for you . . .
Client:	I shouldn't have to work hard to put things right. You don't need to go on, I get the picture. I just seem to have a lot of problems and I'm getting overwhelmed by them.
Therapist:	I understand that, but the good news is that there is probably a theme which ties all these beliefs together.
Client:	I'm not sure what you mean.
Therapist:	Well, when we sift through these beliefs, they always seem to involve you complaining about something. What do you think is the essence of these complaints?

Client:	I suppose if I'm honest with you, I'm always moaning when I have to struggle in any way or work hard, especially with something I don't like.
Therapist:	The theme seems to be of having a smooth path through life. Would you agree?
Client:	Yes, I would. That does feel right.
Therapist:	So what might be the core belief from which these ideas stem?
Client:	'That other people, life itself, should make things easy and trouble free for me'.
Therapist:	And when things aren't made easy for you?
Client:	I can't bear all the hassle and discomfort involved. That's why I'm always getting angry or depressed over it.
Therapist:	Now that we've revealed this core belief, we can be more ambitious in therapy: if you forcefully dispute this belief you will be tackling simultaneously a number of problems rather than examining each one consecutively. Does that make sense?
Client:	It does now that I can see how they are linked. We are now going to work from the centre outwards rather than inwards to the centre. Is that right?
Therapist:	Precisely.
Client:	That helps me to feel less overwhelmed.

This dialogue demonstrates the therapist switching the therapeutic focus to deeper cognitive structures in order to show the client the wellspring of his situationally specific irrational ideas. This new focus allows for extensive and rapid progress as the client learns how to restructure radically and constructively his disturbance-inducing philosophy of living. Though not highlighted in the excerpt, it is wise for the therapist not to assume the presence of only one core irrational belief – a few others might also be present. In the above example, it may well be that the client has a core belief of self-condemnation or ego disturbance (e.g. 'I'm an utter failure') because of his inability to tolerate discomfort in his life and this idea accounts for his depression.

When clients are reluctant to take the reins of therapy

As therapist directiveness begins to fade, so clients are encouraged to take the lead in using the 'ABC's of REBT for self-analysis and change as well as setting and reviewing their homework assignments. However, some clients are reluctant to grasp the nettle of practising self-therapy. Reasons for this include fear of failure in their new role and discomfort tolerance beliefs regarding the additional and more demanding work now involved. This phase heralds the beginning of the end of therapy and some clients do not wish to acknowledge this and, instead, want to prolong therapy. Resistance to becoming a self-therapist is perceived by clients as the therapist abdicating responsibility for them. Whatever the reason, the therapist needs to draw out and challenge the ideas blocking this necessary shift in therapeutic responsibility; such ideas will be frequently linked to clients' presenting problems, e.g. 'I can't cope with anything on my own'.

Dealing with client resistance in the ending phase

During the ending phase of therapy, therapists and clients agree to work towards termination by decreasing session frequency or setting a fixed date for the final session. Clients review the course of therapy and what they have learnt from it, focusing on future problem-solving as a self-therapist using REBT skills and dealing with termination issues. In this section, we address a number of client roadblocks in the final phase of therapy.

When clients want to end therapy prematurely

Ellis (1972) suggested that many clients leave therapy when there has been an elevation in their mood, external circumstances have improved, some measure of hope or optimism has returned or they just feel better generally. Though all of these changes are to be welcomed, they are likely to be relatively short-lived because clients have terminated before they have adequately dealt with the irrational ideas underlying their presenting problems. REBT calls this process of change only 'feeling better' but not 'getting better':

Client:	I believe it's the right time to leave as I'm much better now.
Therapist:	Is that because you really can accept yourself without a man in your life and can be relatively happy on your own? Or have circumstances changed in your life?
Client:	Oh yeah, I do believe that stuff now but as it happens, I met this man and the chemistry between us is just perfect. We're both very happy and I don't need therapy any longer.
Therapist:	I don't want to dampen your happiness, but you have been through this same situation a number of times and when your partner leaves, you end up in suicidal despair.
Client:	This time will be different because our relationship will just keep on going. I know it will.

Therapist: My strong hunch is that you have paid lip service to rational ideas while still seeking the same old solutions to your problems. If the relationship does fall apart, I fear you may end up in hospital again after an overdose. I sincerely hope I'm wrong.

Client: So what do you want me to do – get rid of him?

Therapist: Of course not. Enjoy the relationship and stay in therapy a bit longer.

Client: What for?

Therapist: To really absorb and act on the idea of self-acceptance whether or not you are in a relationship. Self-acceptance is a form of protection against emotional distress.

Client: The relationship will protect me.

Therapist: Only when things are going right; if things go wrong you will be exposed again to the ideas that you're nothing without a man, life has no meaning on your own. Self-acceptance is the genuine protection against those ideas.

Client: Well, I don't agree and, anyway, my mind is made up.

Therapist: If you start slipping back or things are going wrong, please contact me again. The door is always open for you.

Client: Okay, I'll bear that in mind.

In this illustration, the therapist is encouraging the client to stay in therapy in order to understand the following:

1   Her disturbance-producing ideas remain intact as she has not challenged and changed them. Therefore these ideas are likely to be reactivated if her present relationship runs into trouble or ends.
2   By still clinging to her self-defeating ways, she has demonstrated that therapy has had little, if any, impact on her so far. Hence the therapist's advice for her to remain in therapy.
3   The rationale for this is that she can both enjoy the relationship and at the same time learn to develop a rational or healthy outlook about it based on self-acceptance. This new attitude will provide emotional stability for her in or out of relationships.
4   Although she is leaving therapy against the therapist's advice to pursue her 'love slobbism' (dire needs for love and approval), the therapist encourages her to return to therapy for further exploration of her problems if, as the therapist anticipates, they reoccur.

Some clients may wish to terminate therapy when they have achieved some progress in tackling their presenting problems. While they have identified and successfully challenged 'musturbatory' demands in specific situations, e.g. 'I must not make mistakes when I lecture to students', it is doubtful if these REBT gains will translate into a deeper and more pervasive approach to tackling emotional distress in various life situations because core irrational beliefs have not yet been excavated, e.g. 'I have to be perfect in everything I do'. This rationale may keep in therapy some of these clients as they are excited or intrigued by the prospect of greatly reducing their general level of disturbability in life. However, if therapy is terminated at this point, these clients can be reminded that they can return to therapy if they wish to extend their therapeutic progress.

When clients are reluctant to end therapy

Instead of prematurely ending therapy or not staying on in order to realise greater therapeutic benefits, some clients will want to stay in therapy as long as possible. This 'longevity in therapy' plea is clinically counter-productive as progress already made may begin to erode as clients look for ways to delay striking out on their own. This may occur because clients believe that they must feel completely confident about coping on their own, conditions in their life have to be perfect before leaving therapy or their problems should be completely resolved first.

If severing the therapeutic relationship 'does become a major issue, then the client is not ready to terminate, for this is an indication that the client relies on the therapist [or therapy] to fulfil some perceived need – perhaps approval, reassurance, or freedom from responsibility' (Wessler and Wessler 1980: 182). In the above examples, the therapist can challenge these termination-blocking ideas by stating that increased rather than complete confidence about problem-solving is most likely to be achieved once the client has left therapy and not remained indefinitely within it; creating 'perfect' or, more realistically, favourable conditions in one's life requires consistent hard work and determination that lingering in therapy will not provide – clients may be distracting themselves with Utopian fantasies rather than focusing on practical realities; as the therapist has consistently pointed out, managing one's problems and not completely resolving them is the benchmark for decisions about terminating therapy. Frequently under-lying this reluctance to leave therapy is the fear of failing as a self-therapist.

When clients think that they can't stand on their own two feet

The ultimate aim of an REBT therapist is to become redundant as clients develop competence and confidence in tackling their present and future problems. For some clients, this new role will provide a feeling of exhilaration, for others it will fill them with a sense of dread particularly if they have experienced a relapse prior to termination. The reactivation of clients' presenting symptoms as therapy nears the end of its course

> is not a phenomenon unique to RE[B]T, nor is it anything to become alarmed about. The most useful thing for the therapist to do when these fears arise is to simply help clients discover what they are telling themselves to become upset and to work these notions through.
>
> (Grieger and Boyd 1980: 190)

Client: I was really pleased with my progress but now it's all in ruins. How can I possibly leave therapy now? This proves I won't be able to do it on my own unless I can keep on coming back to you.

Therapist: How is your progress as a self-therapist destroyed because of a setback?

Client: I thought my public speaking anxiety was under control and then last week I nearly died of stage fright.

Therapist: We've discussed many times that change involves both progress and setbacks. Now let's get to work sorting out this stage fright. What were you telling yourself to bring back your anxiety?

Client: Same old thing – that I've got to give a perfect performance in order to gain the audience's approval?

Therapist: So your irrational ideas are still fighting a strong rearguard action. Therefore you are still having trouble at times believing your new rational ideas.

Client: They don't always feel so convincing when I'm in front of an audience.

Therapist: Therefore what needs to be done?

Client: I knew you would say that. More hard work and practice: keep on forcefully disputing my ideas until I only feel concerned about public speaking.

Therapist: That's right. Always use the 'ABC's of REBT to analyse your anxiety or any other emotional problem in your life. Now you got yourself quite upset over this relapse – are there any irrational ideas lurking in the background about your progress?

Client: I didn't think so until last week, but now I realise I'm demanding perfect progress. I don't want to lose your approval or my own if things go wrong.

Therapist: As you know, you've never had my approval or disapproval but my unconditional acceptance as a fallible

human being. You obviously don't give it to yourself all
the time.

Client: Well, this approval thing gets in the way.

Therapist: How can you deal with it? Approval is a key theme that
connects your problems.

Client: Challenge up the musts. I must challenge the musts
(laughs).

Therapist: You don't seem agitated now. What thoughts are going
through your mind?

Client: The setback doesn't seem so serious now it's been put
into perspective. I'm feeling quite confident now about
becoming a self-therapist. The dread and despair seem to
have gone.

Therapist: Yet another example of how your thinking creates your
feelings. So to recap: what does progress as a self-
therapist actually mean?

Client: It means lots of hard work to maintain my gains from
therapy, there will be mistakes and setbacks but these
will be useful to learn from if I can keep a problem-
solving focus. And as you keep on telling me: don't take
myself or these perfectionistic ideas too seriously.

Therapist: Good. Now shall we make the next session the last one?

Client: Agreed.

In the above extract, important points to consider are the following:

1   The setback near the end of therapy is not the real problem but the
client's awfulising belief about it – all her therapeutic gains have been
wiped out because of the recrudescence of her performance anxiety.
Therefore she concludes she cannot leave therapy at this juncture.

2   Strengthening rational ideas while attenuating irrational ones requires
consistent and persistent hard work and practice in all problem situations in her life. The 'ABC' model is a lifelong tool to understand and
remediate emotional disturbance.

3   Another block to standing on her own feet is her unrealistic notion that
progress must be perfect and, like her performance anxiety, making
self-acceptance conditional upon it. Even near the end of therapy, the
therapist keeps on encouraging the client to draw out further cognitive
data to understand how she impedes herself from experiencing greater
change.

4   A positive change in her mood is contrasted with her earlier despair in
order to demonstrate the thinking–feeling link. REBT therapists are
always on the lookout for ways of reinforcing this link.

5   As part of standard REBT practice, the client is asked for feedback on the issues raised in this extract to show she has understood the realistic expectations of self-therapy. This is confirmed by her ready agreement to terminate therapy at the next session.

When clients struggle with ambivalence about therapy's end

Some clients are eager to strike out on their own but also feel sad about ending what they consider to have been an important relationship in their lives. They may believe that feeling sad is a sign of weakness or 'not being rational' and therefore attempt to suppress this emotion in the final session while struggling to put on a brave face. It is important that therapists are alert to clues that such clients are struggling with these feelings and tease out the possible irrational ideas underlying them:

Therapist: I'm glad you are looking forward to standing alone, but I detect in some of your facial expressions and the way you're interacting with me today a certain sadness. Would this be true?

Client: No, I feel fine.

Therapist: Would you tell me if you were feeling sad?

Client: *(sighs deeply)* I don't want to admit it, but I do feel sad.

Therapist: What's the problem with that?

Client: Well, if I'm feeling sad then I really can't be that rational. I should be feeling really confident about everything now.

Therapist: Doesn't REBT emphasise feeling healthy negative emotions such as sadness? I feel sad about the end of the relationship, but I certainly do not see myself as irrational because of it.

Client: I know there's nothing wrong with sadness or any other healthy negative emotion. We've gone over it enough times but I still believe I shouldn't feel sad . . .

Therapist: Because . . .?

Client: I'm not sure.

Therapist: You mentioned it earlier.

Client: I've got to feel confident all the time.

Therapist: And feeling sad is . . .?

Client: . . . is a sign of weakness, failure.

Therapist: So you've got some lingering irrational ideas to winkle out and you've shown with previous problems that you have the REBT skills to do it. Now why is feeling sad a sign of weakness?

Client: Well, I should be upbeat and confident at the last session. Show the world I mean business.

Therapist: But you're not showing the world a rational role model because you are trying to suppress your healthy sadness at the loss of an important relationship in your life. Suppressed feelings may cause trouble for you.

Client: They already are – I'm screwing up the last session.

Therapist: I wouldn't agree with that. Like every other problem you've had in therapy, we're bringing a problem-solving focus to bear on it.

Client: Okay, so I've got a few blindspots left and some disputing to do.

Therapist: So what homework can you set yourself that we can review at the three-month follow-up session?

Client: Well, I can read again some of those REBT books, as I've obviously overlooked something.

Therapist: And your sadness?

Client: *(hesitantly)* Start expressing it?

Therapist: Good. Let me get the ball rolling by expressing mine and then going on to my feelings of pleasure at the great progress you've made in therapy.

Client: Thanks. That will give me the push I need.

The REBT therapist maintains a problem-solving focus right to the end of therapy and draws out the client's avoidance of expressing her sadness about termination. Her irrational ideas underlying her avoidance are pinpointed for her to dispute. Her self-assigned homework is further reading to correct her misunderstanding of REBT rationality with regard to the expression of healthy negative emotions. Despite the emergence of these problems in the last session, the therapist does not extend therapy but suggests that these problems can be reviewed at the three-month follow-up. This will be a long enough period to give a good indication of how she is coping as a self-therapist. In order to encourage her to express her suppressed feelings, the therapist employs self-disclosure to reveal his own sadness at no longer seeing her and thereby acts as a rational role model for her. What he also wants to discuss, of course, is her considerable progress because 'RE[B]T terminations are primarily pleasant events' (Wessler and Wessler 1980: 182).

The five chapters in Part I of the book have focused on client-created problems in therapy and what methods REBT therapists can employ to overcome them. Now we turn our attention in Part II to resistance induced by therapists that block or impede therapeutic progress and what remedial steps they can take.

Part II

Therapist resistance

Chapter 7

Dealing with therapist resistance in the bonds domain of the working alliance

Some REBT therapists can easily slip into blaming clients for difficulties in building a therapeutic alliance (e.g. 'They're being resistant') because they are unaware of or reluctant to look at their own ideas and behaviour which contribute to a stagnant relationship. This may be due to, among other factors, therapists holding irrational beliefs, clinical inexperience, an unvarying therapeutic style or diminishing the importance of the relationship in effecting constructive change. These and other therapist problems will now be discussed.

When therapists are overly concerned with getting down to work

REBT is generally a robust, no-nonsense approach to emotional problem-solving which seeks to elicit and challenge as quickly as possible clients' disturbance-creating ideas; so REBT therapists usually do not feel sorry for or 'mollycoddle' their clients. Facing up to and coping with the rigours of life will bring more constructive gains for clients than dollops of sympathy from therapists. However, some REBT practitioners may apply this hard-headed approach insensitively, indiscriminately or too forcefully and thereby stymie the development of a working alliance as clients shrink away from such an onslaught. A few clients might leave therapy after the first session because of it. Reinforcing these problems, therapists might start asking clients how they are upsetting themselves over this hard-headed therapeutic approach before discussing the principle of emotional responsibility (see Chapter 2). Clients may understandably feel bewildered or angry because they perceive they are being blamed for their reactions which they believe are caused by the therapist's manner.

While REBT therapists favour a 'let's get on with it' business-like approach to therapy, this has to be tempered with their clients' level of emotional distress or fragility, their expectations of therapy and preferences for a particular type of relationship. Therapists need to calibrate the pace of therapy to their clients' learning styles, allowing sufficient but not excessive time to talk about their problems. Such considerations, among others, will help to build rapport with clients and thereby make therapeutic progress more likely because they believe that the therapist has a genuine interest in helping them. Therefore therapists should not be in a hurry or appear to be impatient but 'relax. It is not necessary to solve the patient's problems right away' (Walen et al. 1992: 44).

Instead of rushing in to tackle the clients' presenting problems, some therapists might take the opposite tack of focusing too much on nurturing the relationship at the expense of problem assessment. This may stem from their belief that the client–therapist relationship is a sacred one and therefore they spend inordinate amounts of time demonstrating empathy, showing respect and offering unconditional positive regard (or, from the REBT viewpoint, unconditional acceptance). Only when the relationship has been developed through this process can therapists turn their attention to their clients' problems. Grieger and Boyd (1980) call this the 'relationship myth' and state that it has no independent existence or function. Developing a working alliance and establishing an early but unhurried problem-solving focus are not mutually exclusive activities, but complementary tasks that can convince clients of the therapist's expertise and trustworthiness.

When therapists lack empathy

Empathy is the therapist's ability to understand and communicate a client's viewpoint accurately. Walen et al. (1992) suggest that empathy is one of two factors – the other is the degree of attitudinal change that has occurred – that largely account for significant improvements in a client's mood during the course of a session. This important factor may be overlooked or paid lip service to by some REBT therapists' eagerness to impress clients with their extensive range of problem-solving techniques or clever arguments. Other therapists may see clients as merely the objects of their impersonal contemplation – another problem to unravel, another test of their clinical acumen. In both these cases, therapy is viewed as a primarily technical endeavour rather than a human one; hence the lack of empathy. Therefore clients may understandably recoil from therapists whose preoccupation is playing with their 'box of tricks' or whose manner indicates that they are being viewed through a microscope.

Empathy is an important quality that therapists need to display in order to help build rapport with clients and thereby increase the chances of effecting constructive change. REBT therapists demonstrate two kinds of empathy: affective – they communicate that they understand how clients feel (e.g. 'You must have been really hurt when you didn't get that promotion after all your years of loyal service') and philosophical – they also show clients the probable ideas underlying their feelings (e.g. 'Do you believe that your boss let you down or betrayed you and that such treatment from him was totally undeserved?'). Clients are often impressed by this double-barrelled empathic approach as the therapist has not only pinpointed the relevant feeling but also echoed their thoughts. Compassion combined with clinical competence helps to cement the therapeutic alliance.

It may be that some therapists have an emotional problem about showing empathy. They feel it, but find it hard to show it. This issue needs to be discussed in supervision and in personal therapy if it endures.

When therapists need to be respected and loved by clients

Therapists are obviously not immune from irrational ideas in general and therapy-related ones in particular. Ellis (1985, 2002) identified several irrational beliefs, including the one that therapists need to be respected and loved by their clients, that therapists may subscribe to and thereby interfere with their clients' progress. The following dialogue illustrates how therapeutic inefficiency occurs when therapists have approval needs:

Supervisor:	Listening to your therapy tapes, I am constantly struck by the easy ride you're giving to the client.
Therapist:	I'm not sure what you mean by that.
Supervisor:	Take homework, for example: he said he didn't get round to doing it and you passed up the opportunity to find out why.
Therapist:	I believed what he said.
Supervisor:	But that doesn't help him or you to elicit the cognitive blocks that prevented him from doing it.
Therapist:	I didn't think it was important to press him at that time.
Supervisor:	Because to do so . . .?
Therapist:	He would get angry, that's why. He often gets angry.
Supervisor:	I agree that angry clients are usually difficult to deal with but you seem to be avoiding dealing with it.
Therapist:	I would deal with his anger if he would stop being angry!
Supervisor:	If you did it that way, you wouldn't tap into his anger-producing cognitions. What are his goals for change?
Therapist:	To overcome his procrastination and anger.
Supervisor:	Do you think you are making any progress with him?
Therapist:	A little.
Supervisor:	I'm also aware from the tapes that you placate him when things start to get uncomfortable and, at one point, he said you were of no help to him. What was your reply again?
Therapist:	'I'm sorry you feel like that'.

Supervisor: What could have been a more therapeutic response?

Therapist: I suppose I could have asked him why he felt like that.

Supervisor: Did you really want to hear his reply?

Therapist: I wasn't too keen to hear it. There's no point having my nose rubbed in it if he thinks I'm no good.

Supervisor: Why do you think you're soft-pedalling with him all the time?

Therapist: *(hesitantly)* I suppose, and I don't like to admit it, I'm afraid of him not liking me. If I push him in therapy he might end up hating me.

Supervisor: He might hate you for the opposite reasons – that you're not helping him to achieve his goals because you're afraid to confront him. Now why do you need his approval?

Therapist: Because without it, this means I'm a bad therapist and an unlikable person.

Supervisor: Therefore therapy is being driven for your benefit, not his. Do you want to retain this belief?

Therapist: No, I don't. I know it's getting in the way of his progress and mine.

Supervisor: So what are you going to do about it?

Therapist: What I should be doing with him: examining an irrational idea from all sides, forcefully disputing it to develop the rational alternative instead.

Supervisor: Which would be?

Therapist: Self-acceptance, no matter what he thinks of me.

Supervisor: When you've developed that belief, how will therapy be different?

Therapist: I'll be focused on encouraging him to deal with his problems and I won't be avoiding confronting him if it seems therapeutically necessary.

Supervisor: Good. Struggling with your problems on your own for a while may provide you with some insights as to what your clients are going through. It's a valuable learning experience.

Therapist: I'm already feeling more confident about the next therapy session.

In this supervision extract, important points to consider are the following:

1   REBT practitioners are not noted for their soothing approach to problem-solving, yet the therapist adopts it to sidestep dealing with the client's homework avoidance, angry outbursts and any other difficult or painful issue that arises. This alerts the supervisor to the probability that the therapist has some operative irrational beliefs.

2   The supervisor's use of such terms as 'easy ride' and 'soft-pedalling' suggest that her hypothesis is that the therapist has approval needs which he subsequently confirms (looking for an 'easy time' in therapy may also indicate low frustration tolerance beliefs).

3   In his desperation to be liked by the client, the therapist has lost his clinical focus and thereby therapy has foundered. In making the irrational belief explicit, the therapist now has the opportunity to put therapy back on track if he undisturbs himself first.

4   The supervisor gets the therapist to describe how he would act differently and efficiently in therapy if he learnt self-acceptance as a further inducement to remove his irrational thinking.

5   Also the supervisor echoes Ellis's (1985: 170) point that 'if you try to change yourself, at first, without guidance and support from another therapist, you may be able to appreciate better the struggles of your own clients when they strive for self-change'.

When therapists create an aura of omniscience

This occurs when therapists convince themselves that their particular brand of psychotherapy is able to explain all aspects of psychological disturbance and its amelioration rather than viewing it as an incomplete and provisional account of these processes. Armed with such an understanding of human behaviour that is not liable to be wrong, they conduct therapy with an Olympian disregard of or a condescension to clients' explanations of their problems:

> *Therapist:*   Do you know why you get so upset when your husband pays no attention to you?
>
> *Client:*   Well, it's only natural if he ignores me when I want a cuddle and a bit of affection.
>
> *Therapist:*   No, that doesn't really account for it. Shall I tell you why?
>
> *Client:*   I'd like to find out if I'm doing the wrong things.
>
> *Therapist:*   Because you're demanding that he must show you affection in order to prove that he still loves you. For without his love you see yourself as worthless.
>
> *Client:*   I don't see it like that.
>
> *Therapist:*   Not yet, but you will in time.

The therapist has no real interest in the client's replies to his questions or the client's comments: these are just used as springboards for the therapist to display his god-like wisdom. Instead of creating a genuinely therapeutic and collaborative relationship, the therapist's conception of it is that of deity and devotee.

In order to avoid developing pretensions to divinity, REBT therapists should do the following:

- acknowledge their own frequent fallibility and, if clinically relevant, share this with their clients
- develop scepticism towards REBT and thereby be aware of its limitations and weaknesses
- employ humour against themselves if they start to yearn for infallibility
- show their clients that by helping them (i.e. the clients) they have gained for themselves further therapeutic skills and experience
- let clients arrive at their own insights into their problems through Socratic questioning and avoid handing them down on tablets of stone.

In the above dialogue, even if the therapist's hypothesis is correct, there are more client-friendly and introspective ways of confirming it.

Guarding against injudicious therapist self-disclosure

Injudicious use of therapist self-disclosure may occur because therapists do not adhere to the 'one rule that seems inviolate . . . the therapist is there to give therapy, not to get it. Therapists who share problems in hopes of getting them solved cheat the clients' (Wessler and Wessler 1980: 170). Therapists who use therapy for their own needs rather than their clients' probably subscribe to a major therapist irrational idea: 'Because I am a person in my own right, I must be able to enjoy myself during therapy sessions and to use these sessions to solve my personal problems as well as to help my clients' (Ellis 2002: 207). As the therapist guides the course of therapy and takes the lead in developing the therapeutic alliance, these crucial activities will be undermined as the therapist's attention and energy is diverted into exploring his or her own problems.

Another reason for inappropriate self-disclosure is not so much a working through of the therapist's problems, but a narcissistic assumption that the therapist's own life experiences and difficulties will be of universal interest and relevance, e.g. 'My own experiences, while not similar to yours, will nevertheless be of real help to you'. Or the therapist has been afflicted with every known problem and is quick to share this with the client but comes across as falsely empathic, e.g. 'I know exactly how you feel. I went through the same thing when it happened to me'. Clients may not appreciate being so well understood so quickly and therefore feel they are not being listened to or that the uniqueness of their problems is being devalued.

Whatever the reasons for the therapist's lack of verbal restraint, the only valid use of self-disclosure is when it is clinically relevant: therapists say that they have experienced a problem and accompanying irrational ideas similar to those of the client's and how they eventually prevailed through a variety of disputing methods. Clinical relevance is ascertained through feedback from clients – if they derive no benefit from such information, then therapists should discontinue the use of this technique.

To disclose or not to disclose

Therapist disclosure may be initiated by clients in an attempt to determine if the therapist can really understand their problems, e.g. 'Have you ever been an alcoholic?' The therapist difficulty here is that a reply of 'Yes' can cement the working alliance because the client believes he has found a kindred spirit who can help him, or destroy it because such a revelation has lost the respect of the client, who was seeking a relationship based on the therapist's expertise untainted by personal experience of his problem. On the other hand, a reply of 'No' may lose the client who wants to see a former-addict-turned-therapist, but relieve the client who believes that a true professional understands but avoids the pitfalls of her clients. There is no easy answer to this dilemma except to answer honestly to such self-revelatory questions, and tackle the reasons why some clients will want to leave therapy on the basis of the therapist's reply.

Dealing with the 'neurotic agreement in psychotherapy'

The 'neurotic agreement in psychotherapy' is a term used by Hauck (1966) to describe a therapist's failure or reluctance to challenge her client's irrational ideas because she holds the same ideas, e.g. 'I must have a romantic relationship in my life in order to feel worthwhile'. Knowing that her own challenges to the client's irrationality will not be particularly convincing and wanting to avoid seeing herself reflected in the client's problem, the clinical focus is switched to other, possibly less important, issues. This results in the therapeutic alliance working at less than optimum effectiveness.

Another form of therapist avoidance which impairs the alliance is the delay in 'getting down to business' because the therapist enjoys the client's company and wants to prolong it, e.g. 'I see so many difficult or obnoxious clients that when I find someone I really like, I deserve to have an easy and pleasurable time in therapy'. This easygoing approach of the therapist's may dovetail with the client's discomfort intolerance problems (e.g. 'I can't stand hard work') to produce a relationship based on short-range hedonism and not on a business-like approach to problem-solving.

In both cases, the therapists are putting their own interests first and thereby leaving important client problems unexamined. By disputing the irrational ideas underpinning their conditional self-acceptance and deservingness, the therapists will not only undisturb themselves about these issues but also return therapy to where it belongs – firmly focused on their clients' disturbances.

When therapists are intransigent

Sometimes therapists can dogmatically insist that their hypotheses or interpretations of the clients' problems are correct and therefore are not prepared to consider any disagreements from the clients, e.g. 'You're still demanding today that your parents should have stayed together when you were young and thereby none of your future problems would have occurred. You are refusing to accept this truth'. In fact, the more their clients 'resist', the more convinced the therapists are of their perceptual accuracy. Such conflict can obviously lead to an impasse in therapy or to early termination. The reasons for the therapist's intransigence can be uncovered in supervision:

Supervisor: Why have you turned what should be a tentative and flexible hypothesis into a rigid one?

Therapist: I know I'm right about this client. I feel it so strongly.

Supervisor: As you know, feelings are not facts and therefore are unreliable guides to the accuracy of any particular interpretation: why must you be right?

Therapist: Because it will prove that I am a highly competent therapist who can see through the client's smokescreen.

Supervisor: But the client does not agree with your interpretation and I doubt if she sees you as highly competent.

Therapist: Well, that just proves how resistant she is being.

Supervisor: Even if you are right, why does she have to agree with you?

Therapist: Because she is still disturbed about her parents' divorce when she was a little girl, so why can't she admit it and be honest?

Supervisor: There appear to be two irrational or therapy-blocking ideas at work here. The first one is that your hypothesis must be right and if it is not, you will see yourself as a poor or lousy therapist. The second one is that you can't stand it when clients deny their disturbances. What do you think about my hypotheses?

Therapist: *(pauses)* I notice you're offering them to me rather than imposing them. I'm reluctant to say it, but they do have the ring of truth about them.

Supervisor: Okay, let's take the first idea. Who defines you as a lousy therapist if your hypothesis is wrong?

Therapist: I do.

Supervisor: Being wrong is not a sign of a lousy therapist but what . . .?

Therapist: It's a sign of being an open-minded, flexible, scientific REBT practitioner who is not afraid to discard his assumptions if they're wrong.

Supervisor: Exactly. Your present anti-scientific stance is more likely to drive clients out of therapy rather than keep them in it. So what are you going to do about it?

Therapist: Start by admitting that my hypothesis may well be wrong and examining the data with the client in order to confirm, revise or reject it.

Supervisor: Remember, hypothesis testing occurs throughout the course of therapy and not just at the beginning. Now if you follow the actual practice of REBT, you will more likely become a skilled therapist.

Therapist: That's what I want.

Supervisor: Then keep your ego out of therapy and you'll find that you're much less disturbable and thereby of much more help to the clients. Now your second irrational idea – why does she have to admit that she is disturbed over this issue?

Therapist: Because if she admits it, she can deal with it. By not doing so, she's pretending everything is all right. I can't stand the pretence.

Supervisor: It seems you're more interested in destroying her supposed pretence rather than dispassionately looking for evidence that it exists. Why can't she keep up this pretence throughout therapy if she wants to?

Therapist: Because it rankles so. I know she's doing it but she won't admit it.

Supervisor: It seems to me that your ego is again on the line – in order to prove you're a smart therapist and this client can't pull the wool over your eyes, you have to be the winner in this battle of wills. Does that sound plausible?

Therapist: (sighs) Yeah, the ego thing is getting in the way again.

Supervisor: If clients do want to play games or pretend everything is okay – and I'm not saying this client is – they lose out because they remain emotionally disturbed, but you don't have to disturb yourself over it. Now I suggest for homework that you list the short- and long-term advantages and disadvantages of ego-driven therapy. Okay?

Therapist: I think that will help me to gain more objectivity about my behaviour in therapy as well as to become more clinically competent. I can see more clearly now how I'm blocking myself and therapy.

Supervisor: Good. We'll review your progress at the next session.

In this extract from supervision, the supervisor is showing the therapist the following points:

1   The therapist's self-disturbance arises from his rigid ideas about the client's problems rather than the client's purported resistance to his interpretations. His insistence on proving himself right is driving therapy into a cul-de-sac and he is displaying all the qualities that are antithetical to the practice of good REBT.

2   Hypotheses are not copper-bottomed facts but only provisional explanations that can be confirmed or repudiated. Teaching by example, the supervisor offers his own hypothesis to the therapist that each irrational belief involves nailing his credibility to the mast – to admit he might be wrong would signal his failure as a therapist.

3   The therapist agrees with the supervisor's assumptions and is encouraged to look at disinterested ways of gathering assessment information and thereby avoiding power struggles with his client. The supervisor's injunction 'to keep your ego out of therapy' means that the therapist's fortunes will not be rising and falling like the stock exchange depending on how the client is faring, responding or behaving.

4   Being less disturbable, this will enable him to improve his clinical skills and thereby become a competent therapist – the homework task (and others of similar ilk) will help him to reach this goal whereas his own battering ram approach to therapy blocked him from achieving it.

Guarding against the inappropriate use of humour

Ellis (1985) frequently stated that one of the major causes of emotional disturbance is when individuals take themselves, their problems and life *too* seriously. Therefore the use of humour can be an effective intervention in helping clients to combat their disturbance-producing ideas, but is not meant to be directed at the clients themselves. However, some therapists might believe that the general use of humour is in itself therapeutic and always aim for a 'fun-filled hour', or they become so enamoured with their putative wit that they are oblivious to its grating effect upon the client. Other therapists' inappropriate use of humour may stem from a major therapist irrational belief that 'I must be able to enjoy myself during therapy sessions' (Ellis 1985, 2002). The net result of such behaviour is that clients may feel they are being laughed at, their problems trivialised or they are supposed to be the admiring spectators of the therapist's comic performance.

When the therapist has made a humorous challenge to a client's irrational idea, e.g. the client says that her drinking 'crept up on me' and the therapist mimics her statement by using a bottle to creep up his body and put itself into his mouth, he needs to gain immediate feedback from the client as to her interpretation of his behaviour. Did she see the clinical relevance of his act? Did the humour help or hinder the issue of personal responsibility for one's problems? Was the humour used in a constructive or insulting way? If the client's reactions are generally negative to such questions, the further use of humour should be ruled out.

Being careful about the use of profane language

Albert Ellis, the founder of REBT, is well known for his use of swearwords, but this is not a requirement to practise as an REBT therapist. Ellis's use of profanity is not gratuitous but serves to, among other things, build rapport with certain clients (e.g. a person whose conversation is splattered with expletives) in order to strengthen the therapeutic alliance as well as to highlight certain points, e.g. 'Why the FUCK do you always have to succeed?' As with humour, profanity is aimed at the client's self-defeating thinking and not at the client.

Some therapists may think that profanity is an important part of an REBT therapist's repertoire in their fight against irrational beliefs and, in a misguided attempt to emulate Ellis, arbitrarily introduce swearing into therapy in order to invigorate it, 'grab the client's attention' or indulge themselves. This may well have the opposite effect upon some clients, who believe they could not reveal intimate details about themselves to such 'a foulmouthed person' and consequently terminate therapy. Therapists should note whether the client uses swearwords as an indicator that profanity might be warranted or pay attention to the client's preferences for a particular type of relationship, e.g. a formal or down-to-earth one, in order to determine the content of the language they will use.

The concept of 'shithood' is frequently used in REBT and refers to individuals who see themselves as completely worthless, inadequate, incompetent, etc. These epithets may be synonymous with shithood in the minds of REBT therapists but not necessarily in their clients:

Client: I see myself as a total failure. It's been like that for a long time. I try to fight against it but nothing works.

> *Therapist:*   Okay, so you see yourself as a complete shit. Now what
> are the factors that lead you to believe . . .
> *Client:*   Hold on a minute! I said I saw myself as a failure, not a
> shit. If I want to be insulted I can stay at home and do it
> myself.

To avoid such a blunder, therapists should employ only clients' terms of
self-depreciation in their efforts to understand clients' perceptions of reality.
In the above example, the client may have been struggling to maintain a
sense of dignity in the face of repeated failure which the use of the word
'shit' may rob him of. The concept of 'shithood' can be introduced into
therapy for clients' consideration and not suddenly unleashed upon them.

Guarding against making moral judgements

Ellis (1985: 28) suggested that 'a trait that many therapists possess and that
blocks them in helping clients is their moralism: the profound tendency to
condemn themselves and others for evil or stupid acts'. Such moralism may
lead to explicit criticism of the client, e.g. 'How in heaven's name are we
supposed to make progress with your problems when you keep on turning
up late?' or non-verbal signals of condemnation such as drumming one's
fingers on the table, not smiling, looking impatient, not listening. This kind
of therapist behaviour will often help clients to reinforce their self-damning
tendencies and thereby they end up even more disturbed than they were at
the outset of therapy. This outcome makes it highly likely that some of
these clients will resist therapy. The therapist's moralistic attitudes are
examined in the following dialogue:

> *Therapist:*   He's hopeless. We waste so much therapy time with his
> lateness when we could be tackling his problems.
> *Supervisor:*   So you believe he should be behaving in the right and
> proper fashion by being punctual. He should be acting
> responsibly.
> *Therapist:*   Exactly. If he wants help, he should get to therapy on
> time.
> *Supervisor:*   Now something strikes me as very odd: if he's emo-
> tionally disturbed, this is obviously affecting his time-
> keeping yet you demand responsible behaviour, so he
> will have to undisturb himself first in order to be punc-
> tual. So how is he supposed to achieve that when by your
> own account he's becoming more not less disturbed?
> *Therapist:*   I really don't know. He's pathetic.

Supervisor: Damning him is not going to make him feel better or get to therapy on time. He's a fallible not a damnable human being. Now why does he have to do the right thing rather than it would be preferable if he did it?

Therapist: Because I would turn up on time if I wanted help, so he too should make the effort.

Supervisor: But you are imposing your moral values on him and thereby clouding your clinical judgement. You're also depriving him of his individuality by demanding he act like you. Do you want to truly help him or just get him to jump through your moral hoops?

Therapist: I want to help him, of course.

Supervisor: Now why does he have to get to therapy on time?

Therapist: He doesn't, but I still think poor timekeeping is nothing to admire.

Supervisor: I'm not asking you to admire it, and you can point out to him in a non-damning way that it is interfering with reaching his goals. Now you will need to change the way you relate to him if you want to achieve progress.

Therapist: You mean offer him unconditional acceptance as a fallible human being.

Supervisor: That's exactly what REBT advocates. Now if you work hard to achieve this, how might therapy be different?

Therapist: Well, I'd stop moralising and looking down on him. We'd probably have a more relaxed time in therapy.

Supervisor: And he may well feel you are now on his side rather than always disapproving of him. Now what would you do about his timekeeping?

Therapist: Look at the reasons for his lack of punctuality and take constructive steps to tackle it.

Supervisor: Now how can disturbed clients suddenly undisturb themselves to get to therapy on time?

Therapist: *(laughs)* It sounds silly now. If he could do that he probably wouldn't need to see me in the first place.

Supervisor: Probably not. Now how would you react if I damned you for damning the client?

Therapist: I'd get angry or feel bad.

Supervisor: Would you be eager to come to supervision?

Therapist: I'd look for ways to avoid it or, I hate to say it, get here late.

Supervisor: None of us likes to feel the moral lash across our backs and it doesn't usually produce improved behaviour.

Therapist: Well, I'll try to keep the moralising to my own life then.

> *Supervisor:* You might find that if you brought some flexibility to your own moral standards, you wouldn't be so harsh on the client when he fell below the standards you demand of yourself.
>
> *Therapist:* That's true. I give myself a hard time as well as him.
>
> *Supervisor:* He's not the only one then who needs to receive unconditional acceptance. Within such a context, you can non-damningly challenge his as well as your own behaviour.
>
> *Therapist:* There's a lot to think about today.
>
> *Supervisor:* And put into practice. We'll see how you've got on at the next session.
>
> *Therapist:* Okay.

Important points to consider in this extract are the following:

1 The only judgements to be made in therapy are clinical not moral ones. Judging clients on the basis of their bad or irresponsible behaviour militates against building a therapeutic alliance, but the acts themselves can be judged as to whether they help or hinder clients to achieve their goals. Demanding morally correct or rational behaviour from disturbed individuals is in itself a sign of psychological disturbance or, at least, muddled thinking.

2 The supervisor asks the therapist to envisage the probable benefits that she and her client will enjoy if she offers the client unconditional acceptance rather than moral disapproval. In such a non-judgemental climate, therapy can revert to its proper focus on the client's problems starting with his poor timekeeping.

3 The supervisor encourages the therapist to see therapy from the client's viewpoint by asking her how she would react if he condemned her for condemning the client. This altered perspective prompts in the therapist the beginnings of an empathic understanding of the client's feelings.

4 Inflicting the 'moral lash' on ourselves or others does not usually lead to better behaviour as we avoid trying to understand these failings and, instead, only condemn them and ourselves. Therefore if the therapist introduces flexibility and self-acceptance into her own moral values, she will be more likely to show compassion towards the client and thereby forge a genuine working alliance.

When therapists lecture clients

Some therapists may indulge in long or too frequent lectures on various aspects of REBT without obtaining feedback from clients. Their eagerness for didactic presentations will probably dull their sensitivity to cues that clients are not listening to them:

> Therapist: Now I've described in some detail the various criteria that suggest a belief is irrational. Do you understand that?
>
> Client: (wearily) Yes.
>
> Therapist: Good. Now let's look at how we go about disputing irrational beliefs.

Clients can become resentful of such an incessant lecturing style and yearn for the end of the session or start daydreaming because they feel uninvolved in therapy. Generally speaking, too much didacticism from the therapist can inhibit clients' ability to think for themselves, turn them into passive rather than active collaborators in therapy and bring about only superficial changes in their problems.

If therapists are going to give lectures, these should be small, concise and infrequent, and after each one they should obtain feedback from their clients that they have made themselves understood, e.g. 'Can you put into your own words the importance of self-acceptance?' Therapists can also monitor their therapy tapes for evidence of counterproductive lecturing.

Guarding against using a monolithic interactional style

Some therapists use an unvarying interactional style with their clients. Instead of being responsive to their clients' preferences for a particular bond (e.g. informal and humorous; formal and serious), therapists are reluctant or unable to modulate their interactional style. This may lead to a clash of styles as their standard no-nonsense, 'let's get on with it' approach is constantly halted by their clients' requests for a quieter and more reflective manner. If clients' interpersonal behaviour is also inflexible, little therapeutic progress can be imagined.

Kwee and Lazarus (1986) suggest that therapists adopt the role of an 'authentic chameleon' which would allow them to display the most helpful facets of their personality in building rapport with a particular client while remaining genuine in the process. Flexibility is the hallmark of the 'authentic chameleon' as the therapist adapts to and blends in with the requirements of the therapeutic alliance at any given time. The only caveat to this approach is if the client's bond preferences reinforce existing problems, e.g. wanting excessive warmth from the therapist to sustain the client's approval needs. If some therapists are reluctant to adopt this role, possible irrational attitudes can be revealed and challenged, e.g. 'Why should I have to pander to what he wants' or 'I won't feel like myself in therapy and therefore I'll be very uncomfortable'. For those therapists who are unfamiliar with this role or unable to fulfil it at present, they can practise varying their interactional styles with their supervisor or others, e.g. family, friends or colleagues.

Dealing with countertransference

The term 'countertransference' is used to denote the feelings and attitudes of the therapist towards the client. These may be transferred on to the client from the therapist's reactions to significant others in the therapist's life, e.g. 'I can't stand people like my mother who endlessly whinge and whine'. The therapist's barely suppressed hostility towards or impatience with the client is highly unlikely to engender a therapeutic milieu:

Supervisor: You are obviously more focused on what you despise about the client than you are on helping her.

Therapist: I know. As soon as she starts moaning, she reminds me of my mother's behaviour and this sets me on edge.

Supervisor: What's the irrational belief at work here?

Therapist: Well, I suppose she should bloody well stop moaning, otherwise I can't bear it.

Supervisor: Now if you vigorously challenged this belief and therefore you could bear the client's moaning, how would this change your interaction with her?

Therapist: I'd be much calmer with her and I would pay close attention to the content of her moaning in order to uncover the beliefs maintaining it. At present, I switch off.

Supervisor: So you would become emotionally undisturbed and clinically focused because you would tell yourself . . .?

Therapist: She should be that way because she is that way. As soon as I accept the reality of the situation, I might be able to help her do something about it and, if I can't, I don't have to disturb myself about that either.

Supervisor: Good. If you wish, you might also apply this approach to your mother. Desirable changes can then be brought about in both relationships.

Therapist: I really do want to improve my performance in therapy and get on better with my mother, so I will give myself a rational inoculation to fight off my 'I-can't-stand-it-itis'.

Supervisor: We'll see if it's working when we next listen to your therapy tapes.

The therapist's reaction to the client may provide useful information about the impact the client may have on other people, e.g. 'I wonder if my anxiety around him is reflected in other people's attitudes to him?' With this kind of reaction, Walen et al. (1992: 246) observe that countertransference 'enables you [the therapist] to use yourself as a monitoring device'. For example, the therapist dreads the appointment time because she will have to face the client's obnoxious behaviour; she feels as if she is walking on eggshells during therapy and experiences tremendous relief at the end of each session. The therapist's irrational belief in this case might be: 'I must avoid at all costs him losing his temper. If he does, it will be awful'. Once the therapist's belief has been identified, challenged and changed, she can then from a non-disturbed viewpoint disclose to the client the unpleasant effect he has upon her and, by extension, others in his life. Such information can help the client to develop more constructive and rewarding ways of behaving in relationships.

Therapists may develop non-countertransference relationship problems as when, for example, they find themselves sexually attracted to some of their clients. Instead of establishing an early problem-solving focus, the therapist may spend an inordinate amount of time building up the supposedly therapeutic relationship, indulging in mild flirtation and generally having a good time. Therapy is prolonged for the therapist's benefit while solving the client's problems is put on a slow track. Although the therapist may well be reluctant to, he needs to give himself the disputing equivalent of a cold shower:

> 'I'm her therapist, not a potential lover. It would have been nice if I had met her socially but as I didn't, too bad. I'm going to focus my mind on her problems and not on her body. If I can't make the adjustment, then I should refer her to someone who can.'

When therapists believe that they have to be outstanding

Ellis (1985, 2002) identified the following therapist irrational belief: 'I must be an outstanding therapist, clearly better than other therapists I know or hear about.' Therapists who hold this belief may be frantic to succeed with clients who have not made progress with a string of previous therapists or are deemed to be 'therapy proof'; agree to unrealistic client goals (e.g. 'I never want to experience another panic attack'); or refuse to acknowledge the limited gains that some or many clients will only achieve as they struggle to wring the last drop of progress out of them. In addition, they may deny they have any emotional problems because this is incompatible with being an 'outstanding therapist'. These various problems result in therapy being driven by the therapist's vanity and panic to succeed – the very opposite of therapeutic efficiency and possibly leading to therapist burnout.

Without encouraging such therapists to lower their standards, the supervisor can help them to transmute this irrational belief into a rational one, surrender their godlike pretensions and acknowledge their fallibility. With this philosophical change, vanity can be replaced by humility and panic by calm deliberation. Such methods will help to avoid burnout and, instead, encourage therapists to strive for the highest possible level of clinical competence.

In this chapter, we have looked at ways of dealing with therapist-created resistances in the bonds domain of the working alliance. We now turn the spotlight on therapist resistance in the views domain of the alliance and particularly therapists' doubts or reservations about the 'ABC' model of emotional disturbance.

Chapter 8

Dealing with therapist resistance in the views domain of the working alliance

We mentioned in Chapter 2 that one of us (WD) added a fourth domain to Bordin's (1979) tripartite view of the working alliance. This domain is referred to as 'views' in that they describe the ideas that therapists and clients hold about therapy (Dryden 2006, 2011). These ideas concern

- the practicalities of therapy (e.g. fees, frequency of sessions, the therapist's cancellation policy)
- confidentiality and its limits
- how the client's problems are conceptualised and how treatment of these problems is conceived.

In Chapter 2, we outlined how therapists are advised to respond to client resistance in the views domain of the alliance and in this chapter we focus on therapist resistance to accepting or teaching clients the 'ABC's of REBT. However, we also discuss more generally about spotting and dealing with therapist resistance in the views domain of the alliance point.

Avoiding being dogmatic about what therapy should be about

REBT therapists tend to see clients as experts on their own experience and themselves as experts on REBT and the conduct of therapy. That being said, perhaps the principle that REBT values above all others is anti-dogmatism or flexibility. This means that while therapists may have a clear idea of their clients' problems and how these can best be tackled, how many sessions clients need and how often they need to meet, it is important that therapists hold and convey to clients that they hold flexible ideas on such points. Let's illustrate this point by comparing an REBT therapist who has rigid ideas about how many sessions a client needs with the same therapist who has flexible ideas about this issue.

Client:	Can I ask you a question about therapy?
Therapist:	Sure.
Client:	How many sessions do you think I need?
Therapist:	Well, based on what you have told me, I would say twenty sessions would be necessary to deal with the problems you outlined.
Client:	Oh! That is quite a lot.
Therapist:	Well, that is what's required
Client:	*(hesitantly)* Well, I will have to think about that.

Note here that the therapist did not even ask the client for her views on the issue. He answers the question honestly, but gave himself and the client no room for manoeuvre (a sure sign of rigidity) and no space for negotiation.

Now let's see what happens when the therapist is flexible about the issue:

Client:	Can I ask you a question about therapy?
Therapist:	Sure.
Client:	How many sessions do you think I need?
Therapist:	Well, based on what you have told me, I would say twenty sessions would be necessary to deal with the problems you outlined.
Client:	Oh! That is quite a lot.
Therapist:	You seem quite shocked?
Client:	Well, I know I have a lot of issues to deal with, but I am concerned about the cost of therapy.
Therapist:	I can understand that. Based on what I've said and what you can afford, do you have a suggestion about the number of sessions?
Client:	Well, I think about five.
Therapist:	Well, if that is all you can afford, let's go with that. We will need to be clear what problems we can realistically tackle in the time though.
Client:	I appreciate that. Perhaps I could afford a little more . . . say eight sessions?
Therapist:	Shall we agree on eight sessions? If later, you want to change that, let's discuss the issue. Okay?
Client:	Okay, and thanks for being flexible.

In the second sequence, the therapist is flexible and is thus able to invite the client to give an opinion. This leads to a productive negotiation and an agreement to eight sessions which is probably eight sessions more than the client would have signed up for in the first sequence.

Let us make one important point. Being flexible does not preclude therapists from having strong views and from expressing them when called for. It also does not preclude therapists refusing to work with clients who want something unethical (e.g. therapy with absolute confidentiality when the therapist cannot offer this). However, flexibility does mean that therapists can make compromises when their ideal views on therapy are not shared by their clients.

Dealing with therapists' resistance to accepting or teaching the 'ABC' model

The 'ABC' model represents the cornerstone of REBT theory and practice and asserts that individuals largely disturb themselves by the beliefs and attitudes they hold about adverse life events rather than by the events themselves, e.g. someone blames his depression on the breakup of his marriage and not on his uncompromising view that his wife should never have left him. This view of the causation of emotional disturbance is opposed by other therapy approaches, flies in the face of what many people would see as sheer common sense and out-of-step with societal trends which increasingly encourage people to blame others for their problems (and sue them if possible). In Chapter 2 we looked at clients' resistances to accepting the 'ABC' model. Therapists also struggle at times in teaching the model to their clients because they have doubts (sometimes grave ones) about its applicability to every human problem including their own, its lack of subtlety or complexity in explaining human behaviour and its remorselessness in uncovering self-induced disturbance through irrational thinking. This chapter examines these and other problems and suggest ways in which therapist doubts can be addressed.

When therapists think that their clients' anger is self-created, but their own anger isn't

Therapists can often work hard to convince clients of their self-created disturbance yet in their own lives distance themselves from this view because they consider their own problems to be of a different or higher order than those of the clients they counsel. With these therapists, the 'ABC' model usually stays in the therapy room. In the following dialogue, the supervisor attempts to understand the therapist's reluctance to apply the model to her own problems (here and elsewhere throughout this part of the book which focuses on therapists' difficulties, supervision is conducted for educational and not therapeutic purposes):

Supervisor: You've said that when you use the 'ABC' model with your client, it has great conceptual clarity for you in understanding how he makes himself angry. Now why does this clarity fade when you consider your own anger?

Therapist: Well, the client keeps on disturbing himself because he's demanding that his train, bus, tube, whatever, should always be on time especially when he has to get to meetings. As this is not the case in life, it's easy to see what's going on.

Supervisor: And in your case . . .?

Therapist: It's much more complex and resists an easy 'ABC' explanation.

Supervisor: In what way?

Therapist: My anger is created by the injustices in the world such as experiments on animals, racial discrimination, famine in the Third World. These are major issues in life, not whether my train is late or not.

Supervisor: Well, the train being late might be a major issue for the client if he's got an important meeting to attend, but you see your anger as righteous or noble rather than small-minded.

Therapist: Yeah, that's a good way of putting it.

Supervisor: These injustices do obviously exist, so what is your attitude to them? Some people wouldn't get angry over them because they couldn't care less.

Therapist: I know what you're trying to manoeuvre me to say: that these injustices absolutely shouldn't exist in the world.

Supervisor: I'm just trying to tease out what your attitude is in order to compare it with your client's. Because, as you know, REBT believes that demandingness is at the core of emotional disturbance.

Therapist: It's hard to explain my attitude without that word 'should' getting in the way.

Supervisor: Well, just say what's in your mind.

Therapist: Okay. These injustices should not be allowed to exist. They violate my principles of what should constitute a fair and just world.

Supervisor: Would you agree that your and your client's anger both stem from the same philosophical source?

Therapist: Yes, reluctantly. I know we're both demanding that what exists at any given time should not exist: his train being late, my injustices occurring.

Supervisor: Exactly. You're both refusing to accept empirical reality. Now if you both gave up your demandingness, obviously these things would still occur, but what might be some of the benefits?

Therapist: Well, I'll probably generate more light and less heat.

Supervisor: In what way?

Therapist: Less ranting and raving for a start. I'd spend more time collecting signatures for petitions, canvassing for support, letter writing, peaceful protests. That sort of thing.

Supervisor: And for the client?

Therapist: He wouldn't suffer double jeopardy: not only is his train late but also he gets to meetings in a foul mood and can't concentrate on them. He could prepare on the train in a constructive way.

Supervisor: Good. Do you now accept that, in essence, you disturb yourself in the same way as your client?

Therapist: Yes, I do but I still see my anger as more justifiable than my client's.

Supervisor: Well, however you describe your anger, it still has the same potentially destructive effects on you as your client. We can continue this discussion at our next session.

Therapist: I'll look forward to that.

In this extract from supervision, the supervisor makes a number of important points:

1   The 'ABC' model can be used to understand the causation and maintenance of anyone's anger and whether it is labelled 'small minded' or 'noble' is irrelevant from the REBT viewpoint. Anger is anger and stems from the same ideological roots of dogmatic musts and shoulds.

2   Even though the therapist believes she is being manoeuvred into saying what she believes the supervisor wants to hear, she eventually cannot avoid revealing her anger-producing 'shoulds' about injustices in the world. This confirms her implicit absolutist philosophy while the client's disturbance-creating ideas were easy to detect as they were explicitly stated.

3   Both therapist and client are refusing to acknowledge that what exists is bound to exist given the conditions that are present at that moment – this is one of two definitions of acceptance in REBT. Therefore both of them are disturbing themselves because they do not accept empirical reality.

4   The supervisor draws out from the therapist the benefits of acceptance for herself and her client. This acts as an inducement for the therapist

to work harder on both herself to give up her anger as well as on the client to surrender his.

5   The therapist still clings to the idea that her anger is more 'justifiable' than the client's, but the supervisor points out that the potentially destructive effects of sustained anger do not discriminate between individuals or the labels they use.

When clients hold that nothing goes through their mind and therapists agree

Some REBT therapists struggle unsuccessfully to tease out their clients' disturbance-inducing cognitions, e.g. 'He says the same thing each time: "Nothing goes through my mind – my anxiety just comes out of the blue". I think he's probably right'. This apparent conversion to the client's viewpoint may be due to, among other factors, lack of therapist skill or creativity in uncovering anxiogenic thinking, poor training or education in understanding anxiety states, or discomfort intolerance beliefs that this task is proving too difficult for the therapist. If the therapist persists in agreeing with the client, the latter will leave therapy with his anxiety intact rather than with a set of strategies and techniques to tackle it.

Hauck (1980) urges REBT therapists not to lose faith in their theory just because clients claim their minds are 'empty'. Therefore they should non-dogmatically persist in locating the relevant disturbance-producing data; additionally, they can offer clients hypotheses about their problems in an effort to encourage them to become more cognitively aware. With regard to the example of anxiety, therapists can familiarise themselves with the cognitive model of panic (Clark 1986) and its emphasis on the catastrophic misinterpretation of bodily sensations. By learning about seemingly innocuous triggers (e.g. palpitations or dizziness from drinking coffee, exercise, getting up suddenly, or fleeting images) and their link with panic-stricken thinking, therapists can begin to tackle their clients' insistence that their anxiety comes 'out of the blue'. Also therapists can combat their own discomfort intolerance beliefs that trying to establish the presence of the 'B' in the 'ABC' model is too much hard work. By being creatively persistent in their use of techniques, therapists can force apart the interlocked 'A' and 'C' elements to reveal to the client his anxiety-provoking thinking as well as develop for themselves discomfort tolerance in tackling the client's problems.

When therapists think that the 'ABC' model is crudely reductionist

Some REBT therapists believe that the 'ABC' model is an unsubtle or crude means of understanding emotional disturbance because all the therapist really wants to know is: "Where's the must"? No matter what the presenting problem is or the level of emotional distress displayed, all the therapist is concerned about is demonstrating to clients the presence of an implicit or explicit absolutist philosophy of living underlying their problems. This can give the impression that REBT places all clients on a Procrustean bed and thereby discredits the idea of the uniqueness of each client and the complexity of human behaviour. These and other worries are explored in the following dialogue:

Therapist: It seems to me that we are just imposing our views on the client.

Supervisor: Why imposing our views rather them offering them?

Therapist: Well, imposing or offering, it doesn't seem to matter really as it all comes down in the end to a 'must' or a 'should'.

Supervisor: If you want to construct a working alliance then offering a viewpoint to the client, not imposing it, is a crucial step as well as asking the client what she thinks of your theory. Obviously REBT does provide a clear account of emotional disturbance and sees demandingness at the core of it. Now why is REBT 'imposing' its view more than other therapeutic approaches?

Therapist: I don't know because I haven't trained in other approaches, but I expect they have their own theories they want clients to accept. To me, REBT seems crude and mechanistic in the way it unravels clients' problems. It seems a blunt instrument to use on clients.

Supervisor: Can you think of a specific case example we can examine?

Therapist: Yes I can. This woman had great doubts about marrying a man she had been going out with for a long time. Also she couldn't make up her mind about a career change. So she was procrastinating and experiencing a lot of anxiety.

Supervisor: What was your hypothesis about her presenting problems?

Therapist: That she must be absolutely certain in both cases that she was making the right decision, otherwise her life would be awful, she would never recover from the mistakes she had made. I presented this to her halfway through the first session.

Supervisor: What was her response?

Therapist: That it was too simple an explanation. REBT wasn't rich or sophisticated enough to explore her problems in

sufficient depth. There were lots of nuances and subtle-
ties to discuss.

Supervisor: Did you agree with her at this point?

Therapist: I did. I felt a bit silly reducing these complex problems
down to a few sentences. So I just sat back and let her
explore the highways and byways of her problems.

Supervisor: And where did it all eventually lead?

Therapist: Right back to my original hypothesis: that she had to be
absolutely certain she was making the right decisions;
hence the procrastination and anxiety.

Supervisor: So why are you not pleased that REBT was right in this
case?

Therapist: It's the crude reductionism of the model that still
troubles me. I got it right, but too quickly.

Supervisor: Is that because you believe that complex, long-standing
problems have to have complex causes and complex
solutions; otherwise you are not really doing 'proper
therapy'?

Therapist: Yes, that's it. You've put your finger on it.

Supervisor: Now if you believe that powerful ideas have a tremendous
influence on people's feelings and behaviours, that they
are maintaining the emotional distress, surely by iso-
lating, revealing and disputing those ideas you're helping
to end the client's suffering as quickly as possible?
Shouldn't that be the aim of all therapies?

Therapist: Of course, but the fact that I helped her to tackle her
problems relatively quickly still leaves me feeling that
I've provided her with only superficial solutions.

Supervisor: And what did she think?

Therapist: She was pleased. She thought her demands for utter
certainty were, after all, the nub of the problem.

Supervisor: You see, some other therapies would inch forward
through the dense undergrowth of clients' problems, so
to speak, and thereby take a long time to reach the
clearing or centre of their problems. Now REBT therapists, armed with their hypotheses derived from its
theory, would avoid the undergrowth and parachute
straight into the clearing. Hence the speed and the depth
of REBT practice.

Therapist: That's assuming, of course, you've picked the right
clearing or haven't drifted into the undergrowth.

Supervisor: Right. If your hypothesis is wrong, then you discard it
and start collecting more information in order to

formulate another one. It's about being open-minded, flexible in order to confirm, revise or throw out hypotheses in the light of incoming information.

Therapist: And what happens if the client doesn't agree that there is a 'must' or 'should' implicated in her problems? Aren't REBT therapists stuck then?

Supervisor: No. We certainly don't insist that there has to be a 'must' or 'should' involved, but we would assume that it's highly likely. If a therapist did translate non-devout REBT theory into rigid practice, he wouldn't be doing REBT as taught by Albert Ellis, but his own dogmatic brand of it. But to answer your question directly: if we couldn't find a 'must' or 'should' or the client disagreed with our interpretations, we would challenge and help change those disturbance-creating ideas chosen by the client as heavily implicated in her problems.

Therapist: So in terms of speed and depth, REBT therapists are quickly sorting out the 'ABC' elements of the client's problems but particularly listening out for the irrational beliefs without insisting that they have to be there.

Supervisor: Exactly. We are genuinely providing individual assessment and treatment programmes. REBT is definitely not a sausage machine.

Therapist: Okay, but it still seems strange that words like 'must' and 'should' can have the potential to create emotional disturbance.

Supervisor: It's not necessarily the words themselves but the absolutist, disturbance-producing philosophies that lie behind those words that, as you correctly said, we listen out for. I am persuaded that REBT theory has great explanatory power in its view of emotional disturbance, but I hold this view non-dogmatically.

Therapist: I don't have that faith yet but I'm certainly not against gaining more conviction in its theory and practice.

Supervisor: And how can you achieve that?

Therapist: More discussions with you, other REBT therapists, reading, workshops, training, that sort of thing.

Supervisor: What about therapy itself?

Therapist: Act in therapy as if I believe what I'm teaching.

Supervisor: And this will assist you to become both confident and competent in its practice without surrendering your scepticism about it.

Therapist: Good. That sounds like a compromise I can live with.

> *Supervisor:* If you acted in therapy like you didn't believe it, how can you expect the client to? You would have a self-fulfilling prophecy on your hands.
>
> *Therapist:* Yes, that's much clearer now. I think part of the problem is my narrow view of REBT and thereby blaming it for my deficiencies in really understanding its theory and practice.
>
> *Supervisor:* I agree and hope we can rectify that. I look forward to our next sessions as these discussions with you help to keep me on my toes and refine my own ideas about REBT.
>
> *Therapist:* I've enjoyed today's supervision. It's been productive.

In this extract from supervision, important points to consider are the following:

1   Offering a viewpoint on emotional disturbance and seeking clients' opinions of it is definitely not the same thing as imposing it. The therapist's inability to see this difference is due to his crude understanding of REBT theory rather than residing in the theory itself. The apparent simplicity of the 'ABC' model in quickly conceptualising clients' problems does not necessarily make it 'mechanistic' or a 'blunt instrument'; it can rapidly bring order into the chaos of some clients' lives (for a highly detailed account of the 'ABC' model, see Ellis 1991).

2   The therapist's unease about presenting his hypothesis regarding the client's irrational ideas before he has heard the full story indicates that he is prey to the 'big picture trap' (Grieger and Boyd 1980: 77) whereby some therapists 'insist on obtaining a total picture of the client's past, present and future before beginning an intervention program'. Even when the client confirms the therapist's initial hypothesis, he still believes he is therapeutically short-changing her as musturbatory (musts) thinking is insufficiently credible or complex as an explanation for her problems. The therapist therefore subscribes to another myth that complex problems have to have complex causes and solutions in order for therapeutic justice or efficacy to be seen to be done.

3   That REBT seeks to pluck the cognitive essence (dogmatic thinking) out of clients' problems, without becoming entangled in the thickets of their accounts of them, is a major feature of its therapeutic efficiency (speed and depth) as well as a target of frequent criticism for its oversimplicity (see Ziegler 1989).

4   While REBT does aver that absolutist thinking in the form of musts, shoulds, have to's, got to's, oughts, is at the heart of emotional disturbance, it does not absolutely insist on this viewpoint. If, for

whatever reason, musts and shoulds are not located, REBT switches its focus to clients' inferences and idiosyncratic attitudes regarding their problems. This form of therapy is known as general REBT (see Ellis and Dryden 1997). Therefore REBT does provide an individually tailored treatment programme and not a 'sausage machine' for turning out REBT clones.

5   Some REBT therapists' uncertainties and difficulties about applying the 'ABC' model arise from their own misunderstanding of or inability to grasp the tenets of REBT. While most, if not all, theoretical systems have some measure of innate confusion or contradiction, it is an easy step to blame the theory because the therapist lacks competence and confidence in its practice.

6   To rectify this problem, the therapist is encouraged to develop a more informed and balanced picture of REBT through further training, reading, discussions with more experienced therapists, etc., to enhance his practice. As the supervisor points out, this process is not meant to squeeze out his scepticism about REBT. Ellis (1983b) has argued that scepticism towards all things in life, including REBT, is an important sign of mental health.

When therapists think that 'B' means blame in the 'ABC' model

Some REBT therapists believe that responsibility for one's disturbed feelings is synonymous with blaming the individual for having them; therefore they do not place the 'ABC' model of self-created disturbance at the centre of their interactions with clients for fear of being seen to condemn them for their disturbance-creating ideas (for a detailed discussion of emotional responsibility, see Chapter 2). Instead, to avoid any hint of condemnation, they might encourage their clients to think more positively or only challenge their inferences, e.g. 'I can understand why your wife's erratic behaviour is upsetting you and, of course, you're not to blame for the way you feel, but nothing you've said so far indicates she is going to leave you'. This obviously dilutes or undermines the possibility of clients striving for profound philosophical change in their lives because they may leave therapy still believing that others or life events directly cause their emotional problems; in other words, they remain 'A'–'C' thinkers. Ironically, in the therapist's efforts to eschew assigning responsibility or blame to the client for his presenting emotional problems, the therapist may well strengthen his proclivities to blame others for them.

REBT powerfully distinguishes between encouraging responsibility for self-created disturbance, e.g. 'I make myself angry because of my demands that my boss absolutely shouldn't behave in the way that he does', and avoiding any form of global condemnation of the client for having such feelings. If there is any condemnation, it usually comes from the client and not the therapist, e.g. 'I'm totally inadequate for my inability to control my anger'. When therapists have clearly understood this important distinction between responsibility and blame, they can then confidently teach it to their clients. Thus the 'ABC' model is returned to its rightful place at the centre of therapy.

When therapists don't want to minimise adversities at 'A'

Advancing the principle of emotional responsibility when clients are still reeling from the impact of unpleasant or harsh activating events may strike some REBT therapists as insensitive, if not downright callous, e.g. 'How in heaven's name can I tell him that he largely makes himself depressed over losing his job and his wife leaving him? I feel like such a cold bastard for even suggesting it'. In these circumstances, such therapists will allow clients to express their feelings at great length over adverse A's rather than zero in on their disturbance-inducing ideas. In not wanting to minimise the 'A' in the client's eyes, they commit the mistake of making it all-important and thereby reinforcing the client's sense of helplessness or misery in the face of such events. It is the beliefs of the events at 'B' that now become minimised: 'AbC'.

While REBT therapists accept the considerable impact that unpleasant activating events have in contributing to the creation of negative emotional states, nevertheless, it is the client's appraisal of these events that ultimately determines whether the client will experience an unhealthy or healthy negative emotion, e.g. depression or sadness respectively. As Burns (1980) points out:

> Sadness is a normal emotion created by realistic perceptions that describe a negative event involving loss or disappointment in an undistorted way. Depression is an illness that *always* results from thoughts that are distorted in some way.
>
> (Burns 1980: 207)

In the above example, the client's depression largely arises from his irrational thinking, e.g. 'This double blow absolutely should not have happened to me. My life is finished, destroyed, over'. Once the therapist has grasped this fact, she can help the client to accept and adjust to the grim reality of painful events. In this way the therapist truly helps the client to reduce or eventually remove his suffering.

When therapists hold that clients' feelings are determined by others' abominable behaviour

When an individual sets out to wreak as much emotional havoc as possible on someone else, it is axiomatic for some REBT therapists that the recipient of such malice cannot be held responsible for their client's resulting emotional disturbance. For example, a woman becomes angry (e.g. 'Why is he doing this to me?') and depressed (e.g. 'I'm powerless to do anything about it') over her ex-partner's continual allegations to her friends and work colleagues that she is a slut, an alcoholic, has AIDS, neglects her children, etc. Such behaviour is understandably difficult to bear and therapy allows her to ventilate her feelings, but the therapist does not suggest ways in which she can modify her disturbed feelings because the therapist, like the client, sees them as caused by someone else and therefore she has no control over them. The focus in therapy is on practical solutions to her emotional distress, e.g. seeking a court injunction to keep her ex-partner away from her. If the ex-partner stops what he is doing, she can feel better and 'breathe easily again'.

Although it is not an easy issue to address in therapy, the client does have some control over her emotional response to her ex-partner's thoroughly abominable behaviour – she can reduce the frequency, intensity and duration of her depression and anger by constructing rational ideas about his behaviour, e.g. 'I'm giving him power over me. If I fight back instead of fall apart, I will take away his pleasure in seeing me suffer'; 'I know that his poisonous allegations are false and that's what really matters irrespective of what others think'; 'Why should I continue to disturb myself about his disturbed behaviour? It just keeps on confirming how right I was to leave him'.

Through such scrutiny, the therapist can help the client both to develop both greater emotional stability and to pursue more vigorously practical solutions in order to counteract her ex-partner's behaviour. Even if there is no cessation of his behaviour in the short term, the client's regained fortitude will allow her to withstand his rumour-mongering as well as experience some measure of happiness in her life. All these possibilities for constructive change will probably be lost if the therapist rules out any emotional responsibility on the client's part.

When therapists think that the use of the 'ABC' model adds insult to injury

Some REBT therapists believe there are certain life events which are so appalling, tragic or overwhelming that not only should use of the 'ABC' model be suspended, but also even to contemplate using it would add to the violation or suffering that the client has already experienced. These life events would include rape, attempted murder, being held hostage, trapped in a car crash or witnessing the violent deaths of others. In the face of such events, the therapist believes that the client is totally incapable of exercising any degree of control or choice over his emotional state. The 'ABC' model may have had great utility with most of the therapist's previous clients but, in this particular case, the therapist's approach is to be very supportive, let the client 'talk it through' and hope that the passage of time heals his wounds:

Therapist: What else can I do?

Supervisor: The 'ABC' model is as applicable here as anywhere else.

Therapist: How can it be after what he has suffered? He was savagely beaten. He spent weeks in hospital.

Supervisor: How is he now?

Therapist: As you would expect, very bitter, angry, anxious, depressed. He doesn't go out very much; he is wary of people in general.

Supervisor: Why do you say 'As you would expect'? Do you not believe that some individuals, even if only a few, might react differently to a savage attack upon them?

Therapist: I would feel exactly the same way if it happened to me. It seems to me that it would be a universal response to such a terrible incident. He can't help his feelings – the attack directly caused them.

Supervisor: Your sense of fatalism, which may well be reinforcing the client's, blinds you to the obvious truth that it wouldn't be a universal response. I have been reading recently of the appalling suffering of British prisoners of war in Japanese prison camps during the Second World War. What comes across time and time again in these old soldiers' accounts is that the Japanese guards may have broken their bodies, but they fought back in their own ways and refused to let the guards break their spirit. These are awe-inspiring accounts of courage and resilience. The same theme rings out each time: the indomitability of the human spirit even under the harshest of conditions.

Therapist: I understand what you're saying but it seems that you're trying to trivialise his present suffering or even blame him for it.

Supervisor: I'm certainly not trying to do that, but to point out to you that his suffering is being exacerbated or made worse by his presently held beliefs following the attack. This is definitely not to blame him for holding such beliefs, but to indicate that those beliefs are owned by him, his responsibility.

Therapist: But he didn't beat himself up. The attack created those beliefs.

Supervisor: Your client's physical injuries are totally caused by the attacker and I hope he gets a long prison sentence for his crime. In addition, it could also be argued that your client's initial disturbed feelings can be attributed to the attack – particularly as this attack was of a very savage nature. However, he has introduced some ideas into his thinking that, so to speak, were not present when he was attacked and are now intensifying and prolonging his disturbed feelings.

Therapist: You've lost me. What are you talking about?

Supervisor: Okay. Take his anxiety: what is he most anxious about?

Therapist: He's terrified of being attacked again and, from the REBT viewpoint, he's demanding it must never happen again. He's afraid to go out and has turned himself into a prisoner in his own home.

Supervisor: So this is the attitude, with regard to his anxiety, that he has constructed from the attack. Is this a realistic attitude that is going to help him live a relatively normal life again?

Therapist: Probably not.

Supervisor: We know that his demands cannot be met. Even being a recluse cannot guarantee his safety – someone could break into his house and attack him. And if he doesn't modify his attitude, what might happen to him if he is attacked again?

Therapist: I expect he may well fall apart and never recover.

Supervisor: Do you still believe that the 'ABC' model does not apply in this case?

Therapist: I'm beginning to be persuaded.

Supervisor: Okay. What is he bitter about?

Therapist: He believes that he cannot trust anyone again. Everyone has to be held at arm's length. This has made him socially isolated.

Supervisor: Did the attacker make him think that or is that belief his responsibility?

Therapist: Well, the attack would probably make most people more wary . . .

Supervisor: That's understandable and I'm not debating that, but would every person attacked hold the same belief?

Therapist: I don't suppose they would.

Supervisor: A friend of my sister's was quite badly attacked a few years ago but, generally speaking, she was still quite friendly and open to most people she met.

Therapist: With that example you're trying to emphasise the 'B' again in the 'ABC' model.

Supervisor: Of course. It's not a model you can wheel out for use with some events and then put away in storage when other events become too distressing for you. The model applies whatever the situation.

Therapist: What about his depression then? He feels utterly powerless to put his life back on the rails because he says the attack destroyed his dignity and self-respect.

Supervisor: Well, no matter what happened to him, only he can ultimately deprive himself of his dignity and self-respect. I come back to those prisoners of war: they may have walked out of those camps severely emaciated and beaten but, for some of them, their dignity as human beings was still intact.

Therapist: So when my client says the attack made him worthless, that's his conclusion about the event and, as you said earlier, not part of the event itself.

Supervisor: That's right. Even if the attacker explicitly told him that he wanted him to feel worthless as a result of the beating, that could only occur only if your client agreed with the attacker's intentions.

Therapist: These are very difficult and contentious issues to try to convey to clients. My client might feel he is being assaulted for a second time – this time by his therapist.

Supervisor: That certainly is a danger. It depends how you handle it. These issues need to be addressed with a great deal of tact and sensitivity, but addressed they have to be if you want to help your client to put his life back on the rails. In essence, your job is to help him bear what he perceives is unbearable – show him his cognitive contribution to making things unbearable. At present, you're not helping him do that because you totally believe the attack is responsible for his suffering and that's why little, if any, progress is being made.

Therapist: Okay, let me try to summarise what you've been saying: my client believes the attack has rendered him thoroughly miserable, powerless to effect any constructive change in his life. My task is to teach him how to empower himself through challenging and changing some of the disturbance-prolonging ideas that he has brought to this event, but were not implicit in the event itself.

Supervisor: Exactly. Which, in turn, will help to modify his present emotional disturbance. Are you now sufficiently motivated and confident in applying the 'ABC' model to this client's problems?

Therapist: Well, I will admit that my own 'A'–'C' thinking about the attack left me feeling as powerless as the client at times, so I'm more convinced now that the model can be applied even in this case.

Supervisor: Well, I hope to hear it being applied with gentle conviction in your therapy tapes. For homework, I would suggest that you read some books about individuals who have coped with great adversity in their life. You might be more persuaded then of my arguments.

Therapist: Yes, I will. That might help to remove my remaining doubts about this issue.

Supervisor: You can still have doubts about the model without impairing or undermining your clinical competence. Please remember that. Okay, I'll see you in two weeks then.

In this supervision extract, the supervisor is teaching the therapist the following:

1   Her rejection of the 'ABC' model in this case is based on her erroneous assumption that everyone would react in exactly the same way to a savage beating – the opposite of REBT theory and practice which she is supposed to be teaching the client. Understanding the client's viewpoint is not the same thing as supporting it. The supervisor's use of the prisoners of war example buttresses the point that no matter how appalling are the events, the individual's reaction to them is still mediated by his belief system.

2   If the therapist wants to help the client recover from the attack, she has to engage in the delicate and probably very difficult task of assisting him to identify those ideas that he has constructed following the attack. These ideas form part of the factors prolonging his suffering. This strategy runs the very considerable risk of appearing to blame the client for his emotional distress which the therapist believes, at this stage in supervision, would be the case.

3   It is important for the therapist to separate the various elements involved in the attack and its aftermath in order for the client (and herself) to understand how the principle of emotional responsibility fits into this case. The attack caused the client's physical injuries and the

initial overwhelming feelings of emotional disturbance (though not all REBT therapists would agree with this latter point), but the maintenance of this disturbance is considerably helped by the client's irrational ideas that are created after the violent assault and not part of or intrinsic to the original event.

4   The therapist should examine the long-term harmful effects upon the client if he does not modify his disturbance-prolonging ideas, e.g. forever dreading another attack and turning into a recluse in the mistaken belief that this will guarantee his future safety, never trusting anyone again and thereby reinforcing his social isolation. These long-term effects may turn out to be even more damaging than the attack itself.

5   The 'ABC' paradigm of emotional disturbance is not to be used or discarded depending on the severity of the client's presenting problems. It is the centrepiece of REBT theory and practice. Avoiding its use is due to the therapist's lack of faith in its applicability in distressing cases rather than the model's inability to show clients how to reduce or remove their distress. Of course, how the model is introduced to clients can be a major factor in building or breaking a therapeutic alliance. If the model is insensitively or brusquely presented to the client, he may well think he is being assaulted again.

6   The therapist has to address the issue of emotional responsibility if the client is to empower himself and put his life back on the rails. Excessive sensitivity or tact on the therapist's part, though appearing to be the right way to behave with this client, will actually be therapeutically ineffective as this will not be encouraging him to 'bear the unbearable'.

7   Although the therapist still has considerable doubts about the model's applicability in this case, this need not preclude her from teaching with 'gentle conviction' the 'ABC's of REBT to her client. The point is helping the client to see how he can help himself through attitudinal change rather than waiting first for the therapist 'to see the light'. The supervisor suggests that she reads some accounts of people coping with great adversity in order to underscore the arguments the supervisor has been advancing.

When the therapist fears that telling a client that he disturbs himself, the client will leave therapy

Some clients, particularly angry ones, are so utterly convinced that other people or events do cause their emotional problems that for the therapist to suggest otherwise could bring therapy to an immediate end, e.g. 'My boss makes me very angry when he insults me. I also get very angry if some smart-arse says I'm overreacting. I won't tolerate such remarks'. Those therapists who are anxious rather than concerned about this occurring face a number of difficulties: disagreeing with the client's view of emotional causation risks losing the client's approval as well as hastening premature termination; agreeing with the client will probably strengthen the client's disturbance-producing beliefs and transform the therapist into a sycophant; confronting the client will trigger the therapist's own discomfort intolerance beliefs about the need for comfort in therapy; worrying about what other therapists might think of them if their client 'storms out of therapy'; seeing themselves as weak and incompetent for not presenting the 'ABC' model 'come what may' and thereby sullying their integrity as a therapist. Such internal conflict is likely to lead to indecision or paralysis on the therapist's part which will allow the client, without little interruption, to expound upon the righteousness of his anger.

Before therapists can focus their clinical attention on tackling the client's anger, they need to challenge and change their own self-defeating attitudes. By surrendering their approval and comfort needs, therapists can develop both self-acceptance and discomfort tolerance and thereby present the self-induced disturbance model in the teeth of the client's refusal to consider it or threatened rejection of them. By keeping their ego out of therapy, therapists have no personal interest in whether the client continually rejects or eventually accepts the model, but they do their professional best to show the client that there might be a more constructive way of dealing with the boss without losing control. By not wilting under intimidation or shrinking from confrontation, therapists can demonstrate to the client how to be assertive and determined rather than disturbed under pressure, e.g. 'Would you like to handle your boss's insults with aplomb and thereby deny him the satisfaction of seeing you crumble in his presence?' Finally, therapists can learn to rectify shortfalls in their professional integrity without condemning themselves for any shortfall. Through such methods, the therapist can maintain a non-disturbed viewpoint throughout therapy no matter how long the client stays for.

When therapists think that it does not matter if clients change beliefs or behaviour as it all leads to the same result

Thinking that it does not matter if clients change beliefs or behaviour rests on the assumption that behavioural change is as equally effective as ideological disputing in effecting profound philosophical change (giving up rigid and unqualified demands). REBT therapists who adhere to this point of view incorrectly infer that because maladaptive behaviour has been replaced with adaptive behaviour, concomitant philosophical change has automatically occurred. As they do not investigate if this change has actually taken place, or do so only in a cursory way, they are in danger of terminating therapy while their clients' disturbance-producing ideas are still intact:

Therapist:	My client has got over his public speaking anxiety. In fact, I can't keep him away from giving talks.
Supervisor:	What was the belief he was challenging?
Therapist:	'I must always give a good performance otherwise I'm a failure'. That belief has been successfully challenged.
Supervisor:	What was the strategy?
Therapist:	Get him to do as many talks as possible. Everyone says how good he is at it. His anxiety has disappeared.
Supervisor:	How do you know that his belief has been eradicated?
Therapist:	The proof is in the pudding – no anxiety and lots of successful talks.
Supervisor:	I'm glad that things are going so well for him, but have you really searched to see if that belief is still there? It might just be dormant.
Therapist:	No, I haven't. It just seemed so obvious that it must have gone because the client was so happy with his progress.
Supervisor:	Well, the danger is that if he does give a bad or poor performance, that belief will be reactivated and his anxiety will return, leading to avoidance of further public speaking. By not really checking to see if he still held that belief in spite of his progress, you have left him vulnerable.
Therapist:	But his fears may never come to pass.
Supervisor:	True, but it's better if therapy is based on enduring rather than conditional change.
Therapist:	That's a good point. I'm only offering him the former. Come to think of it now, his anxiety is still with him.
Supervisor:	What evidence do you have for that?
Therapist:	I suggested to him a few weeks ago that he did an imagery exercise in which he saw himself giving a poor speech in order to cope with it. He became very agitated and didn't want to do it. He said, 'Why spoil a good thing? Everything is going fine'. I agreed with him and felt silly for suggesting it.
Supervisor:	Okay, well suggest it again, but this time within the context of a powerful clinical rationale. Which is . . .?
Therapist:	That behavioural-based change is more limited than philosophical change because it does not provide him with any coping responses if his fears are realised. Even if they are not, I would expect that some measure of anxiety precedes every talk.
Supervisor:	Good. You can check out that last point with him.

The supervisor points out to the therapist that cognitive change does not necessarily keep in step with behavioural change like an obedient dog with its owner. The unexamined and therefore unpredictable cognitive content of the client's adaptive behaviour may precipitate the re-emergence of his anxiety if he falls below his current high standards of public speaking. REBT therapists should remember that behavioural tasks are used to implement philosophical change and are not used on their own as the main modality of such change.

In this chapter, we have looked at therapist resistance in the views domain of the working alliance and particularly at the often considerable problems and doubts that therapists have in using the 'ABC' model with their clients as well as in their own lives. We now turn our attention to the many stumbling blocks that therapists experience in executing the tasks that will help their clients realise their goals for change.

Chapter 9

Dealing with therapist resistance in the goals domain of the working alliance

When clients come to therapy, they are generally in a disturbed frame of mind. They want to get relief from their psychological pain and are generally not interested in the issues that REBT therapists are concerned with when it comes to goals. Indeed REBT therapists have a lot to consider when it comes to the goals domain of the alliance and, as such, there is much scope for therapists. In this chapter we consider therapist resistance in the goals domain in two main areas:

- Resistance due to therapist ignorance and skills deficits
- Resistance due to therapist personal issues.

Resistance due to therapist ignorance and skills deficits

What do REBT therapists need to know about goals and goal-setting to be proficient in this area of the working alliance? In our view, here are the key areas of goal-related knowledge that REBT therapists should ideally have at their fingertips.

Negotiate goals, don't set them unilaterally or take them at face value

When we listen to REBT therapists and trainees talk about their clients' goals, we are struck by the language that they use. Phrases like 'I got my client to see that she needed to . . .' and 'I set his goals . . .' may reveal a unilateral attitude when it comes to eliciting clients' goals. It is important that goal-setting is a collaborative exercise and that goals are negotiated rather than unilaterally set perhaps on the basis of REBT theory. Therapists need to remember that REBT theory suggests interventions and it should not be used as gospel!

Some therapists may cause problems by taking clients' goals at face value. As we shall see, when clients articulate their goals for change, they indicate a variety of problematic objectives. For example, they want others to change or they wish to feel indifferent in the face of adversity. Unless therapists intervene and show their clients the difficulties with such goals, they will help to induce later resistance, albeit unwittingly.

So rather than unilaterally setting goals for clients, on the one hand, or accepting such goals at face value, on the other, it is important that therapists engage clients in process of negotiation with respect to their goals.

Goals should be specified by clients themselves and not by interested parties

It sometimes happens that clients are 'sent' to therapy by their partners, family or employers. When this happens, it is important that REBT therapists take time to disentangle what others want clients to achieve from therapy from what clients want to achieve for themselves. In the first vignette, the therapist accepts at face value the goal that someone else has set for the client:

Therapist:	So, what would you like to achieve by coming to see me?
Client:	Well, my wife thinks I need to spend more time with her.
Therapist:	Okay, so let me help you to do that. Where shall we start?
Client:	Ummm. I don't know.

The therapist should have approached it differently by engaging the client in a discussion about his goals as shown below:

Therapist:	So, what would you like to achieve by coming to see me?
Client:	Well, my wife thinks I need to spend more time with her.
Therapist:	And what do you think about her goal for you?
Client:	I can understand that from her point of view.
Therapist:	What about from your point of view?
Client:	Well, I would like that too, but my wife is so angry these days.
Therapist:	How do you handle her anger?
Client:	By withdrawing from her.
Therapist:	So, on the one hand you share your wife's goal about spending more time together, but on the other hand, you withdraw from her when she gets angry. Would you like to handle your wife's anger differently?
Client:	Yes, I would.
Therapist:	How would you like to respond differently to her when she gets angry?

In the above sequence, the therapist does the following:

1   The therapist acknowledges that in response to the question about what the client wanted to achieve, the client mentioned his wife's goal for him.
2   The therapist asked the client what the latter thought of his wife's goal and elicited ambivalence: part of the client shared his wife's goal, but another part voiced an obstacle.
3   The therapist asked the client if he wanted to deal with the obstacle and when the client responded that he did, the therapist asked for the client's goal in this respect.

Both therapist and client still have much work to do in the area of the client's goals, but they now are both focused on what the client wants rather than what his wife wants.

Helping clients to set goals at two different goal-setting stages

There are usually two goal-setting stages in the initial assessment of clients' problems:

1   When clients state their problem and goal in general terms (the 'problem and goal as defined').
2   After the problem has been explored in 'ABC' terms and the problem and goal have now been made specific (the 'problem and goal as assessed').

If therapists set goals only with relation to clients' problems as defined and not in relation to problems as assessed, they will not help their clients know where they going with the latter:

Therapist:	What problem are you seeking help for?
Client:	My progress at work is being hampered because I don't do enough presentations. I try and find ways not to give them.
Therapist:	What do you want to achieve from coming to see me?
Client:	To give more presentations at work.
Therapist:	What stops you from doing this?
Client:	I am anxious.
Therapist:	Anxious about what?
Client:	About being seen as incompetent by my boss.

> *Therapist:*   What would be a constructive response to the possibility that he might think that you are incompetent?
>
> *Client:*   To be bothered about that but not anxious about it.

In this interchange the therapist does the following:

1   The therapist discovers that the goal in relation to the problem as defined is to give more presentations at work.
2   By asking the client to elaborate on the obstacle to doing that already, the therapist works with the client to identify the goal in relation to the problem as assessed, which is to be bothered about being seen as incompetent by his boss, but not to be anxious about it.

Negotiate goals with reference to clients' psychological problems before goals with reference to practical problems

Clients come to therapy because they disturb themselves about the practical problems that they face in their lives. Thus, a client may have been made redundant and feels depressed about losing her job. She comes to therapy with two types of problems: an emotional problem (i.e. depression) and a practical problem (i.e. she does not have a job). In cases where clients have practical problems and emotional problems about these practical problems and their therapists ask them for their therapeutic goals, they may well specify solving their problems as their goals rather than dealing with their emotional problems.

If therapists go along with their clients' wishes on this point, that will be laying the foundation for client resistance to change later since the presence of emotional problems will interfere with their attempts to solve their practical problems and also, if they solve their practical problems, they may well lose interest in dealing with their emotional problems. In our example, if the therapist goes along with the client's nominated goal with respect to her practical problem (e.g. to find a new job) and she finds a job, she will not be motivated to work on her emotional problem (i.e. depression) and to set a goal with respect to this problem. This may not matter much to the client in the immediate term since she has solved her practical problem about which she depressed herself, but she has not learned to deal effectively with similar future adversities.

When clients have emotional problems about their practical problems and they nominate goals with respect to the latter, but not the former, here is how we suggest that REBT therapists can respond:

Therapist:	So you have been made redundant and feel depressed about that. Is that correct?
Client:	Yes, it is.
Therapist:	What would you like to achieve by seeing me?
Client:	I would like you to help me to find a new job.
Therapist:	Do you think that your feelings of depression will help us do this or hinder us?
Client:	I think it might hinder us.
Therapist:	In what way?
Client:	Well, if I'm depressed, I may not come across well at interview and this may affect my chances of getting a job.
Therapist:	Good point. Given this, what would you like to achieve with respect to your depression?
Client:	I want to overcome my depression.
Therapist:	Well, we are now focused on your feelings, so let's look at this issue a little more clearly.

Here, the therapist has done the following;

1   The therapist begins by acknowledging that the client has stated that she wants to get a new job, which is a goal related to her practical problem.
2   The therapist then focuses the client's attention on her emotional problem and asks her Socratically if she thinks that the existence of this problem will help or hinder her in her quest to solve her practical problem.
3   The client can see that the existence of her emotional problem will hinder her from solving her practical problem.
4   The therapist then asks the client to nominate a goal with respect to her emotional problem.

While the client's response shows the therapist that she has more work to do on this issue with the client, the latter is now focused on a goal with respect to her emotional problem.

Convert vague goals into 'smart' goals

When therapists ask clients at the outset of therapy what they want to achieve from the process, clients often give a vague answer such as 'to be happy' or 'to get over my anxiety'. Like other approaches within the CBT therapeutic tradition, REBT recommends that practitioners help clients specify goals that are 'SMART' (S = specific; M = measurable; A=

achievable; R = realistic and T = time-bound).[1] Therapists contribute to resistance in REBT when they do not help clients to convert their vague goals into 'smart' goals or when they do not have the skills to do this. If you suspect that you fall in the latter category, we suggest that you play audio-recordings of your attempts to help your clients convert their vague goals into 'smart' goals so that you can get feedback on your skills in this area.

Here is an example of a therapist who is skilled in helping her client convert a vague goal into a specific goal:

Therapist: What would you like to achieve by coming to see me?
Client: I want to be happier than I am now.
Therapist: What would be different in your life if you were happier?
Client: I would have more friends.
Therapist: What obstacle exists to you having more friends at the moment?
Client: I get anxious around people, so I tend to avoid social gatherings or I don't speak much when I am with others.
Therapist: What are you most anxious about when you are with people?
Client: That they might think I'm boring.
Therapist: If you could handle being thought boring more adaptively, would that help you with your anxiety?
Client: Yes it would, but is that possible?
Therapist: Yes it is. So, if I could help you to feel concerned, but not anxious about being thought boring and to be more responsive in social situations would that be something that you would be interested in?
Client: Definitely.

In this interchange, the therapist helps the client in the following ways:

1 The therapist takes the client's vague goal (i.e. to be happier) and begins to make it more concrete by asking: 'What would be different in your life if you were happier?' and 'What obstacle exists to you having more friends at the moment?'
2 The client then refers to an unhealthy negative emotion at 'C' (i.e. anxiety) and the therapist immediately seeks to discover the client's 'A': 'What are you most anxious about when you are with people?'

---

1 'Time-bound' means that the client has sufficient time to achieve the goal.

3   The therapist takes the client's 'A' (i.e. 'That they might think I'm boring') and suggests an emotional goal it (i.e. concern) and a behavioural goal (i.e. to be more responsive in social situations).

4   Note that in a fairly short period, the therapist has helped the client move from a vague goal (to be happier) to a much more concrete goal (to be concerned, but not anxious about being thought boring in social situations and to be more responsive in social situations.

5   While the client's behavioural goal will be clarified later, much good therapeutic work has been done in a short period of time.

The above interchange shows how REBT therapists can help clients convert vague goals into specific goals. Don't forget though that there are four other components to consider. We suggest, therefore that in order to minimise client resistance to change that therapists do the following:

- *Ensure that clients' goals are measurable ('M')*. It is important that clients have clear criteria to judge whether or not they have achieved their goals and ways of determining their progress towards their goals. Helping clients to measure progress and success is important here.
- *Ensure that clients' goals are achievable ('A')*. If clients cannot achieve their goals, good REBT therapists will not accept them as goals and will help clients to understand why and to reformulate their goals so that they are achievable.
- *Ensure that clients' goals are realistic ('R')*. Sometimes clients say that they don't want to be anxious again, and want to set this as a goal for therapy. Such a goal is unrealistic since it is not within the capability of humans to reach a stage where they will not ever experience anxiety (or any other unhealthy negative emotion). Helping clients to see this and to set goals that are realistic will foster the working alliance not only in the goals domain, but across the board.
- *Ensure that clients' goals are time-bound ('T')*. A client's goal may be specific, measurable, achievable and realistic, but it may not meet the criterion of being time-bound. Thus, the client may wish to achieve a certain goal by a certain time and this deadline may make the goal achievable. In which case, the competent REBT practitioner will not accept it since doing so would be a recipe for client failure. Therefore, helping clients to be mindful of time when setting goals is an important consideration.

Help clients to specify their emotional problems before helping them specify their goals

As clients' goals are closely allied to their problems, therapists can obstruct clients' progress by not helping them to specify their goals. By doing so, clients not only can see a clear connection between their problems and their goals, but also are shown the components of their goals. The therapist in the above exchange did some of this work, but in this section, we want to discuss how this can be done more formally.

Putting a client's problems into the REBT framework

In order to help clients put their problems into the REBT framework, the therapist elicits the following information from the client:

1   The context in which the problem typically occurs, if relevant.
2   The main inferential theme at 'A' about which the client disturbs himself.
3   The client's unhealthy negative emotion (UNE) at 'C'.
4   The client's dysfunctional behaviour or action tendency at 'C'.
5   The client's grossly distorted subsequent thinking at 'C', if relevant.

Here is an example of a client's problem that has been put into the REBT framework:

> Whenever people are late for a meeting with me [context], I get unhealthily angry [UNE at 'C'] about their lack of respect for me ['A']. I only wait for them for a minute [behavioural 'C'] but think about how I can get my revenge on them [thinking 'C'].

Putting a client's goals into the REBT framework

The therapist modifies the above schema and uses it to help the client to set goals as follows:

1   The context in which the problem typically occurs, if relevant.
2   The main inferential theme at 'A' about which the client disturbs himself.
3   The client's alternative healthy negative emotion (HNE) at 'C'.
4   The client's alternative functional behaviour or action tendency at 'C'.
5   The client's realistic subsequent thinking at 'C', if relevant.

You will see from the above that the context and main inferential theme at 'A' are common between the client's problem and his goal. What is different are the three components at 'C'.

Here is an example of a client's goal problem that has been put into the REBT framework:

Whenever people are late for a meeting with me [context], I want to feel healthily angry rather than unhealthily angry [HNE is the desired new 'C'] about their lack of respect for me ['A']. I will wait for them for twenty minutes rather than leave after a minute [new behavioural 'C'] and rather than think about how I can get my revenge on them, I will think about how to assert myself with them when they turn up [new thinking 'C'].

When clients nominate understanding goals

Clients may think that the purpose of psychotherapy is to provide them with insight into their problems and when they have such insight, change will naturally follow. REBT puts forward a different model of change (Ellis 1963; Dryden and Neenan 2004b). This model argues that there are two forms of insight: *intellectual insight*, where clients understand why and how they disturb themselves and what they need to undisturb themselves, and *emotional insight*, where they act on this understanding and get the benefits of doing so.

It follows from this that when clients nominate insight goals (e.g. 'I want to understand why I get so anxious about giving presentations'), REBT therapists need to determine if that is all they want (i.e. intellectual insight) or if they want what they see to be the psychological benefits of such understanding (i.e. emotional insight). REBT therapists who do not clarify this issue for themselves and for their clients are at risk of accepting intellectual insight goals which, if achieved, will not help clients deal effectively with their emotional problems which will predictably lead to resistance. Note how the therapist in the following exchange helps the client move from an 'intellectual insight' goal to an 'emotional insight' goal:

Therapist:	So, you are anxious about giving presentations at work. What would you like to achieve from seeing me?
Client:	I want to understand why I get so anxious about giving presentations.
Therapist:	Would you like to have such understanding and still be anxious about giving presentations, or do you want to have such understanding and learn to overcome your anxiety?
Client:	*(laughing)* The latter, of course.
Therapist:	Then what do you hope such insight would lead to?
Client:	Not being anxious about making the presentations.
Therapist:	What are you most anxious about with respect to giving presentations?
Client:	Saying or doing something stupid.

> *Therapist:* Well, I guess that is always a possibility, but if I could help you to be concerned, but not anxious, about saying or doing something stupid when you give presentations, would you be interested in that as a goal?
>
> *Client:* Definitely.
>
> *Therapist:* So let me be clear that I understand you. You don't just want to understand why you get anxious, about giving presentations, you want to be concerned, but not anxious about the possibility of saying or doing something stupid while you give presentations. Is that right?
>
> *Client:* Exactly right.

The therapist in the above interchange does the following;

1   She takes the client's expressed 'intellectual insight' goal and asks him if he wants to achieve this goal and still be anxious or overcome his anxiety. She does this to show that there is a difference between intellectual insight goals and dealing effectively with anxiety.

2   Once the client has indicated that he wants more than intellectual understanding, the therapist does a brief assessment on his anxiety and discovers that he is most anxious (at 'C') about the possibility of saying or doing something stupid (at 'A').

3   She then puts forward concern as a healthy negative emotional alternative to anxiety as a possible emotional goal given the existence of the possibility of saying or doing something stupid at 'A', a suggestion that the client accepts.

4   The therapist closes by summarising what they have done and stresses that the client's goal will be related to emotional insight and not just intellectual insight.

Some clients may put forward intellectual insight goals related to their past (e.g. 'I want to understand what has happened in the past which has resulted in me getting so anxious about presentations'). If a client nominates such a goal, the therapist is advised to respond as follows: as shown above, the therapist should enquire whether or not the client hopes that such insight will lead to overcoming anxiety. If so, the therapist should respond as the therapist did in the above example; the therapist needs to help the client understand the REBT view on the role of the past in present emotional problems. This position is as follows:

• The past may contribute to the client's present problems, but does not cause them.

• It is possible to have the same current problem with a variety of past experiences.

• In order to overcome the current problem, the client needs to identify, challenge and change the irrational beliefs that are deemed to underpin the problem and to act and think in ways that are consistent with the client's alternative rational beliefs.

If the therapist does not take the above steps, it is unlikely that mere understanding of the past will help the client overcome his current problem and resistance will, in all probability, ensue.

When negotiating clients' goals, make sure that these goals are not contaminated by client disturbance

We have made the point throughout this chapter that a major task of REBT therapists in the goals domain of the working alliance is to help clients set goals with respect to their emotional problems. Having said that, therapists need to be mindful that clients' states of emotional disturbance may contaminate the goal-setting process. Typical examples of this would be:

• a person with anorexia who wants to set 'losing weight' as a therapeutic goal
• a person with anxiety of losing control who wants to set 'self-control' as a goal.

While the first example is obvious, the second example is less so. People with a fear of losing self-control often think that the only way to gain self-control is to apply methods which will result in self-control. Indeed this solution is part of the problem, given that the real issue that needs to be addressed is helping them to deal with times when they do not feel in self-control. Helping such clients to set a goal such as 'being concerned, but not anxious about losing self-control' is a more productive therapeutic goal then 'gaining self-control' for such clients, given that this goal is not contaminated by the problem.

Clients' goals should be relevant to their stage of change

We have made the point above that clients' emotional state may impact negatively on goal-setting. It is also important that therapists help clients set goals according to the stage of change. Dryden (2001) distinguishes between overcoming disturbance ('OD') goals and personal development ('PD') goals. It is clear that therapists can contribute to the resistance process if they set 'PD' goals when clients are emotionally disturbed. For example, accepting a 'PD' goal such as 'I want to be more loving with my partner' when that person is experiencing unhealthy anger towards his partner will generally not be helpful to the client since his disturbance (unhealthy anger) will interfere markedly with his 'PD' goal (i.e. being more loving). In this case the therapist's task is to help the client see that he is much more likely to achieve his 'PD' goal once he has dealt with his emotional problem and in this respect the therapist needs to help the client to set an 'OD' goal.

However, some REBT therapists wrongly think that REBT is concerned only with helping clients deal with their emotional problems and struggle when clients want to set and pursue 'PD' goals when they have met their 'OD' goals. Such therapists tend to continue to search for problems of emotional disturbance and don't realise that they are still practising REBT when they set and help clients pursue their 'PD' goals.

It is worth remembering, then, that REBT can help clients deal with their emotional problems and help them to develop themselves in relevant areas once they have overcome these emotional problems.

When negotiating clients' goals, help them to specify the presence of an emotional state, not the absence of one

Often when clients have been helped to identify their emotional problem and are asked what their goals are in respect to this problem, they reply that they don't want to experience that problem. If therapists accept this answer uncritically, they are again laying the foundations for later therapy resistance:

Supervisor: I noticed that when you asked your client what she wanted to achieve with respect to her anxiety about being criticised, she replied that she did not want to be anxious and you seemed to accept this as a valid goal.

Therapist: That's correct, I did.

Supervisor: Can you see any problems with accepting it?

Therapist: No, it seems okay to me.

Supervisor: Okay, bear with me if you will and I will demonstrate what's wrong with it. I want you to imagine that you are a train ticket seller and I am a passenger wishing to buy a ticket. Okay?

Therapist: Okay. Hello madam, where would you like to go?

Supervisor: Hello. I don't want to travel to Bath.

Therapist: Okay, but where do you want to buy a ticket for?

Supervisor: I don't want to buy a ticket for Bath.

Therapist: *(laughing)* Okay, I get the point.

Supervisor: Which is?

> *Therapist:*   When a client indicates that she does not want to feel anxious, neither of us knows what she does see as her emotional goal.
> *Supervisor:*   And therefore?
> *Therapist:*   And therefore, it's my job to help her to specify that goal.

1   In the above interchange, the supervisor resists the temptation to make two points didactically to the therapist, as follows:

- 'Not feeling anxious' is not a viable goal in REBT since it lacks a specific direction.
- It is the therapist's responsibility to help the client to specify such a direction.

2   Instead, the supervisor uses an analogous role-play situation which helps the therapist to understand both points.

Goals in the face of adversity need to be negative and healthy (not indifference, happiness or a less intense version of a disturbed emotion)

One of the aspects of REBT theory that clients and therapists new to REBT struggle with is the concept of healthy negative emotions (HNEs). These healthy negative emotions (at 'C') are deemed to stem from rational beliefs (at 'B') about adversities (at 'A'). Thus, when clients are disturbed (i.e. experience unhealthy negative emotions or UNEs) about these adversities, the task of REBT therapists is to encourage their clients to work towards experiencing HNEs about the same adversities.

However, clients often have other ideas. Thus, instead of HNEs, clients might nominate emotional goals that are characterised by:

- *Indifference:* this is problematic because in order to achieve it, clients would have to believe: 'I don't care that this adversity happened'.
- *Happiness:* this is problematic because in order to achieve it, clients would have to believe: 'I am pleased that this adversity happened'.
- *A less intense version of a disturbed emotion* (e.g. less anxious): this is problematic because it still involves clients holding irrational beliefs, albeit with less intensity than hitherto.

Therapists who uncritically accept such unrealistic goals serve only to create conditions which lead to resistance later in the therapy process. Here is an example of a therapist who does not uncritically accept a goal of indifference:

Therapist: So to recap, you feel unhealthily envious whenever your friends have something that you want, but don't have. Is that right?

Client: Right.

Therapist: And what is your goal when you are faced with friends having something that you want, but don't have?

Client: To be indifferent about this.

Therapist: Okay, let me ask you something that may seem off track, but isn't. Okay?

Client: Okay.

Therapist: On Saturday, Albion Rovers are playing Montrose in the Scottish third division. Who do you want to win?

Client: I don't care.

Therapist: Because it doesn't matter to you who wins?

Client: That's right.

Therapist: Now does it matter to you if you don't have something that you prize that your friends have?

Client: Yes, it does.

Therapist: So in order for you to be indifferent about this, you have to persuade yourself that it does not matter to you when it does. How are you going to do that?

Client: I don't know. I don't think I can do that.

Therapist: Well, you could lie to yourself.

Client: But I still won't believe it.

Therapist: I guess your choice then is to feel unhealthily envious about your friends having something that you prize, but don't have, or to feel healthily envious about this. Which would you like?

Client: Healthy envy . . . I think, but what is the difference between the two?

Here, the therapist helps the client in the following ways:

1   Having established that the client feels unhealthy envy about his friends having something that he prizes, but does not have, the therapist asks him to nominate an emotional goal about this adversity. The client nominates 'indifference' as his feeling goal.

2   The therapist then goes about showing the client in a Socratic manner that when one is truly indifferent about something, the object of indifference is of no consequence to the client.

3   Given this the therapist shows the client that he can choose to feel healthy envy about his friends having something that he prizes, but does not have, or to feel unhealthy envy about it.

4   The segment closes at the point at which the therapist is about to show the client the difference between healthy envy and unhealthy envy.

Emotional goals should be accompanied by behavioural and thinking goals at 'C'

As we have seen above, one of the tasks of REBT therapists is to help clients to make keen discriminations about salient items such as unhealthy negative emotions and healthy negative emotions. One of the ways of doing this is to invoke the behavioural and thinking accompaniments of both sets of negative emotions. It follows from this that clients' goals about adversities should specify not only the presence of healthy negative emotions but also their behavioural and thinking accompaniments (for a formal way of doing this, see p. 153).

Goals need to be within the control of clients

When therapists ask their clients what they want to achieve from REBT, it often happens that clients nominate goals that are, in fact, outside of their sphere of control. These often refer to changes in others or to changes in life's circumstances. In providing an example of each below, we will comment on what is problematic about them from an REBT perspective.

- 'My goal is for my mother to be more loving to me'
  This goal implies a change in the mother's behaviour which the client would infer as more loving. As his mother's behaviour is under her control and not his, this is a problematic goal.
- 'My goal is to get promotion'
  While getting promotion will be partly down to factors within the client's control (e.g. his performance in his present role, how he prepares his application form for promotion and how he performs at interview), it also involves factors outside his control (e.g. what the promotion appointments board thinks about his current job performance, application form and performance at interview and what criteria they choose to set concerning who is to be promoted). Given the latter, this is a problematic goal.

Therapists who accept such goals uncritically will be promising more than REBT can deliver and thus, the foundation for later resistance is set.

When clients nominate goals that are outside their control, therapists should respond to this, show them the problematic nature of such goals and refocus clients' attention on factors that are within their control. The following shows an REBT therapist doing this:

Therapist:	What would you like to achieve from therapy?
Client:	My goal is for my mother to be more loving towards me.
Therapist:	If she was more loving to you, what would she be doing that she is not doing now?
Client:	She would phone me more often and show a genuine interest in what I'm doing.
Therapist:	Knowing your mother as you do, what's the best way you can bring this to her attention so that you increase the chances of getting what you want?
Client:	By being nice to her myself, buying her a present and then bringing the matter up with her gently.
Therapist:	Have you done that?
Client:	No.
Therapist:	Why not?
Client:	Because I am angry with her for not being loving.
Therapist:	I see. Here's my thought about your goal and what you've just said. I think the main problem here is that you are waiting angrily for your mother to change before you do anything that will increase your chances of getting what you want.
Client:	Put like that, I can see what you mean.
Therapist:	So does it make sense that we address your anger so that you can do what may result in your mother being more loving?
Client:	Good idea.
Therapist:	I'll help you to specify your goal with respect to this in a minute. One other thing, if you are nice to your mother, buy her present and then bring up the issue up with her gently, does that increase your chances of her being loving or does it guarantee success?
Client:	It increases the chances, but doesn't guarantee it.
Therapist:	Why is that?
Client:	Well, even if I do all those things, my mother may still decide not to be loving.
Therapist:	That's right, that's why in REBT we help clients set goals that are within their control, In your case, this is the obstacle that you have to doing what would increase your chances of success. But as you rightly note, there will be no guarantee of success. Incidentally, how would you feel if your mother continues to be unloving despite your attempts to influence her?
Client:	I'd be devastated.
Therapist:	What's your goal here?

Client:	Not to be devastated.
Therapist:	But to feel what instead?
Client:	Sad.
Therapist:	So to recap, you have two goals that are within your control. First, you want to address your anger to doing certain things that will increase your chances of getting a more loving response from your mother, and second, you want to feel sad, but not devastated, if your mother continues to be unloving despite your best efforts. Is that accurate?
Client:	Yes.
Therapist:	Okay, let's first talk about your goal with respect to your anger about your mother not making the first move.

In the above exchange, the therapist has done the following:

1 The therapist helps the client to be more specific about what would constitute 'loving' behaviour from his mother. The therapist asks the client what's the best way he can bring this to his mother's attention to increase the chances of getting what he wants. In doing this, the therapist focuses on what is in the client's control, i.e. his behaviour.

2 The therapist then discovers that the client has not done what he thinks will best influence his mother and enquires as to the reason. Having ascertained that the client is angrily waiting for his mother to make the first move, the therapist agrees with the client that this is an obstacle to changing his own behaviour and that this needs addressing, and notes that they will set a goal with respect to this problem shortly.

3 The therapist then helps the client to see that even if he acts in a way designed to influence his mother to be more loving towards him, the mother may still decide not to respond in the desired manner. This is an important point. While the therapist may accept as goals behaviour designed to influence another person to change, because such behaviour is within the clients' control, it is important that clients realise that such influence attempts may fail. The therapist in the above interchange does this and elicits the client's feeling about his mother not changing. Realising that his response represents an emotional problem, the therapist helps the client to set a goal with respect to the problem there and then. The fact that the therapist has not helped the client to set a concrete goal with respect to his anger is that doing so requires more work than setting a goal with respect to the client feeling devastated about his mother not changing. At the end the therapist initiates goal-setting with respect to the client's anger.

Helping clients to get a good balance between short-term goals and long-term goals

REBT argues that we are likely to be at our happiest when we achieve a balance between enjoying the pleasures of the moment and planning constructively for the future (known as long-range hedonism). Clients often pursue short-term goals (e.g. avoidance of discomfort) which sabotage their long-term goals (e.g. overcoming their anxiety). On the other hand, some REBT therapists and particularly trainees focus only on long-term goals, thereby implying that short-term goals are unimportant or self-defeating:

> *Trainee:*   You're falling behind with your studies because you go to too many parties. Is that right?
>
> *Client:*   Yes.
>
> *Trainee:*   So pleasure always first, then work a distant second, and sometimes you never get down to it at all.
>
> *Client:*   A good party versus studying alone on some boring subject. No contest.
>
> *Trainee:*   Do you want to pass your exams? *(client nods)* Then I would suggest you stop all party-going and concentrate on hard study. When the exams are out of the way, then go to parties. Does that sound like a worthwhile goal to work for?
>
> *Client:*   Are you joking about the goal? Stop all party-going?
>
> *[The client is not interested in the goal as it is extreme (i.e. all work and no play) and hardly likely to motivate him to change.]*

In the following extract, the therapist looks at a goal that involves both work and play:

> *Therapist:*   What about study during the week and parties only at the weekend, but you don't go to the parties when you don't study?
>
> *Client:*   Yes, I can live with that.
>
> *Therapist:*   So let's look at developing an attitude that will help you to study more and party less.

When REBT therapists help their clients to reach a balance between pursuing both short- and long-term goals, they minimise resistance to change. If they expect clients to delay gratification completely, they will encounter resistance.

Monitoring goals with clients

We hope that we have conveyed so far the intricacies and complexities of negotiating goals with clients. We have to add to this one even more complicating factor: clients' goals change over time. Therapists who assume that goals properly negotiated at the outset of therapy remain unchanged over the course of therapy are more likely to foster therapy resistance than therapists who monitor clients' goals and deal with changing goals.

Therapists can monitor clients' goals formally at agreed review sessions or informally when it appears that their goals may have shifted. In whichever way clients' goals are monitored, REBT is more effective when geared towards clients' current goals than when geared towards goals identified at the outset of therapy.

There is one rider to this. Some clients claim that their goals have changed in order to avoid working towards any particular goal because they fear failure, for example. Given this, it is important for therapists to assess why clients modify their goals.

Eliciting from clients a commitment to achieve their goals

Stating a goal is not the same as being committed to achieving it. To be committed to change means undertaking willingly the hard work involved in reaching the goal and seeing clearly the benefits to be gained when the goal is achieved. Therapists who assume that clients will, as a matter of course, put in the effort and hard work to achieve their goals once they have agreed these goals with their therapists are likely to be naive.

In our view, a commitment to achieve a therapeutic goal involves the following stages:

1 A clear statement of the goal and its benefits. If one is ambivalent about achieving the goal, it is important to carry out a cost-benefit analysis to increase motivation to change.
2 A plan of what one needs to do to achieve the goal. This includes the realisation that repetition of the activities made explicit in the plan is an integral part of change.
3 A verbal declaration that one will execute the plan.
4 Executing the plan.

Seasoned REBT therapists realise that difficulties can occur at each of the four stages listed above and deal with them when they become manifest. Novice and naive REBT therapists assume, for example, that if clients declare that they will execute their plan, then they will do so. Sadly, this is a recipe for therapeutic resistance!

Resistance due to therapist personal issues

So far in this chapter, we have discussed the knowledge and skills that therapists need to in order to minimise the existence of resistance in the goals domain of the working alliance. It is a premise of this book, however, that knowledge and skills do not guarantee that these will be implemented by REBT therapists. Practitioners may have a number of personal issues, the existence of which may well impede them from carrying out what they know is good practice in negotiating clients' goals using the skills that are in their skill repertoire. Thus, in this section of the chapter, we will consider some of these impeding personal factors.

Dealing with discomfort intolerance beliefs

As should be apparent from the discussion of the knowledge and skills that REBT therapists need to minimise resistance in the goals domain of the working alliance, negotiating effective goals with clients in REBT can be a lengthy and painstaking business. Therapists with discomfort intolerance beliefs about therapy may well decide to opt out of the fray and go along with poor client goals (if indeed they ask clients about their goals at all!) all for an easy life.

While this can be picked up in supervision, it is recognised by seasoned REBT supervisors that therapists who have discomfort intolerance beliefs about therapy may well also have discomfort intolerance beliefs about supervision. The latter results in taking to supervision cases where one is doing well and therapy is going smoothly, so that supervisors tend to give positive feedback and certainly do not challenge supervisees since they have nothing to challenge them on!

One way round this for supervisors is to implement a technique which one of us (WD) calls the 'lucky dip' technique, although it can easily be called the 'unlucky dip' technique for reasons that will soon become clear. In this technique, the supervisor asks the therapist to bring to therapy audio-recordings of a number of therapy sessions and the supervisor picks one at random to play in the supervision session.[2]

In the following session, the supervisor has, for a while, harboured the suspicion that the therapist she is supervising has 'faked good' in presenting only cases and recordings of sessions that are going well and smoothly. She has asked the therapist to bring in fifteen of his audio-recordings and has selected one to play. In playing the recording, it is clear that the therapist has accepted a goal put forward by his client that indicates the absence of

---

2 Of course the therapist can choose to bring only recordings of good sessions, although if they have to bring along a large sample of such sessions, this self-selection bias is minimised.

an unhealthy negative emotion rather than the presence of a healthy negative emotion. The therapist is an experienced practitioner and certainly has the knowledge and skills to deal with this common problem in the goals domain in the working alliance. The supervisor handles the situation in the following manner:

Supervisor: When your client said that her goal was not to feel anxious about sitting exams, I'm puzzled as to why you let that go. What error have you made in letting that issue go?

Therapist: I have not helped her to set a specific healthy negative emotion about sitting exams.

Supervisor: I was sure that you knew that and that you know how best to address it. Am I right in that?

Therapist: Yes, you are.

Supervisor: So, I'm curious why you didn't do it?

Therapist: I guess it didn't occur to me.

Supervisor: So, if you had thought about it at the time, you would have done it?

Therapist: I'm not sure.

Supervisor: How so?

Therapist: Well, it's hard work negotiating appropriate goals with clients and it was the end of a long hard day and . . .

Supervisor: So what conditions would have had to be present for you to have negotiated an appropriate goal with your client?

Therapist: Okay, okay, I get the point. I was saying that it was too much of a pain to do it.

Supervisor: Would you do the same all over again?

Therapist: Well, I might if I don't deal with my discomfort intolerance belief.

Supervisor: So, I guess the issue is whether you are going to do that?

Therapist: You know I have been resting on my laurels too much recently. When you asked me to bring me to bring in a big sample of my recordings, I felt myself really resisting the idea. But now the issue is out in the open, I am going to tackle my discomfort intolerance beliefs.

Supervisor: How can I best help you do that?

In this interchange, the supervisor has helped the therapist to realise that the reason that he did not help the client to set a suitable goal was not because he lacked the knowledge or the skill to do it, but because he held a discomfort intolerance belief about the effort and discomfort that doing so would have entailed. The therapist realises that this is a more general issue for him and decides with determination to address it. Note that throughout this sequence, the supervisor took a Socratic, non-challenging stance. She did so because the therapist is experienced and does not need an active-directive approach. The supervisor helped the therapist understand what was happening and when he did so, his commitment to change was apparent. If the supervisor needed to be more challenging, she would have been, thus modelling a discomfort tolerance attitude.

Dealing with need for clients' approval

Helping clients to reformulate their initially stated goals for change not only is hard work, but also may antagonise some clients no matter how delicately the therapist may raise and discuss the issue. In order to practise REBT effectively, practitioners not only need to do so while tolerating the discomfort of the slings and arrows of outrageous therapy fortune, but also need to show themselves that they don't have to have their clients' approval while doing REBT. In the first exchange below, the therapist backs away from sticking with the goal negotiation process when the client gets cross, while in the second exchange he persists:

Excerpt 1

Therapist:	So you are anxious about being boring when you are out on dates? How would you like me to help you with this problem?
Client:	I want you to help me to not be anxious about this.
Therapist:	Given that being seen as boring is a negative event for you, you need to feel something, and not being anxious means that you would not have any feelings.
Client:	Why are you being so pedantic? You know what I mean, you are just being picky.
Therapist:	Sorry about that. It's not my intention to be picky. Okay, let me help you to not be anxious about being thought boring.

Excerpt 2

Therapist:	So you are anxious about being boring when you are out on dates? How would you like me to help you with this problem?

Client:	I want you to help me to not be anxious about this.
Therapist:	Given that being seen as boring is a negative event for you, you need to feel something, and not being anxious means that you would not have any feelings.
Client:	Why are you being so pedantic? You know what I mean, you are just being picky.
Therapist:	Sorry about that. It's not my intention to be picky. However, if I don't help you to set a goal that you can see and work towards, you may well not deal as effectively with your anxiety problem as you would if I did help you to set a suitable goal. Can you see that?
Client:	Well, I still think you are being picky.
Therapist:	But are you prepared to bear with my pickiness as you see it, if doing so helps me to help you more effectively?
Client:	Okay.

Therapists who believe that they need to have their clients' approval tend to give in to clients' wishes without much of a struggle (as demonstrated in the first excerpt above). In doing so they fail to persist with a useful therapeutic strategy as the therapist did in the second excerpt. It follows, therefore, that REBT therapists should advisedly practise REBT preferring, but not needing their clients' approval. Unless doing so will unduly threaten the working alliance, we recommend that REBT therapists prioritise good REBT over getting client approval if the two are likely to conflict.

Dealing with shame

Novice REBT therapists are often over-concerned about showing their clients that they are incompetent. They think that if they say to clients that they are not sure how to respond for the best in therapy and that they need to get advice from their supervisor, the client will look down on them and they will feel shame as a result. Consequently, they tend to go along with their clients' problematic goals either because although they know that they are problematic they don't know why or because they know why these goals are problematic, but don't how best to deal with them.

When learning REBT, it is important to do so from the standpoint of unconditional self-acceptance (USA) belief. Trainees who say to clients in effect: 'At my stage of training I am not sure about how to set a goal with you on this problem, but I will find out and get back to you' are doing the following:

• They are getting the most out of the learning process. Hiding one's ignorance does not promote learning and growth as a therapist.

- They will learn how to set goals and thus induce less resistance in their clients than trainees who try to bluff their way through therapy.
- They serve as a good role model for clients who believe that their own self-esteem is based on knowing all the answers.
- If a client does openly mock them for displaying ignorance, they can practise maintaining their USA belief in the face of this adversity.

In short, practising REBT to avoid shame will promote resistance in therapy, while practising REBT from the standpoint of USA will help to minimise such resistance.

Clients and therapists have tasks to undertake if clients are to achieve their goals. In Chapter 10 we outline and discuss the many resistances to change that can occur in the tasks domain of the working alliance and how these can best be addressed.

Dealing with therapist resistance in the tasks domain of the working alliance

In Chapter 5, we examined the blocks that clients have in carrying out their goal-directed tasks. While REBT therapists may continually remind clients of their therapeutic responsibility in effecting constructive change (e.g. 'If you don't put into practice what is taught in the sessions you won't make much progress'), they may forget, ignore, fail to understand or pay lip service to the fact that they have their own form of therapeutic responsibility to adhere to. This comprises a number of tasks throughout the course of therapy which are designed to help clients to achieve, ideally, the highest possible degree of change in their lives. The reasons for therapists' lack of diligence in applying themselves to these tasks will now be explored.

When therapists don't investigate clients' anticipations of and preferences for therapy

Some REBT therapists might automatically assume that providing clients with rapid relief from their presenting problems is the main order of business and spending time on teasing out clients' expectations of therapy is holding up the momentum of therapy. Also they may believe that exploring such issues is largely irrelevant, because no matter what the clients say they are still going to be taught the 'ABC's of REBT. Therefore sounding confident and authoritative is what really counts in clients' eyes and, as this approach will impress them, they will quickly 'fall into line'. A few therapists might resent dwelling on clients' anticipations of and preferences for therapy because 'they [clients] should be grateful that someone is prepared to help them. I'm not pandering to their whims'. This take-it-or-leave-it approach may alienate more clients than it attracts. The aforementioned therapist attitudes can leave clients confused, overwhelmed, indignant or thinking that they have been devalued – hardly the basis for building a working alliance.

By discovering clients' anticipations of therapy important misconceptions can be corrected, e.g. 'You will be able to cure me'; 'I do all the talking, you just listen and that's how I get better', thereby reducing the potential for client resistance when therapy unfolds in a way they did not envisage. Encouraging clients to express their preferences for a particular therapeutic relationship helps 'to establish and maintain an appropriately bonded relationship that will encourage each individual client to implement his or her goal-directed therapeutic tasks' (Golden and Dryden 1986: 368–9). Such idiosyncratic preferences might include a formal, no-nonsense relationship based on the therapist's expertise or a relaxed, informal one with the therapist seen as a confidant. The point of gathering this information is to create a client-friendly environment which encourages them to address their problems within the 'ABC' model – the manner in which this is done is more important than the speed with which it is carried out.

When therapists don't take care in socialising clients into REBT

It is important for clients to understand both what is expected of them and what lies ahead if they are to participate effectively in REBT, e.g. collaborating with the therapist in the trial and error of emotional problem-solving rather than submissively absorbing the therapist's 'insights'. Instead of detailing what the therapist's and client's respective responsibilities and tasks are as part of structuring the therapy process, the therapist may sum it up ominously: 'There's lots of hard work ahead for both of us'. The therapist's guarantee of hard work but delivered without an accompanying clinical rationale makes the clients' understanding of their expected role in therapy much harder to grasp – like groping forward in the dark. Not providing clients with a general design of therapy might be due to the therapist's own inability to think strategically and, instead of offering guidance, therapy unfolds in an inchoate fashion, e.g. tasks are foisted on clients as the therapist thinks of them, rather than integrated in a systematic way into therapy.

Socialising clients into REBT makes their responsibilities and tasks explicit and lessens the chances of them receiving any unexpected 'shocks'. This approach helps to buttress rather than rupture the working alliance therapeutic alliance. This process can be carried out in the form of a direct address to the client:

> *Therapist:*   Our job in therapy is to identify your key ideas that are at the core of a great deal of your present emotional distress. By examining these ideas, we can work out ways of developing more helpful ones which will, in turn, reduce your distress. In order to bring this about, you will be required to carry out homework tasks designed to increase your confidence and skill in problem-solving.

> The ultimate aim of therapy is for you to become a self-therapist and thereby increase the likelihood of successfully tackling your problems of today tomorrow and the future.

Instead of letting clients swallow undigested their 'job description', it is important for therapists to obtain feedback in order to clarify points and deal with clients' doubts or objections about it (see also Chapter 2). Some therapists may not wish to be so blatant in outlining the client's role in therapy and, instead, signal the collaborative and task-oriented nature of the endeavour by an early problem-solving focus, e.g. 'Okay, what problem shall we look at first?' However, as Dryden and Yankura (1993) point out, clients could become confused if their tasks are introduced into therapy without a supporting rationale.

When therapists are too active and too directive

REBT therapists usually adopt a vigorous and forceful approach to therapy that guides clients to the salient aspects of their presenting problems and is deemed to be more effective in helping clients change than a passive or non-directive style of intervention. Thus they are active in, among other clinical responsibilities, asking questions, gathering information, limiting extraneous material, problem-defining, goal-setting, disputing, negotiating homework assignments – all with the express purpose of directing clients to the cognitive core of their emotional disturbance. Some therapists might pursue the active-directive style too zealously and thereby overlook or pay no attention to their clients' interactional and learning requirements:

Supervisor: How do you think therapy is going for the client?
Therapist: We're really getting down to business. Things are zipping along.
Supervisor: I can believe that. Your tape sounds as if you're roaring through therapy at a hundred miles an hour. Is your client keeping up with you though?
Therapist: I haven't had any complaints from her.
Supervisor: You may not have heard any but have you asked her? In fact, I haven't heard the client say much at all. Has she been flattened by your juggernaut?
Therapist: What do you mean?
Supervisor: I get the impression that the pace of therapy is much too fast for her and she has been left lying in the road behind you.

Therapist: She seems compliant. Nodding in agreement with the points I'm making.

Supervisor: In REBT, we look for genuinely collaborative clients, not compliant ones. You're failing to get feedback in order to establish if she really understands the points you are making, if she is happy with the pace you're setting, if your approach is best suited to her learning needs, and what kind of preferred relationship she would like with you. All these things will help to create an optimal learning environment for her.

Therapist: But it's my natural pace and style in therapy.

Supervisor: But is it hers? Unless you adjust your pace and level of verbal activity to suit your client's, you will probably have a high attrition rate among clients through boredom, confusion, hostility.

Therapist: What's the problem with my 'verbal activity' as you call it?

Supervisor: Instead of asking one question and waiting for an answer, you ask half a dozen and often end up answering them yourself. Therapy sounds like a monologue rather than a dialogue.

Therapist: It seems like my sessions are a catalogue of disasters.

Supervisor: You're obviously trying to help the client, but this would be done better if you slow down, ask one question at a time and follow the other suggestions I've already made.

Therapist: Well, it does make sense: people generally tell me that I talk too fast and show impatience when things are dawdling along.

Supervisor: Okay, so you will need to monitor your speedometer in therapy. Now another problem is that you keep on asking her, '. . . and what are you telling yourself'? Her replies indicate that she is unsure what you mean by that question. Are you automatically assuming that she understands how some of her attitudes are implicated in her emotional problems?

Therapist: Well . . . I have been telling her that there is a connection.

Supervisor: But have you helped her to see this link? You should be teaching her the thinking–feeling link in order to engender greater cognitive awareness on her part. Then that question can be asked with probably much greater effect.

Therapist: *(sighs)* No, I haven't been doing that either.

> *Supervisor:* Right, so you now have a list of activities that I want to hear on your next tape. Remember that therapy is adjusted to dovetail with the client's abilities. Please keep in step with her. Less can be more.
>
> *Therapist:* You mean if I go slower she will probably learn more?
>
> *Supervisor:* Yes. Less active-directiveness on your part can bring more therapeutic benefits for her as she genuinely absorbs what is being taught – more benefits than she is receiving at the moment.
>
> *Therapist:* I'll keep in mind that phrase 'less can be more' to guide my behaviour in therapy.
>
> *Supervisor:* Good.

Working too fast in therapy is a common problem, particularly among novice REBT therapists. They may have seen on video such expert REBT therapists as Albert Ellis, Raymond DiGiuseppe and Richard Wessler set a fast pace with some of their clients and incorrectly assume that this is the standard speed to conduct therapy. What they overlook is that these clients profited from a faster rather than a slower pace and that is why it has been selected for use by Ellis and DiGiuseppe. REBT is primarily a psycho-educational therapy approach and therefore, as the supervisor puts it, the therapist needs 'to create an optimal learning environment for her'. This is achieved by using the client's reactions to therapy to build a learning profile of her, e.g. a slow pace if she keeps on saying 'I'm not sure' after each question, examples to illustrate each point if she is a concrete thinker, diagrams on the board 'as I'm not too good with ideas', the therapist as a friendly face rather than a forbidding one 'to help me feel more at ease when I don't understand what's being said to me'. An active-directive approach means a certain style of therapy, not a predetermined speed at which to conduct it.

When therapists accept vague terms as disturbed emotions

When clients are asked how they feel about unpleasant or adverse events in their lives, they frequently say things like 'terrible', 'bad', 'screwed up', 'rejected', 'a failure', 'stressed out'. Clients may consider these terms to be apt descriptions of their feeling states, but for REBT therapists they are a vague collection of 'A', 'B' and 'C' factors which need to sorted out and slotted into their appropriate places within the model. Some therapists may believe that 'bad' or 'stressed out' are sufficiently precise or descriptive terms to indicate which unhealthy negative emotions the client is suffering from, e.g. 'It sounds to me by what he says that he's depressed and angry'. Also they may be reluctant to 'push' clients to be more specific about their feelings when they are so obviously distressed or unsure themselves, e.g. 'How the hell do I know if I'm depressed or guilty? I just know that I feel bloody terrible'. Lack of specificity in identifying an unhealthy negative emotion may mean, for example, that the therapist is grappling simultaneously with several disturbed emotions and their different belief structures; the therapist is tackling a healthy negative emotion instead of an unhealthy one, e.g. sadness and depression respectively, or the therapist is mistaking an activating event ('A') for a feeling ('C'), e.g. 'I feel frustrated over things'.

Specifying a disturbed negative emotion is the starting point for therapeutic intervention as it provides important cognitive clues to what the client's operative irrational belief might be, e.g. pursuing the central idea or theme in hurt of a perceived injustice to oneself which is totally undeserved eventually leads the therapist to the client's disturbance-inducing belief, such as 'He forgot my birthday, which he absolutely shouldn't have done after all these years of faithful devotion, and this means he doesn't love me any more. I'm worthless'. Each disturbed emotion that the client has can be tackled in a similar and consecutive fashion. Distinguishing between unhealthy and healthy negative emotions reveals that the client's 'pissed off' state is actually annoyance, not anger, and therefore valuable therapy time is not wasted on trying to change the client's healthy feeling. By learning REBT's emotional vocabulary, the therapist can see that frustration is not listed and therefore is usually to be treated as the client's 'A'. Then, the therapist can ask how the client feels about being frustrated – 'Angry!' ('C') – which then sets the stage to uncover the 'B'.

By teaching REBT's taxonomy of unhealthy and healthy negative emotions, the therapist now replaces vagueness with precision in identifying the client's 'C'. Clarifying 'hard to get at' or unclear emotions through various techniques (e.g. the empty chair technique, imagery exercises) enables the clients to uncover their suppressed feelings or bring specificity to their amorphous emotional state. All these techniques, among others, usually allow therapists to pinpoint rapidly clients' disturbed feelings so that their amelioration can occur as early as possible in therapy.

When therapists wrongly assume that they know what clients are disturbed about

In assessing the client's activating event, the therapist is trying to locate the client's most clinically relevant inference of 'A' (sometimes referred to as the critical 'A'), which triggers the client's irrational belief ('B') and which, in turn, largely creates the client's disturbed feeling at 'C'. This process is known as inference chaining and is a skilful and often complicated procedure to carry out (see Dryden and Branch 2008). Therapists who fail to be thorough in investigating the 'A' to locate the triggering inference are not helping their clients to discover what they are most upset about in a given situation. For example, a therapist who states that the client's anxiety is due to the possibility of making factual errors in front of colleagues does not help the client to pursue the implications of such errors in order to come face-to-face with what the client is most anxious about. Such an inadequate analysis often leaves clients believing that 'something is still missing' and the problem remains unresolved.

Burrowing into the 'A' rather than scratching about on the surface of it should be the guiding principle of inference chaining (though, of course, the first inference in the chain could be the critical one):

Therapist:	Let's assume that you do make factual errors in front of your colleagues. Then what?
Client:	I'm supposed to be an expert on the subject and I'm showing myself up as a fool in front of them.
Therapist:	Okay, let's assume that they do see you as a fool rather than as an expert. Then what?
Client:	My professional reputation would be in tatters. Everything I've worked for would be destroyed.
Therapist:	And what would happen next if your reputation was shattered?
Client:	*(crying)* Oh God! I'd want to kill myself. I've never seen it so starkly before. I couldn't stand the humiliation and shame of failure.
Therapist:	So what are you most anxious about – your reputation being shattered or the suicidal thoughts that would occur if this happened?
Client:	My reputation. I must preserve it all costs and that's why I can't allow myself to make any errors.

The therapist's 'Let's assume . . . Then what?' questions lead the client to uncover what she is most anxious about if she makes factual errors in front of her colleagues and the verbalisation of her irrational belief: 'I must preserve my reputation at all costs. I couldn't stand the humiliation and shame of failure'. By pinpointing the critical 'A' and 'springing' the implicit irrational belief, the therapist will now be tackling the core of the client's anxiety rather than probing at its periphery.

When therapists don't attend to clients' secondary problems

One of the distinctive features of REBT is its routine searching for clients' secondary emotional problems about their primary ones, e.g. anxiety about anxiety; shame about feeling depressed; guilt about displaying anger. This procedure is carried out to determine if clients are preoccupied with or distracted by these second-order problems and thereby interferes with them focusing on their first-order ones, e.g. someone who presents with a history of panic attacks is deeply ashamed of his 'unmanly' behaviour and focuses on his self-disgust rather than on the therapist's explanation of the cognitive model of panic. Some therapists may overlook this important aspect of assessment because, among other reasons, they are too eager to get to work on the primary problem, only give cursory attention to any secondary problems that may exist, readily agree when clients deny they exist or do not help them to understand the important role of second-order problems in the perpetuation of their emotional disturbance.

A routine question for teasing out secondary problems is to ask, for example, 'Are there any other feelings that you experience in relation to your panic attacks?' If the client is unsure what the therapist means by this question, the therapist can present a brief explanation of the reasons she is probing for second-order problems. If none is uncovered at this point in therapy, the therapist can remain alert to clues that the client is experiencing them, e.g. the client seems distant or his attention wanders; lack of progress on his primary problem. If secondary problems are identified and deemed to be more clinically significant to work on first, it is important that the therapist presents her rationale to the client for this approach, but without insisting upon it.

When therapists imply that preferences can be equated with passivity

In encouraging clients to surrender their musturbatory (musts) demands, inexperienced REBT therapists often imply that embracing a preferential outlook means being passive, indifferent or resigned in the face of unpleasant events. Needless to say, many clients will be hostile to this suggestion and get the wrong impression of REBT philosophy, e.g. 'You mean I'm just supposed to roll over and play dead when he insults me?'; 'Achieving very high standards is no longer important?' Such therapists may wonder what the 'problem' is when clients resist their viewpoint:

Therapist: She doesn't seem to grasp how preferences will help her.
Supervisor: I'm not surprised. Listening to your tape, I can't hear you advocating preferences, particularly strong ones, in this client's case.
Therapist: But I have been – I keep on reminding her that it doesn't matter if she doesn't reach her high standards.

Supervisor: That isn't a powerful preference but a statement of indifference. Look at it from her viewpoint: she is continually striving to achieve high standards and by giving up her demands, what have you left her with?

Therapist: I suppose mediocrity.

Supervisor: Exactly. No wonder she's giving you a hard time in therapy. Now how can you state a real preference without dropping her standards?

Therapist: 'I passionately want to achieve my very high standards but I don't have to'.

Supervisor: So you are getting her to introduce some flexibility into her thinking about her standards without implying that she has to lower them. What are the benefits of a preferential approach?

Therapist: Well, she can keep on striving to maintain her standards but is no longer anxious about falling below them. If she does fall below them, she can maintain a problem-solving focus and examine what went wrong. With her demands, she usually plunges into doom and gloom and takes longer to achieve her standards again.

Supervisor: Good. That should help to put therapy back on track. Now remember that preferences can be expressed mildly, moderately or powerfully, but don't confuse them with statements of indifference or resignation. Otherwise clients will assume that REBT stands for 'Really Can't Be Bothered Therapy', 'Rarely Emotive Behaviour Therapy' or something like that.

Therapist: Okay, I've really got the difference now.

Supervisor: I'll look forward to listening to your next tape then.

Therapists should pay close attention to how they phrase preferential statements and ensure that they convey the correct message of rational alternatives to demands. Feedback from clients will confirm how successful they have been in this task.

When therapists don't deal with clients' doubts about REBT

It is highly likely that many, if not all, clients will have some doubts, reservations or misconceptions about REBT theory or practice, e.g. 'I can't see what's irrational in demanding that my husband must love me? After all, that's why he married me'. Because they are not openly expressed, some therapists may not search for them and they may see such probing as an onerous or potentially anxiety-provoking task, or blithely believe that therapy is 'progressing nicely'. The danger in not carrying out this activity is that the client's doubts will increase to the extent that the client is focused on them rather than on the therapy itself or that they may overwhelm the client and lead to premature termination.

REBT therapists need to encourage their clients to express openly any doubts or reservations they have about any aspect of therapy. This 'invitation' can be part of clients' induction into REBT. Of course, once this invitation has been issued, therapists should handle any complaints or doubts in an open, respectful and non-defensive manner – therapists who took umbrage at a client's comments would display hypocrisy and would be likely to undermine their stance as a rational role model. Therapists' reluctance to engage in this task may reflect discomfort intolerance beliefs (e.g. 'Therapy is going to be hard enough without encouraging whingeing and whining in the client') or ego anxiety (e.g. 'What if I can't come up with good answers, as I must do, to remove her doubts?'). Unless such therapists challenge and change these ideas, clients' unexamined doubts may well prove a source of resistance later in therapy.

When therapists conclude too quickly that their disputing hasn't worked

Disputing clients' irrational beliefs is a major activity of REBT therapists. The degree of skill, persistence and creativity shown in challenging clients' self-defeating thinking often means the difference between them achieving enduring rather than superficial change in their lives. Ellis (1979, 1985) emphasised the role of force and energy in eradicating often deeply rooted musturbatory ideas. Some therapists, often novice ones, incorrectly believe that a few tilts at an irrational belief will bring it crashing down and its rational alternative will automatically take its place. More commonly, therapists can become disillusioned about making any therapeutic headway when their clients show no signs of surrendering or weakening their irrational beliefs:

Therapist: It's bloody difficult. Nothing seems to work with her.
Supervisor: Remind me of her belief.
Therapist: 'I must be in control at all times otherwise I'm totally inadequate'.
Supervisor: So what disputing strategies are you using with her?
Therapist: The usual ones of logic, empiricism and pragmatism.
Supervisor: 'How does it logically follow . . .?', 'Is it consistent with reality?' and 'Where is it going to get you?' You haven't cracked the case yet?

Therapist: I keep on going over these arguments but she won't budge. She won't take on board rational ideas.

Supervisor: Remember, she doesn't have to budge in order to prove what an outstanding therapist you are. If she remains disturbed, too bad! Also she may have a different conception of what rational means, so you will need to check that out. Now, listening to your tape, your disputes are presented in a monotonous and lacklustre fashion – no matter what she says, you ask her the same three questions.

Therapist: I thought that's what I'm supposed to do?

Supervisor: You can use a wide array of disputes underpinned by those three criteria and also vary your disputing style. For example, she sounds like a lively, humorous woman.

Therapist: She is.

Supervisor: Well, I would inject some humour into the sessions. I would drop books, fall out of my chair, walk into the bookcase, that sort of thing, and then ask her if I'm totally inadequate because I lost control.

Therapist: It might not work.

Supervisor: That's true, but try it anyway. Take risks, be inventive, creative. Don't be afraid to experiment . . .

Therapist: . . . rather than be a stick-in-the-mud, which is what I am.

Supervisor: But you don't have to stay like that. Look for lots of ways of contradicting her belief, such as what's she doing in therapy if she has total control? If she really was in complete control of herself, she wouldn't need to demand it of herself as it would be patently obvious to herself and others.

Therapist: Those arguments seem so obvious when you say them, but they haven't occurred to me. I'm just disputing mechanically without any flair or imagination.

Supervisor: Have you really brought out the heavy price she has to pay for keeping up this facade of total control when the reality is imperfect control? All the strain and anxiety created by this tension? The depression and anger when things go wrong?

Therapist: Well, I do ask her about the practical consequences of hanging on to this belief, but we don't pursue it very far. No, we haven't really spelt it out.

Supervisor: What about homework tasks?

Therapist: To deliberately make a mistake at work and learn to accept herself as a fallible human being.

Supervisor: What happened?

Therapist: She said she wouldn't do it.

Supervisor: Individuals who demand infallibility don't like those feet of clay homework tasks. I would have suggested that she record the mistakes she will inevitably, not deliberately, make to reinforce the point about her fallibility. How old is she?

Therapist: She's 40.

Supervisor: I would keep on pointing out that she's had 40 years of evidence which conclusively disproves her total control idea. How many more years does she need before the point sinks in?

Therapist: She's hard going.

Supervisor: Well, you need to be equally persistent in attacking the ideas but, of course, not her. How are you getting on developing the rational alternative?

Therapist: I'm still disputing her irrational beliefs.

Supervisor: Building up the greater benefits of rational beliefs is part of the disputing process. So how could you try and interest her in them?

Therapist: Well, self-acceptance would be a good thing for her.

Supervisor: Why?

Therapist: Well . . . I'm not sure really.

Supervisor: With self-acceptance, she would give up her anxiety about not being in control at all times. When she did make mistakes, she could quickly bounce back from them because she has kept a problem-solving focus and avoided becoming mired in depression and anger. She would be learning from her mistakes how to develop greater control rather than wasting time and energy on maintaining this facade. That would be a real and realistic sense of control. When you are not afraid of losing control, that's when you really are in control. Keep on repeating to her why you believe these are good ideas to acquire.

Therapist: I'm sure I'll forget all this in the session.

Supervisor: Then suggest that she writes these points down on cards to act as prompts during the session. Have you found out if she has had other deeply held beliefs she eventually discarded?

Therapist: No, I haven't thought of that. Obviously if that has occurred, this might give me some information on how to structure my present disputes.

Supervisor: Exactly. Are you any the wiser now?
Therapist: Yes, I am. I've got to wake my brain up to the great possibilities in disputing.
Supervisor: And stay with them. High frustration tolerance coupled with creativity. Let's hope that your next tape is more exciting than this one and yields some therapeutic movement.
Therapist: I feel more confident now about tackling her irrational ideas.

In this extract from supervision, important points to consider are the following:

1   Disputing is engaged in to persuade clients of the superiority of rational ideas over irrational ones in emotional problem-solving. It is not about a power struggle between the therapist and client where the former has to convince the latter of REBT's 'rational correctness'.
2   The logical, empirical and pragmatic arguments advocated in the REBT literature (Ellis and Dryden 1997; Dryden 2009b) are only the starting point of cognitive intervention and not the whole disputing process itself. Hauck (1980) suggests that one's credibility and strength as an REBT therapist is partly due to the ease with which the therapist can employ a wide range of rational arguments to turn the tide in the client's thinking.
3   Effective disputing involves creativity, humour, risk-taking, persistence, repetition, force and energy, in order to makes one's rational case to the client. Disputing is an ever-improving skill and it would be unwise for any REBT therapist to claim that they have totally mastered it.
4   As a general point, those therapists, novice or experienced, who find disputing unusually difficult to conduct should practise as much as possible with friends and colleagues, join a debating society, watch videos or read transcripts of highly proficient REBT therapists at work, learn how to develop a genuine enthusiasm for analysing argument rather than a programmatic approach to it. In this way, disputing might become more of a pleasure and less of a chore.

When therapists do not work with clients to establish a criterion for client coping

The coping criterion is the point at which clients are managing their problems but not always smoothly or easily. This criterion is used by therapists to determine the right time to switch from one client problem to another. However, some therapists may switch too quickly because they inaccurately infer that once an irrational belief associated with a particular problem has been identified then 'the problem is almost solved'. Therapists may also in a single session switch rapidly between the ego and discomfort aspects of a particular problem without properly investigating either. Jumping from problem to problem in quick succession can leave clients feeling confused, unaware of the crucial role of beliefs in their presenting problems, and inadequately prepared to tackle their emotional difficulties.

In order to establish a genuine coping criterion, therapists need to elicit from clients that they understand and agree with the REBT view that demandingness lies at the core of their emotional problems, ensure that clients are equipped with the skills to carry out multimodal tasks in order to dispute their irrational ideas, troubleshoot actual or potential blocks to working through their problems, and establish that clients can act according to their rational beliefs. When these conditions have been met, it would be clinically appropriate for the therapist to focus upon another client problem. The previous problem does not at that point slip out of the therapist's vision, but continues to be monitored for signs of client roadblocks or backsliding.

When therapists leave clients marooned at the level of intellectual insight

Ellis (1963) wrote of the distinction between intellectual and emotional insight as it pertains to REBT. The former type of insight refers to rational ideas lightly and intermittently held but with irrational beliefs still exerting a powerful influence; the latter type relates to rational ideas strongly and consistently held with irrational beliefs now attenuated. Getting from intellectual to emotional insight means putting REBT theory into daily hard work and practice. Some therapists may leave clients stranded at intellectual insight (e.g. 'I understand it in my head how these new ideas will help me to overcome my problems . . .') because they believe that insight alone is sufficient to effect enduring change. Therefore therapy slips into a discourse on rational ideas rather than an enactment of them.

In order for clients to reach emotional insight ('. . . and I also now feel these ideas in my gut'), therapists need to encourage them to undertake and experiment with a wide range of homework tasks (e.g. 'stay-in-there' assignments, shame-attacking exercises, rational emotive imagery) in order to internalise a rational outlook. This stage of therapy also involves removing client blocks to achieving emotional insight, such as the 'I won't be me' syndrome (Grieger and Boyd 1980) whereby clients believe that they will lose their identity in the change process, and low frustration tolerance, e.g. 'I want to change but the work involved is too bloody hard!'. Lifelong hard work and continual practice will eventually bridge the 'head–gut' divide.

When therapists negotiate homework tasks that are not therapeutically potent

As discussed above, homework tasks represent the bridge between intellectual and emotional insight. Some clients may not get very far along this bridge or they may take an inordinate amount of time to cross it because the tasks that the therapist has negotiated with them are insufficiently challenging to promote substantial or rapid constructive change. For example, the therapist agrees with the client's 'tiny steps' approach to overcoming her social anxiety, thereby prolonging it rather than encouraging her to stay in social situations as long as possible in order to habituate herself to the discomfort involved. Any therapeutic potency that the task could offer is undermined by the therapist colluding with and probably reinforcing the client's discomfort intolerance beliefs instead of encouraging her to argue forcefully against them.

In planning homework assignments, it is important for the therapist to consider if the designated tasks will help clients to come appreciably closer to their goal, but without discouraging them from undertaking the tasks because they appear too difficult to execute, e.g. clients agree to enter and stay in social situations on alternate nights rather than every night in order to banish their social anxiety. One of us (WD) calls this principle of homework negotiation 'challenging, but not overwhelming' (Dryden 1985). Each task selected should be aimed at weakening clients' irrational ideas while strengthening their rational ones. In this way, homework becomes the real crucible of change rather than anything that happens in the therapist's office.

When therapists fail to uncover core irrational beliefs

As a client's situation-specific irrational beliefs are revealed and challenged (e.g. 'I must give a perfect presentation to my work colleagues'; 'I must not let a friend down when he asks me for a favour'; 'I must not show any weaknesses in front of my children') they usually suggest common themes which frequently coalesce into core irrational beliefs which link the client's problems. In the above example, a core belief might be 'I must have the approval of significant others in my life otherwise I'm worthless'. Working at this fundamental cognitive level can help clients to effect enduring and profound philosophical change in their lives as many problems are tackled simultaneously rather than consecutively. Some therapists may assume that removing or 'knocking down' each irrational belief that appears is profound philosophical change of a sort, but obviously remains a haphazard way of achieving it and leaves clients vulnerable to emotional disturbance in problematic contexts that have not been examined. Also plodding through each problem may give clients tunnel vision rather than offering them a panorama of their problems by tapping into their rules of living or core philosophies.

When clients start working through their problems, it is important for therapists to encourage them to probe for central ideas or themes that recur in each problem dissected:

> *Therapist:* Can you see any connection between giving the perfect work presentation, not letting down a friend, not showing weaknesses in front of your children?
>
> *Client:* Yes, I can. I'm always demanding approval from people I consider important in my life. I wish I could stop doing it.
>
> *Therapist:* What would be the value of working on this core belief rather than asking for more similar problems to explore?
>
> *Client:* If we look at other problems, it will be the same old story of me having to behave in the right way each time. Let's get to the heart of the problem: my need for approval – and the sooner the better.

If clients are unable to identify key themes or ideas in their problems, the therapist can suggest what they might be and seek feedback in order to confirm, modify or reject them.

When therapists hold clients back from becoming their own therapists

As clients develop greater confidence and competence in tackling their problems, the therapist should begin to diminish the level of active-directiveness in order to encourage clients to become their own therapists for present and future emotional problem-solving. Hence clients take on more responsibility for, among other things, agenda setting, undertaking an 'ABC' analysis of their problems, eliciting the disturbance-inducing beliefs, selecting disputing strategies, and devising homework assignments. However, if the therapist does not pull back and continues to play a dominant role in directing therapy, some clients are likely to remain dependent on the therapist to promote therapeutic change and thereby increase the chances of relapse when they leave therapy, remain at the level of intellectual insight rather than internalise a new rational outlook, or prolong therapy to delay standing on their own feet.

Dryden and Neenan (2006) suggest that it is important that therapists give their clients an opportunity to serve as their own therapist as early in the process as is clinically indicated. This can be determined by monitoring how quickly clients accept and act on the principles of emotional and therapeutic responsibility, e.g. a client acknowledges that she makes herself anxious by demanding she must have the right answer if she speaks up in class and suggests that her first homework task is to reply to questions when she is unsure of the answer. As clients take over more of the reins of therapy, the therapist can slip into the role of their consultant or trainer and provide advice on how to improve their problem-solving skills. If a client's progress falters significantly, the therapist can temporarily resume a more active role until the client's obstacles to change have been removed, e.g. the client experiences panic in class when she gets an answer wrong and is reluctant to return; the therapist teaches her how to re-establish cognitive control over her panic and encourages her to return to class.

When therapists take too much credit for clients' progress

As therapy moves towards termination, it is important for therapists to help their clients attribute the majority of their progress to their own efforts rather than to their therapist, e.g. 'I taught you how you mainly created your self-induced disturbances but you did all the hard work between sessions to overcome them. Without that tremendous determination on your part, therapy would have been stuck in the mud'. This kind of summary puts the locus of control and change within the client and is usually a powerful stimulus for clients to maintain their gains after therapy has ended. Some therapists may baulk at giving too much credit to the clients for their progress and diminishing their own contributions to it; instead, these therapists convey to their clients how 'dazzling' they were in orchestrating the process of change and thereby relegating the clients to the sidelines of therapy. Such therapist self-adoration is likely to communicate to the clients that 'you can't do it without me' and, if believed, greatly increase their chances of relapse once therapy has ended.

Therapists who feed their vanity as the omnipotent force of change in others' lives usually have considerable ego problems that they bring into therapy, e.g. 'I need the client to see and acknowledge how great I am in getting them better'. By challenging and changing such beliefs, therapists can remove their ego from therapy and refocus their clinical attention where it belongs – making sure their clients are equipped to be effective problem-solvers. The real satisfaction for REBT therapists is not in blowing their own trumpet, but in seeing their clients acquire a rational outlook that can help to guide them for the rest of their lives.

In this chapter, we have explored therapist blocks to carrying out their various assignments and have suggested methods for removing these obstacles. In Chapter 11 we turn our attention to a diverse collection of therapist problems that usually inhibit or undermine the progress of therapy.

Chapter 11

A compendium of therapist problems

This chapter presents a collection of therapist problems that are driven by ideological rigidity and shows how therapists can often be more resistant than their clients to changing their own irrationalities. As we shall see, some of these irrationalities are easy to uncover, e.g. an angry therapist who demands that his clients must carry out their homework tasks, while others are harder to detect because they are subtly expressed, e.g. a therapist's pleasure in seeing her client every week masks her fear that his absence would prove that she is an awful therapist. Also therapist rigidity may masquerade as force and energy in the process of constructive change: clients are pushed, persuaded, encouraged (pleaded with!), to overcome their problems in order to rescue therapists from their own sense of a 'crushing defeat' if their clients remain emotionally disturbed. These and other issues will now be discussed.

When therapists believe they should have an easy time in therapy

A succession of highly resistant, troublesome, complex or self-sabotaging clients can put a considerable strain on the therapist's resilience or equilibrium, so it is understandable when a therapist desires 'a few easy clients' to usher in a more tranquil period in therapy. However, trouble arises when the therapist transmutes a desire into a demand, e.g. 'Because I want an easy time in therapy, therefore I absolutely must have one' and thereby rapidly diminishes his tolerance for coping with the next recalcitrant or disruptive client. The therapist may signal his discomfort intolerance attitude to such a client with, among other ways, visible displays of anger when the client 'steps out of line', perfunctory disputing, indifference to whether the client carries out her homework tasks. He will probably also experience great relief when the client drops out of therapy – this may confirm from his viewpoint that she lacked commitment to change rather than was discouraged by his abysmal attitude towards her. Her absence now provides him with the easy time in therapy he has been demanding.

Although a clutch of 'easy' clients may provide a welcome interlude in the seemingly never-ending stream of difficult customers (DCs), REBT therapists need to keep on reminding themselves that there is no reason why they must have or deserve an easy time in therapy. Their own disturbed behaviour may reinforce that of a DC and thereby make therapy even tougher than it was already. Such clients present a formidable challenge as they are liable to test the limits of the therapist's competence and patience. This can be viewed by the therapist as a valuable learning experience in order to improve clinical skills and strive for discomfort tolerance. Even though the therapist will generally work much harder with DCs, accepting the reality of their often highly disturbed behaviour will allow the therapist to have an easier time in therapy than would be the case if the therapist continually railed against such behaviour. An easy time in therapy is likely to produce complacent rather than competent and creative therapy. As Hauck (1980: 248) points out, no matter how badly clients behave, 'they are there to stimulate you, to enrich your life, to broaden your horizons . . . [they] are the key to your therapeutic success'. So welcome them into your office!

When therapists believe that they must challenge all their clients' irrational beliefs

While a client may express many irrational (i.e. self-defeating) beliefs during the course of therapy, it does not mean that they are all implicated in the client's presenting problems or all of them have to become the focus of clinical attention simply because they are irrational. The 'musts' and 'shoulds' that REBT therapists target for challenge and change are unconditional ones that underlie the client's emotional disturbance, e.g. the anxiety-inducing belief that 'I must never show any weakness to others as this would be terrible', or the depression-creating belief that 'I should never have lost my job and now I'm worthless'. The experienced REBT therapist keeps in focus the client's key irrationalities and generally avoids examining less important or peripheral ones.

Some REBT therapists, usually novice ones, mistakenly believe that it is their devout mission to uproot all the client's irrational beliefs – or what they perceive to be irrational ones. Any sentence that contains a 'must' or 'should', an 'it's awful' or 'I can't stand it', etc., is immediately disputed, e.g. 'Why must you wash your hair just because it is greasy?'; 'Prove that traffic jams are awful?'; 'Where's the evidence that you can't stand sugar in your coffee?' These are hardly the issues that the client wants to discuss in therapy and she may well become confused by and frustrated with the therapist's relentless attacks upon her every time she mentions one of the aforementioned words or phrases. In attempting to remove all the client's putative irrational thinking, the therapist ends up reinforcing his own genuine irrationalities and diminishing his chances of helping the client to overcome the problems she really wants addressed in therapy.

Such 'knee-jerk' disputing misrepresents REBT. As Walen et al. (1992: 212) point out: 'Remember that these words [and phrases] are harmful because of the concepts that they stand for, not their face value'. Such words and phrases are part of our daily vocabulary and are frequently used in a harmless way – there is usually no absolutist philosophy lurking behind these terms. Even if the client did mean, in the REBT sense, that she cannot stand sugar in her coffee, it is highly unlikely to be clinically relevant to her presenting problems or an issue that she has come to therapy to discuss. By surrendering his own musturbatory approach to therapy – 'I must dispute all musts!' – the therapist gradually gains clinical acuity in determining which terms used by the client are implicated in the emotional problems she wishes to address and therefore are legitimate targets for disputing.

When therapists believe that they must always be rational

Acquiring a rational philosophy of living means reducing one's general level of disturbability, but not completely removing it. This is the message to convey to clients in order to counter any misconceptions they may have that REBT will teach them how to be in emotional control at all times, because each problem they have will be solved by impeccable logical analysis. Therefore human fallibility is an inseparable part of a rational outlook. However, some REBT therapists equate rationality with never again holding irrational ideas or experiencing unhealthy negative emotions. Instead of posing as rational role models for their clients, they are actually exhibiting psychological disturbance in their presence:

> *Supervisor:* Listening to your tapes, I'm greatly struck by your notion of rationality, which seems to imply that all emotional distress has been banished for good. Is this true?
>
> *Therapist:* Well, once you've learnt how to think in a rational manner, there's no reason or excuse for disturbing yourself again.
>
> *Supervisor:* That's a pretty harsh doctrine. Are you teaching that to your client?
>
> *Therapist:* I'm attempting to but she's not very receptive to it. She sees it as something cold and alien to her. I'm hoping to win her over by acting as a role model.
>
> *Supervisor:* As an uncompromising rather than a flexible one. I don't think she's going to be persuaded.

Therapist: We'll see. Anyway, why do you call it harsh? Rational means establishing permanent cognitive control of one's reactions to life events.

Supervisor: The reason I call it harsh is because you are not allowing for human fallibility – that human beings from time to time will slip back into self-defeating patterns of thinking, feeling and behaving. Being rational in REBT terms includes accepting human fallibility. Your view of rationality is not the REBT one and therefore you are misleading the client and yourself.

Therapist: I'm not misleading her or myself. I am trying to teach her to be rational by surrendering all her demands and expressing her goals only in terms of desires and preferences.

Supervisor: And are you also trying to teach her how to cope constructively when she transforms desires into demands and starts disturbing herself again?

Therapist: But that's the point – when she stops making demands all over the place, then she'll stop disturbing herself for good.

Supervisor: If only it was as simple as that. You've fallen into the same trap as some other REBT therapists have done; namely, now that you are an REBT therapist you have to be rational at all times. You said earlier that there is no excuse for becoming disturbed again once you've learnt how to think rationally. Doesn't sound to me as if you're expressing that idea as a preference.

Therapist: I suppose it does sound rather harsh, but I'm trying to follow this philosophy myself as well as offer it to the client.

Supervisor: Well, you had better examine what it is you're offering her. By demanding that you must be rational at all times you are, in fact, being what?

Therapist: Irrational. The opposite of what I preferably should be teaching her.

Supervisor: And yourself. When you are upset, do you tell yourself, for example, that you are only annoyed or concerned when you are actually feeling angry or anxious?

Therapist: I don't like to admit it but that does happen sometimes. If I admit that I'm angry, this means that I'm disturbing myself, which means, in turn, I'm being irrational which I prefer not to be.

Supervisor: Well, you're not expressing it as a preference, but as a demand that you must not be irrational.

Therapist: How do you work that out?

Supervisor: Because if you really followed the preference, you would acknowledge that you still experience unhealthy negative emotions but want to limit their frequency, intensity and duration in your life. Instead you're denying that you feel them because . . .

Therapist: . . . that would mean I'm not thinking rationally, which I must do at all times.

Supervisor: Exactly. Now are you going to teach your client the REBT view of rationality once you've sorted it out in your own mind?

Therapist: I can see now where I've been going wrong, but I'm worried what the client will think when I admit my mistakes.

Supervisor: Because you'll be displaying what as a therapist and human being?

Therapist: *(laughs)* My dreaded fallibility.

Supervisor: Which forms part of a . . .?

Therapist: A truly rational outlook.

Supervisor: You might find your client is now more receptive to REBT as she doesn't feel you're trying to turn her into Mr Spock from 'Star Trek'.

Therapist: I probably do come across in therapy as Mr Logical devoid of all emotion.

Supervisor: Okay, so in your next tapes let me hear you teaching your client proper REBT.

Throughout their training and beyond, REBT therapists are repeatedly taught that a rational philosophy of living is an anti-musturbatory one that includes human fallibility – accepting oneself as a fallible human being is often the phrase that rings the loudest in the clients' ears. Yet some therapists remain deaf to this message and demand that they must be rational at all times and thereby deny their own fallibility. In order for this irrational view of rationality to be detected and challenged, it is important for therapists to have regular supervision. Left unchecked, this anti-REBT stance will help some clients to develop more irrationalities rather than fewer.

When therapists base their self-worth on keeping clients in therapy

A plaintive but silent plea is sometimes made by those therapists who judge their clinical competence on the basis of clients attending therapy every week, e.g. 'My clients must come back to therapy regularly in order for me to see myself as a good and effective therapist'. Attendance is the yardstick of competence not outcome. Because of their need to ensure that clients return, these therapists make therapy as easy and as pleasant as possible for them. Therefore hard work is not on the session agenda. Clients may leave therapy feeling better because of all the positive strokes they have received, but they are highly unlikely to be getting better as their disturbance-creating ideas have been left unexamined and therefore intact.

Clinical competence in REBT is assessed by the reduction in or elimination of the client's emotional disturbance and not by the length of time spent in therapy. When therapists have understood this distinction by tackling their ego problems, they can then focus their clinical attention on teaching their clients to be problem-solvers. This is achieved by clients becoming collaborators in therapy to identify, challenge and change their irrational ideas through a variety of homework tasks. This usually involves clients experiencing the discomfort of hard work and the dogged persistence of the therapist in pushing, persuading and encouraging them to change. Some clients may drop out of therapy as the non-disturbed therapist is no longer bending over backwards to help them feel comfortable or worthwhile. While premature termination is regrettable, helping those clients who remain to realise enduring therapeutic gains is more important than trying to retain all clients in order to achieve only palliative benefits for them.

When therapists think that they must challenge immediately their clients' irrational beliefs

REBT is a highly active-directive form of psychotherapy and seeks to elicit as early as possible the client's irrational beliefs for disputing. Although REBT does have a 'let's get on with it' message to convey to clients, it does recognise that some or most clients will need time to settle into therapy. For them, having an irrational idea disputed as soon as it is uncovered is likely to impair the development of a therapeutic alliance as they feel under attack from the therapist, e.g. 'Why won't he listen to what I have to say instead of trying to shoot me down all the time?' For some REBT therapists, zeroing in on an irrational idea once it is detected is the hallmark of a highly proficient therapist; not a moment must be wasted in getting to grips with the client's emotional distress and rapidly ameliorating it. Also some of these therapists may have self-esteem problems: to hold their disputing fire might indicate to the client that they are unsure of themselves and thereby let the client gain the upper hand.

Immediate disputing of irrational beliefs is not necessarily a sign of a proficient REBT therapist but, more usually, of a hasty and ill-prepared one. Care needs to be taken in constructing a working alliance, inducting clients into REBT, gathering background information, assessing accurately clients' presenting problems, gaining feedback, pinpointing the relevant irrational beliefs to challenge rather than the first ones the clients utter. Once these activities have been accomplished, it is much more likely that the clients will be amenable to having their beliefs disputed. Setting the stage for disputing rather than a headlong rush into it will usually create the impression of clinical competence and remove the need for power struggles, real or imagined. Disputing is not for the therapist's self-satisfaction, but to enable the clients to feel healthy negative emotions as their goals for change.

'It doesn't feel comfortable': when therapists believe that they must be comfortable in therapy

The comment that therapists should be comfortable in therapy seems to be widely expressed by therapists from all kinds of therapy disciplines. The 'it' refers to any difficulty, obstacle, problem, conflict, tension, discomfort, etc. that threatens to destabilise or impair the relatively smooth or harmonious functioning of therapy. In order for therapists not to feel uncomfortable, they implement measures (e.g. placating the client, not discussing painful issues) to defuse or sidestep any looming difficulties. Although REBT therapists are generally a hard-headed and unsentimental bunch who do not usually flinch from dealing with whatever occurs in therapy, some are not immune from the need for comfort in their therapy practice:

Supervisor: Listening to your tapes, you seem to be deliberately deaf to some of the issues that the client wants to talk about.

Therapist: I don't agree. We put on the agenda whatever she wants to talk about.

Supervisor: Such as . . .?

Therapist: We're exploring her depression, which is related to losing her job, her diminishing social circle, nothing seeming to go right in her life. So it's all being covered.

Supervisor: It seems to me there are issues she is not going to offer up easily for discussion but wants them addressed anyway. She refers several times to something that happened with a former boyfriend but, on each occasion, you let it pass.

Therapist: Well, the reason I do that is because when she is ready to tell me, I expect she will.

Supervisor: And you think it is as straightforward as that?

Therapist: You obviously don't.

Supervisor: That's true. My hypothesis about your behaviour is this: that you are aware of avoiding the boyfriend issue because to explore it may detonate all sorts of painful

	issues that would turn therapy into a very uncomfortable experience for you.
Therapist:	There may well be an element of truth in that. On the other hand, I've had very uncomfortable experiences in therapy and haven't tried to run away from them.
Supervisor:	I'm sure that's perfectly true in other cases, but we're trying to find out why this case is different. What do you think the boyfriend issue might be?
Therapist:	Well, I suppose it might be rape or some form of sexual abuse.
Supervisor:	Let's suppose you're right. Now what prevents you from exploring these issues with her?
Therapist:	I'm worried about opening this Pandora's box of emotional pain and not being able to close it again.
Supervisor:	Well, you don't want to close the box, but help her to deal with the problems that emerge from it.
Therapist:	I don't feel I'd be able to cope with it.
Supervisor:	What's the 'it' you believe you can't cope with?
Therapist:	The uncertainty whether I'll be really able to help her. Week after week I'll be listening to this outpouring of unhappiness but not knowing if she's going to get better. That's what I'd feel really uncomfortable about: having to tolerate this uncertainty.
Supervisor:	So this uncomfortable feeling is actually discomfort anxiety: which is about getting into these areas with her and not knowing what the outcome will be and having to tolerate this uncertainty.
Therapist:	Yeah, that's right.
Supervisor:	How would you state the anxiety-producing belief?
Therapist:	Something like 'I absolutely must be certain that I can help her otherwise I won't be able to stand the uncertainty that I might be getting therapy hideously wrong'.
Supervisor:	Okay, which therapist has a guarantee that he or she will have a successful outcome in dealing with these issues?
Therapist:	I know there are no guarantees . . .
Supervisor:	Well, you're demanding one.
Therapist:	What I mean is that more experienced, confident and skilful REBT therapists would know how to handle rape and sexual abuse cases.
Supervisor:	And how did they acquire these qualities?
Therapist:	I know – they had to go through a learning process.
Supervisor:	Which never stops. You apply REBT to this case as any other. I'll assign you reading which covers these areas

and, of course, you're in regular supervision, so I'll be keeping a close eye on your progress or lack of it.

Therapist: I really do want to help her. I'm just worried about if I actually can help her or not.

Supervisor: Neither you nor she will know that until you start finding out. While you delay, her suffering continues.

Therapist: Okay, I'll start in the next session.

Supervisor: Good. Now one last thing to say: your assumption is that the boyfriend issue is related to rape or sexual abuse. It could be something else like her previous boyfriend lied to her about being in love with her. We want to develop a treatment programme based on empirical data not hunches. So what are you going to do with that assumption of yours?

Therapist: Check it out with the client.

Supervisor: Right. I would suggest that you don't actually present it to her, but let her tell her story and silently check it out. It might be the more tactful thing to do in the circumstances. I'll look forward to supervising your next tape.

Therapist: I feel more confident now about bringing it.

Important points to note in this extract from supervision are:

1   The supervisor suggests that there are two kinds of agenda setting: the explicit kind where the client readily offers problems for discussion and a more tacit form that is hinted at by the client. As the therapist is reluctant to acknowledge the client's tacit agenda, this prompts the supervisor to explore the possible reasons for it.

2   The supervisor's hypothesis is that the therapist's avoidance is based on his worry of feeling very uncomfortable when confronted with the client's highly painful emotional issues related to her tacit agenda. The therapist gingerly accepts this hypothesis and suggests that these issues might relate to rape or sexual abuse and therefore 'I don't feel I'd be able to cope with it'.

3   In order to determine what lies at the heart of the therapist's anticipated discomfort in dealing with these issues, the supervisor asks him to clarify what the 'it' refers to – the therapist having to tolerate the great discomfort of not knowing whether he really has the clinical ability to help the client. Then the therapist's discomfort anxiety is crystallised into an irrational belief for disputing.

4   The supervisor points out that the therapist's uncertainty creates one certainty: the client's suffering continues while the therapist searches for a guarantee that his clinical intervention will be successful. In order

to develop greater clinical competence and confidence, the therapist needs to tolerate the uncertainty of treatment outcome while preparing himself to deal as best he can with the problems that arise from tackling the client's tacit agenda.

5   The therapist's assumption that the 'boyfriend issue' refers to rape or sexual abuse is just that – an assumption and therefore needs to be corroborated by the client. Therapy driven by assumption is a poor basis for developing a treatment programme.

When therapists think that they know what's best for their clients

While REBT therapists encourage their clients to strive for elegant or profound philosophical change in their lives (surrendering rigid and unconditional musts and shoulds), they acknowledge that some or most clients will fall short of this goal. Clients will frequently terminate therapy as soon as they feel better because their presenting symptoms have now been reduced or removed. Tracing the largely cognitive roots of these symptoms may seem irrelevant, arduous or too time-consuming to many clients to warrant prolonging therapy. From a pragmatic viewpoint, some change is usually better than no change. However, some REBT therapists may see mere symptom reduction or removal as no change at all and issue dire warnings about the client's imminent relapse, 'skating on thin cognitive ice' or only applying a Band-Aid to the psychic wound rather than treating the wound itself.

Such therapist arrogance is based not only on a 'do as you're told because I know what's best for you' approach, but also on the disdain they feel for those clients who waste the therapist's precious time by entering therapy only to feel better instead of get better, e.g. 'If you just wanted reassurance, you should have spoken to a friend rather than come to therapy. I'm here to offer you real solutions to your problems, not to placate you'. These attitudes will probably hasten the client's departure from therapy; they are highly unlikely to encourage the client to reconsider her decision to terminate.

Such therapists easily forget that the elegant solution in REBT is the preferred goal, not the only goal. Clients are not to be despised because they seek palliative solutions to their problems. To insist that all clients must stay in therapy until their musturbatory thinking has been removed creates the great possibility of the therapist being more disturbed than the clients; therefore the therapist would be attempting to keep clients in therapy in order to teach them an irrational belief system. The therapist's 'I know what's best for you' diktat would now carry a heavy charge of irony.

While REBT therapists would certainly not object to only helping clients to feel better, they can also present to them a persuasive clinical rationale to keep them longer in therapy:

'I'm glad that the reassurance you've received has helped to reduce your anxiety, but the next and even more important stage in therapy is to get rid of that anxiety by showing you how to cope if your fears ever turned out to be true. This stage takes longer but the benefits are usually lifelong. Would you be interested in entering this next stage?'

Even if some therapists do believe that they know what is best for their clients, it is the clients who remain the final arbiter of the degree of change they wish to effect in their lives.

When therapists' personal problems cloud their clinical judgement

REBT therapists strive to keep their egos out of therapy and refrain from making moral judgements about their clients (but not always of their actions or traits). We have already looked at examples where this does not occur. In a similar vein, REBT therapists try to prevent personal problems from infiltrating into and adversely affecting their clinical practice. When this does happen, the client becomes the target of the therapist's hidden agenda:

Supervisor: In listening to your tapes, you seem to be giving your client an inordinately hard time in therapy.

Therapist: In what way?

Supervisor: Well, when he turns up late for appointments, doesn't do his homework, disagrees with you, provides inadequate feedback, has trouble understanding rational concepts. That sort of thing.

Therapist: He's lazy, argumentative and inattentive. He wants to make progress with his problem but without doing any work; so I have to push him.

Supervisor: I agree that some clients require pushing but you seem to be persecuting him. You can barely contain your anger with him.

Therapist: When you say 'persecuting him', you obviously have some hypothesis you're going to present to me about my behaviour.

Supervisor: Correct. I'm in the hypothesis presenting business – I'm an REBT therapist and your clinical supervisor.

Therapist: So what is it then?

Supervisor: There is a personal issue involved which you're taking out on the client.

Therapist: Where's your evidence for that assumption?

Supervisor: Well, you brought to supervision a couple of months ago a client with very similar behavioural problems and I commented on how well you were handling him. You certainly were not hot under the collar then about his behaviour.

Therapist: Well, this client is different, that's why.

Supervisor: Is it the client or is it that your attitude is different this time?

Therapist: I don't know. Maybe I had a bad day or something.

Supervisor: You seem to be getting angry with me asking you these questions. What's going through your mind at the moment?

Therapist: You're implying that I'm being less than professional with this client. I told you, he's bloody difficult! That's the reason.

Supervisor: If I'm wrong about it, am I allowed to imply it as your clinical supervisor? My role as your supervisor is to help you to develop your therapeutic skills as well as to monitor what goes on between you and your client. If I'm right, denying what's actually going on in therapy is not going to help you resolve it. The poor old client receives a double whammy: he's not helped to sort out his problems and he's on the receiving end as you vent your spleen in therapy.

Therapist: *(sighs)* Yes, I am angry. I'm angry that you're right about the personal issue.

Supervisor: And therefore . . .?

Therapist: *(mock anger)* You bloody well shouldn't be right!

Supervisor: Because as I am . . .?

Therapist: Well, this means that I have to admit reluctantly that I am being unprofessional with this client and a few others whose tapes you haven't heard yet. Then I'm angry with myself for being unprofessional in the first place.

Supervisor: Okay, thanks for being honest. As you know, I'm not here to provide personal therapy for you, but obviously I need to consider the impact that your problems are having on your clinical practice. Now let's find out what the attitude is that arises in your private life that you bring into your professional one.

Therapist: Well, my wife and I are arguing all the time, tense silences, doors being slammed, no peace at home at all. I'm glad to come to work for a bit of peace and quiet.

Supervisor: And if you don't get it because your clients are giving you a hard time, what then?

Therapist: *(emphatic)* I'm bloody well not putting up with it! At work as well as at home. You must be joking.

Supervisor: So what's the demand you're making, just to be clear?

Therapist: If I'm having hassle at home, I must have a quiet time at work. I can't stand it when the clients start messing me about. If they make me suffer, then I'm going to make them suffer.

Supervisor: Your use of the word 'suffer' reflects your present emotional disturbance. You're supposed to be creating a therapeutic environment and not a torture chamber.

Therapist: *(wearily)* Yes, I know. I shouldn't be taking it out on them.

Supervisor: So how are you going to stop doing it then?

Therapist: By disconnecting my private life from my professional one. Every day I come to work, I can forcefully remind myself that just because I have turbulence at home, there is no reason why I must have tranquillity at work though, of course, it would be preferable to have it. If things are tough at work and at home, too damn bad.

Supervisor: How can you make things less tough for yourself if your clients are 'messing you about' as you call it?

Therapist: By accepting the reality of their present behaviour and looking at constructive ways of tackling it by examining the reasons why one keeps on turning up late or another doesn't do his homework. In other words, not use my anger to try and bludgeon them into submission, which isn't working anyway.

Supervisor: Now imagine that you have dealt with your anger: how different will your day be?

Therapist: Well, I won't be disturbed in the sessions or while waiting for the next client to show. I won't be consumed by my anger any longer and will have more energy at work for other things.

Supervisor: And how will you be on the way home?

Therapist: I won't be wound up as much and therefore less likely to start sniping as soon as I get home. I'll be much more inclined to try to sort out our relationship. It sounds good talking about it with you.

Supervisor: Okay. Now let's see if you begin to put this new attitude into practice in your next tapes. Remember, there's no evidence that supports your belief that you must have

> what you want either at home, work or anywhere in life, so deal with that 'must'. It's not compatible with effective problem-solving. Good luck. See you in a fortnight.

Important points to note in this extract from supervision are the following:

1   The supervisor is alerted to the possibility that the therapist's actions are driven by personal motives in the way he attacks the client for his recalcitrant behaviour. The supervisor's hypothesis is quickly challenged by the therapist, but the supervisor does not become defensive and simply presents her evidence for the therapist to consider.
2   Even though the therapist admits that the supervisor's hypothesis is correct, and is angry at her accuracy as well as his own unprofessional conduct, the supervisor is not sidetracked into examining these secondary issues but continues to probe for the cognitive source of the therapist's primary anger. This starts in his domestic life and spreads into his professional one.
3   The supervisor's role is not to provide the therapist with personal therapy, but to deal with the clinical impact of his domestic problems. The supervisor uses Socratic questioning in order to allow the therapist to suggest how he can undisturb himself and the likely therapeutic benefits that will be gained.
4   In order to provide an added encouragement to change, the supervisor nudges the therapist to speculate on the possible advantages he may experience in his private life if he acts in a non-disturbed way. The supervisor points out as a summation of the session that musturbatory thinking is an ineffective cognitive tool for solving problems in any sphere of our lives.
5   If the therapist is unable to remove his disturbance-inducing ideas, then a period of personal therapy is advisable. The client would be assigned to another (undisturbed) REBT therapist so that his presenting problems now receive undivided clinical attention.

When therapists believe that they must crush their clients' resistance to prove what strong and determined therapists they are

Ellis (1985, 2002) wrote a book describing common forms of client resistance and the wide range of multimodal techniques that can be used to overcome it. While providing an excellent resource for therapists whose patience and problem-solving skills are sorely taxed by such clients, Ellis acknowledged that for some clients, no amount of therapeutic effort appears to moderate their emotional disturbance. Instead of accepting this grim reality, some REBT therapists see resistance as the client throwing down the gauntlet which they are compelled to pick up to prove how omnipotent they are. Instead of employing creative persistence to break through the client's resistance in order to effect constructive change, they seek to crush resistance as an end in itself to prove 'who is the boss in therapy'. Actually working on the client's problems is often an afterthought or anticlimax for these therapists, while clients who linger in therapy may do so in a state of sullen dejection or obedient passivity. Power without therapeutic purpose is a hollow victory that these therapists are unable to see.

Therapists should remember that tackling client resistance is usually a significant learning experience for them – the more difficult the case, the more that therapists have to stretch themselves to find the right combination of skills and techniques to produce therapeutic movement. Inevitable failure with some clients is not linked to self-depreciation but unconditional self-acceptance as a fallible therapist. Therefore they do not see therapy as a power struggle which they have to win because their ego is on the line. Instead they focus their energies where they clinically belong – overcoming clients' resistance in order to empower them to realise their goals for change. That is the real power that therapists can achieve.

Therapists who think that the concept of fallibility applies to clients and not to themselves

A key teaching of REBT is to encourage clients to accept themselves unconditionally as fallible human beings. If they choose, they can judge, rate or condemn their actions or traits but never themselves. Self-acceptance is the basis for enduring emotional stability in their lives. Although some REBT therapists may be persuasive in urging clients to embrace this concept, they fail to act on it themselves. They refuse or are reluctant to admit they have personal problems or display any perceived weaknesses. This may occur because, among other reasons, they irrationally believe that therapists should be free from problems or flaws, that understanding and practising REBT is a kind of amulet against emotional disturbance or refrain from potentially painful self-examination. While the client accepts the undeniable truth of human fallibility, the therapist flees from his or her fallibility by projecting an image of a calm, too controlled, utterly rational and superior being. This is diametrically opposed to what the therapist is supposed to be teaching the client, who may come to view the therapist as more of a fraud or hypocrite than role model.

Practise what you preach is the guiding principle for such therapists. If clinically relevant, they should use judicious self-disclosure to discuss with clients similar problems they experienced and how they coped with them or poke fun at their behaviour to deflate their pretensions to superior status. Being a psychotherapist may provide greater insight into the wellsprings of human disturbance, but it does not and cannot eradicate our own disturbance-producing tendencies. Certainly REBT makes no claims to do this but it can show individuals how to reduce significantly their general level of disturbability. Self-examination does not have to be too painful a procedure if therapists are prepared to admit their problems and flaws rather than condemn themselves on the basis of them. What therapists can demonstrate to their clients is a kind of highly efficient fallibility, i.e. rapidly correcting mistakes, resolving problems, attacking disturbance-creating ideas, in order to reach their short- and long-term goals. Clients are more likely to respond favourably to this model of human behaviour than the unattainable one that the therapist is fixated with.

In this chapter, we have discussed various forms of ideological rigidity that undermine or impair the progress of therapy. In Chapter 12, the final chapter of this book, we focus upon therapist difficulties that occur in the various stages of the therapeutic process.

A process-orientated view of therapist resistance

In Chapter 6 we examined the problems that clients experience during the beginning, middle and ending phases of therapy. Now we turn the spotlight on some of the problems or pitfalls that therapists encounter during these phases, e.g. in the ending phase, therapists who take too much of the credit for their clients' progress can hinder or undermine their clients' growing confidence as self-therapists. How therapists can make a relatively smooth transition from one phase to another by tackling such obstacles will now be addressed.

When therapists are resistant in the beginning phase

In this phase, the therapist starts to construct a working alliance, undertakes an early problem assessment, teaches the 'ABC's of REBT and negotiates initial homework tasks.

When therapists believe that they have to make sense of it all

When clients are asked to talk about the problems that brought them to therapy, they often do so in a verbose, rambling and emotionally charged way. It would be very surprising if clients described in an orderly fashion the series of events which led to their current predicament. Usually the 'ABC' elements of the clients' presenting problems are intricately interwoven and it is the therapist's task to tease them apart in order to bring clarity to confusion, make order out of chaos. The quicker this is achieved, the quicker that clients can tackle their irrational ideas and thereby reduce their emotional distress. However, some REBT therapists may unnecessarily delay this process because they are reluctant to interrupt clients as they elaborate upon their problems because this might appear insensitive, or they encourage clients to keep on talking as they are unsure when to intervene, or they believe that clients will start to feel better as they 'let it all out' and thereby a natural resolution of their problems will get underway. Such inaction on the part of these therapists may actually fuel their clients' incessant complaining or allow them to slip further into their misery. Instead of enlightenment beginning to dawn after the early sessions of therapy, the clients may be none the wiser about what is ailing them.

It is important for therapists to realise that in REBT, the client follows the therapist's lead rather than vice versa. This is necessary if the client is to learn the 'ABC' model of emotional disturbance and change in order to become a self-therapist. Therefore, the therapist getting to grips with the client's troubles as early as possible is a good role model for clients to follow in their own attempts at problem-solving. The perceived insensitivity that may occur by interrupting the client can be lessened by asking for permission to do it, e.g. 'If you are providing more information than I require to understand your problems, may I interrupt you so that we can begin to work on actually tackling them?' If therapists are unsure when to intervene this may require further skills training in what Grieger and Boyd (1980: 59) call 'listen[ing] for the A's, B's, and C's of client problems', particularly the all-important irrational ideas. The belief that allowing clients to talk endlessly about their problems is somehow curative does not really hold water, as the clients may have been doing this for years and still remain emotionally disturbed. Helping clients to make sense of themselves and their problems through the 'ABC' framework begins as soon as they step into the therapist's office and not at some unspecified time later in therapy.

When therapists think that they have to understand their clients' past in order to understand their present

REBT is largely an ahistorical approach to emotional problem-solving in that it focuses on how clients are maintaining their problems rather than on how they were acquired. REBT therapists who undertake a lengthy historical examination of the clients' problems may well create the impression that the past and not the present is the true focus of therapy:

Supervisor: I've listened to a few of your tapes and the majority of your time is spent dwelling on past events. Is this the best way to help your client? He's still experiencing the guilt today no matter how it started.

Therapist: Well, I suppose if I can understand as fully as possible how the guilt originated and how it developed over the years, fifteen years in fact, only then can I focus on the here-and-now. He certainly wants to talk about the past.

Supervisor: I'm sure he does, but how long will it take before you arrive in the present?

Therapist: It's a complicated process – who knows?

Supervisor: You're making it too complicated. You've trained in REBT yet you're barking up the wrong tree. What do you think I mean by that?

Therapist: I suppose you mean I should focus on what he is still telling himself today about past events in order to keep feeling guilty. Instead, I'm excavating the past as if I'm convinced that's where the answer lies.

Supervisor: Exactly. In REBT, you don't cut the past adrift but link it to the present. The client has been telling himself the same thing for the last fifteen years and therefore the solution to his problems is in surrendering his guilt-inducing beliefs today.

Therapist: I do see that, but I'm worried that the client will think I'm minimising or trivialising past events if I keep on dragging him back to the present.

Supervisor: Have you presented a clear rationale to the client why you would be doing this? In essence, are you teaching him REBT?

Therapist: No, I haven't done that. I suppose I'm just following where he leads.

Supervisor: Well, if you haven't, then he will believe that the past is all-important and continue to go on about it. Now let's get him and you into the present. What is he guilty about?

Therapist: He left his wife about fifteen years ago when they were going through a crisis. They had debts, the house was going to be repossessed, he'd lost his job, they were rowing all the time. It was a real mess. He says that if he can find out why he left, this might ease his guilt.

Supervisor: But not remove it. Why do you think he left?

Therapist: He's already hinted at it several times – he couldn't cope with all the pressure. Thinking about it now, his guilt seems to be getting worse as he keeps on condemning himself as weak and spineless for running out on his wife.

Supervisor: So running out on his wife is his 'A' or activating event. What do you think the belief might be that's maintaining his guilt?

Therapist: Something like 'I absolutely shouldn't have run out on my wife and left her to face all those problems on her own. Because I did, I'm a worthless and rotten person'.

Supervisor: So how do you propose to tackle this belief without slipping back into the past?

Therapist: I'll start by providing him with the clinical rationale that I've failed to do so far.

Supervisor: You'll probably need to do it more than once. Then what?

Therapist: Teach him how to accept the grim reality of what he did fifteen years ago without condemning himself for it.

Supervisor: Does that mean he gets off scot-free?

Therapist: No. He can take responsibility for his perceived bad behaviour and, from a non-disturbed viewpoint, try to understand the reasons for his behaviour. In this way, he is more likely to feel remorse rather than guilt. So he may experience a painful regret for his bad behaviour but will have removed the crushing burden of guilt.

Supervisor: Good. You're doing REBT again. You'll also be showing him that by tackling his irrational beliefs in the present, this will change the way he views the past as he begins to understand how he created and maintained his guilt. So the past is being addressed but without being locked into it.

Therapist: That does make a lot of sense. I've got my bearings back again.

Supervisor: I hope so. In your next tapes, then, I want to hear some here-and-now therapy.

This extract from supervision focuses on what Grieger and Boyd (1980) call 'the past history trap'. This is the widespread belief among therapists (and the wider public) that past events in themselves have an irrevocable and often malign influence upon our present feelings and behaviour. The only way for individuals to break free of this influence is to revisit the past in order to gain insight into the origins of their problems. While not wishing to diminish the impact of unpleasant or adverse past events, REBT argues that the real insight into these events is the irrational beliefs that individuals have constructed from them and carried forward into the present. Therapists can help clients to identify, challenge and change these presently held beliefs 'so that tomorrow's existence can be better than yesterday's. In a sense, the person each day chooses to either hold onto disturbed beliefs or to give them up' (Grieger and Boyd 1980: 76–7).

When therapists fail to help clients to distinguish between healthy and unhealthy negative emotions

REBT divides negative emotions into unhealthy and healthy states with their cognitive correlates of, respectively, demands and preferences. For example, anger, depression and anxiety are underpinned by dogmatic musts and shoulds, while their healthy alternatives of annoyance, sadness and concern are based on desires and wants. Clients are encouraged to adopt this emotional vocabulary in order to reduce or avoid misunderstanding and confusion in describing their feelings and the ones they wish to change (of course, the therapist and client can devise their own taxonomy of negative emotions). Some REBT therapists, particularly novice ones, automatically assume that clients understand the differences between these feeling states and therefore do not investigate the cognitive content of their supposedly non-disturbed emotions:

Client:	I get so annoyed with my boss's obnoxious behaviour. I don't like feeling this way.
Therapist:	You don't have to like it, but what's wrong with feeling annoyed? It's a healthy and natural feeling. You don't want to feel indifferent about his obnoxious behaviour, do you?
Client:	No, I suppose not. I would like to handle my emotional reaction in a more positive way, if that's possible.
Therapist:	Feeling annoyed is fine, that's positive. Maybe it needs a bit of fine-tuning. Probably you're feeling too annoyed.
Client:	Maybe that's it, though I'm not convinced.
Therapist:	Now let's get down to the real business of REBT, which is tackling emotional disturbance. Now when do you feel angry? *(emphasises word)*.
Client:	When I'm annoyed. It's the same thing.
Therapist:	No, you can't feel annoyed when you're angry or vice versa. You're getting confused. I said 'when do you feel angry?', not annoyed.
Client:	I'm not confused. Are you telling me what and how I should feel?
Therapist:	Well, no . . . but in REBT there is a difference between anger and annoyance.
Client:	How am I supposed to work that out – telepathy? Anyway, I don't see any difference.
Therapist:	Oh, I'm sorry for my blunder. I just thought you would realise the difference, that's all.

The therapist makes a cardinal error in not checking the client's under-standing of these emotional states and thereby brushes aside the client's desire to focus on her annoyance with the glib assurance that 'it's a healthy and natural feeling'. The client believes that anger and annoyance are one and the same emotion and resents the therapist's fiat on how she should feel. The therapist's manner is unlikely to be conducive to building a working alliance. In REBT, nothing is taken for granted and therefore its emotional vocabulary is compared with and contrasted to the client's. Seeking an agreed emotional language not only helps to clarify the client's goals for change but also provides her with genuine reassurance that her feelings have not been hijacked by the therapist.

When therapists put words in their clients' mouths

REBT theory asserts that demandingness (musturbation) lies at the core of emotional disturbance. This philosophy of demandingness is usually explicit or implicit in clients' statements about their presenting problems. Stating this view of disturbance is not the same as clients agreeing with it. Like every other concept in REBT, it is offered to clients for their consideration and not their compliance. Because REBT therapists know in advance the musturbatory form of the clients' self-defeating thinking (the assessment will reveal the specific content of this thinking), some therapists cannot resist the temptation to tell clients how they upset themselves rather than let clients decide for themselves if this is indeed the case. Such misguided eagerness often stems from therapists' urgent needs to display their 'superior' insights into the clients' problems, therapists' belief that proficiency is equated with didacticism, and therapists' impatience to hurry therapy along as they assume that 'getting to the musts' is the overriding imperative. The following dialogue illustrates some of these points:

> *Client:* I'm always a little anxious when I meet new people. Maybe it's because they might find me a bit boring and not like me.
>
> *Therapist:* You are more than a little anxious. You have a specific statement in your head which goes something like this: 'I absolutely must not be seen as boring, otherwise I will lose people's approval. It would be terrible to be rejected'. That's what you're probably telling yourself and which is driving your anxiety.
>
> *Client:* I can't hear myself saying that in those situations.
>
> *Therapist:* Only because it's outside of your current awareness, but I'll help you to find it quickly. We don't want to waste time beating around the bush when I've already given you the answer.
>
> *Client:* So that's what I'm saying to myself then?
>
> *Therapist:* Yeah, that's your statement you need to address immediately. Everything else is secondary.

The therapist might as well hold up cue cards for the client to read. His behaviour in therapy is more prescriptive than proficient. There is no evidence of the therapist encouraging the client through Socratic questioning to develop greater cognitive awareness in order for her to discover if dogmatism is at the root of her anxiogenic thinking. It is far better for the client to reach her own insights than for her to be told what these are. Of course, some clients will not be persuaded of or agree with the disturbance-producing potential of absolute musts and shoulds and therefore this is no insight for them. In that case, therapists should focus on these key ideas that these clients believe are the real source of their problems. The belief that telling clients how they are upsetting themselves will produce quicker progress is usually counterproductive, because they may pay only lip service to the therapist's pronouncements, become resistant to his patronising manner or feel excluded from what should be a collaborative endeavour. If therapists resist the temptation to put words in clients' mouths, they will be better able to defend themselves against the accusation that all they want to do is turn out REBT clones and not independent thinkers (see Chapter 5).

When therapists are resistant in the middle phase

During the middle phase, the therapist helps clients to internalise their newly acquired rational beliefs and weaken their lingering but often still powerfully held irrational ones. This is carried out by the therapist encouraging (sometimes persuading) clients to use multimodal methods of disputing their disturbance-creating ideas in a variety of problematic contexts. Also the therapist will be on the lookout for the presence of core irrational beliefs that link the client's problems. Therapist difficulties encountered in this phase will now be explored.

When therapists do not warn clients about the possibility of relapse

Clients can often make quick, even spectacular, progress in the early stages of therapy and therefore conclude that their problems are 'licked'. Some REBT therapists might be so enamoured with their own 'brilliance' for effecting such rapid change that they fail to mention to the clients that progress is usually accompanied by backsliding or relapse. On the other hand, this point may well be deliberately overlooked as these therapists do not want to introduce a discordant note into a, so far, highly successful and enjoyable therapeutic alliance. When clients typically experience a re-emergence of their emotional disturbance, the shock and despair they may feel could have been lessened (or even removed) if the therapist had properly instructed them in the likely process of change.

Discussing the probability that there will be some episodes of relapse in a client's overall progress allows the therapist to inject a note of realism, but not fatalism, into therapy:

'As I'm sure you're aware, progress is very often two steps forward and one step back. This certainly does not mean that you can never overcome your problem. What it does mean is that every time you step backward you will need to redouble your efforts to move forward again'.

As with every problem considered in REBT, therapists encourage their clients to use the 'ABC' model to pinpoint the cognitive source of their backsliding (see Dryden 2009b, 2009c). If clients are making good or excellent progress, therapists should be exploring the factors that account for it and not be distracted by self-admiration as an 'outstanding therapist'; this can quickly turn to self-depreciation if clients encounter obstacles or their progress starts to unravel. Therapists should be mindful that an enjoyable relationship is not necessarily a therapeutic one as difficult or contentious, but important issues can be skirted in order to keep therapy 'upbeat'. Also while therapeutic success is to be applauded, it needs to be tempered with caution as progress is rarely sustained indefinitely.

When therapists find it difficult to hold their tongues

While greater use of short didactic presentations of REBT concepts are usually made in the early stages of therapy as clients are socialised into REBT, their frequent use during the middle phase of therapy is contra-indicated, because this may undermine or impair the development of the client's role as a self-therapist. A client's ability to think through problems usually varies in inverse ratio to the amount of lecturing that the therapist does. Too much of it can help to turn clients into passive partners in therapy who parrot REBT tenets, rather than active and increasingly independently minded problem-solvers.

Dryden and Neenan's (2006) advice to REBT therapists to 'let your clients' brains take the strain' means a corresponding decrease in their own level of verbal activity. Instead of lectures, therapists should use Socratic dialogue as much as possible, e.g. 'What are the implications for you if change is based on self-esteem rather than self-acceptance?'; 'How were you able to stay in that situation when only a few weeks ago you would have fled from it?' Therapists cannot do the thinking for their clients once they have left therapy, so while they remain in it, clients need to be encouraged to take cognitive control of the change process. One of us (MN) has had clients who complain at the end of a session that they have done so much thinking that 'my brain hurts'. At least their cognitive wheels are still turning and not stopped because the therapist would not let them get a word in edgeways.

When therapists are intimidated by how much clients know about REBT

Some clients, perhaps only a small number, become erudite in the theory and practice of REBT and give unfailingly 'correct' answers to every question posed by the therapist. This may convince the latter that therapy is on track for a highly successful outcome:

Supervisor: Listening to the tapes, it sounds like you have an REBT expert on your hands.

Therapist: She's brilliant. She's read lots of books on REBT, listened to all of Ellis's audiotapes. I can't catch her out on anything. She's always rational. She points out mistakes I make in applying REBT.

Supervisor: What's her presenting problem?

Therapist: She's afraid of being rejected if she enters into romantic relationships, but she's worked it out logically in her own mind, so she's really over the problem.

Supervisor: Well, I'm not so sure. Has she carried out any homework tasks to face her fear of rejection?

Therapist: No, but then you see, she doesn't really need to as she's worked out why she's afraid of rejection and thereby resolved it.

Supervisor: How has she done that?

Therapist: By convincing herself that she doesn't need other people's approval or love and therefore can accept herself under all conditions. Obviously you don't agree.

Supervisor: I'm suspicious. Listening to her, I think she is pseudo-rational.

Therapist: Which is . . .?

Supervisor: A kind of false or pretended acceptance of REBT's rational philosophy of living. The reason I'm suspicious is because she knows all the theory but is not putting any of it into practice.

Therapist: But she knows more about REBT than I do!

Supervisor: This might be true on the theory side but she's not acting on it. That's where your clinical focus should be. What's blocking her from carrying out the homework tasks?

Therapist: I'm not sure really. I suppose I've let myself be dazzled by her vast knowledge of REBT.

Supervisor: Vast but empty, as no action appears to flow from it. Let's consider some hypotheses. First, she genuinely believes that insight alone is sufficient to promote enduring change.

Therapist: So she can solve her problems without getting out of her armchair.

Supervisor: Right. Second, she has discomfort intolerance beliefs.

Therapist: That change is too hard, uncomfortable, frustrating. That sort of thing.

Supervisor: That's right. Third, and this is more uncommon, she has a kind of narcissistic reluctance to be judged by others as she believes she is superior to them. By not entering into relationships and the possibility of rejection, she thus preserves her self-image.

Therapist: Now that the dazzle is fading, I can see more clearly her homework avoidance. She always opts for further reading but no action.

Supervisor: Continually remind her what the 'B' in REBT stands for: behaviour, forcefully acting against her irrational beliefs if she truly wishes to live by a rational outlook. It doesn't mean more beavering through REBT books. If she's such an expert, why hasn't she followed through on it?

Therapist: It's been a very eye-opening session. Thanks. I'd never heard of pseudo-rationality before.

Supervisor: Keep it in mind for future sessions with her. If she starts to dazzle you again, wear sunglasses.

Therapist: Okay.

Because the therapist is overawed by the client's impressive grasp of REBT theory, he fails to notice that she is, in fact, not crossing the bridge between intellectual and emotional insight, i.e. rational principles are understood in the client's head, but not acted upon. The supervisor suggests several hypotheses that may underpin her behavioural avoidance as a way of changing the therapist from admirer to sceptic. The therapist has forgotten to ask the most basic question, namely, 'If she is so incredibly knowledgeable about REBT, why isn't she acting according to her rational beliefs?' This should have alerted him to the possibility that the client is only pseudo-rational in her attempts at problem-solving; or, as he said he was unfamiliar with the term, to the discrepancy between thought and deed. The therapist needs to dispute the client's behavioural avoidance ideas in order to help her internalise the REBT view of genuine rationality.

When therapists hold discomfort intolerance beliefs about their clients' discomfort intolerance

After some initial success in confronting their problems, many clients begin to realise that the path of progress is much longer and rockier than they had expected. Disillusionment can begin to set in along with resistance to working hard to maintain current progress and dealing with other problem areas in their lives. Also relapses are experienced. Clients can endlessly complain about how difficult and uncomfortable therapy is. The danger is that the therapist becomes so fed up with the client's incessant whining that she displays her own discomfort intolerance:

Therapist:	Are you ever going to stop moaning every week? Whine, whine, whine, just because things are getting tougher now.
Client:	I can't help it. Nothing is going right at the moment. I didn't think that sorting my problems out would be this hard. Things were going well for a while.
Therapist:	Well, that's what change is all about. What did you expect – an easy ride?
Client:	It would help. Anyway, you're supposed to be more sympathetic. You're supposed to be helping me!
Therapist:	You're not exactly helping me with all this moaning, are you? Now I don't want to hear any more of it. I'm not an agony aunt, I'm a therapist, so you come here to work, not whinge. Got it?
Client:	Got what? I can't help it if I find things difficult. I can't cope without a drink. You know what happens to me when I'm under any pressure. That's why I'm in therapy.
Therapist:	Oh, for Christ's sake, give me strength.

The therapist's discomfort intolerance is just as marked as the client's. Therapy has ground to a halt. Each is looking to the other to get it moving again: the client expects the therapist to be more sympathetic to his plight while the therapist believes that the proper focus of therapy is problem-solving and not whingeing. The proper focus of therapy is tackling all problems that occur, including the client's whingeing and the therapist's 'I don't want to hear any more of it' tantrums. Therefore the therapist needs to undisturb herself first about the client's moaning and thereby begin to develop discomfort tolerance:

> 'He should be whingeing and whining because that's the way he undoubtedly is at the moment. I certainly don't like listening to it but I can tolerate it. He can learn to acquire discomfort tolerance just like me and therapy can become more productive again.'

Instead of appealing to a higher power for forbearance, the therapist has found it closer to home by following the rational principles that presently elude the client.

When therapists engage too much in intellectual discussion with their clients

As clients begin to develop a greater understanding of REBT, their questions, criticisms or observations of its theory and practice can have a corresponding level of sophistication, e.g. 'Surely if our actions are an indivisible part of ourselves, then in judging the action we are also judging ourselves? This undermines the notion of unconditional self-acceptance'. While these and other questions obviously need to be addressed, for some therapists they become the trigger for turning therapy into a seminar on the philosophical foundations of REBT (and possibly satisfying their need to display their true vocation as a professional philosopher or be seen as a 'deep thinker'). While the client's intellect might be stimulated by such discussion, it is also highly likely that therapy will get bogged down in overly lengthy theorising rather than acting as a platform for concerted action against the client's self-defeating thoughts, feelings and behaviours.

Philosophical discussion should be relatively brief and, whenever possible, directly related to the client's presenting problems:

> 'Your actions can never represent or equal your true complexity as a human being. Judging yourself on the basis of your actions is an insult to this complexity and a potential pathway to emotional disturbance. In your case, condemning yourself as an utter failure for losing your job largely accounts for your present depression.'

It is important that feedback is obtained to determine if the client not only understands the points made but also agrees with them. Philosophical discussion can be a highly enjoyable aspect of therapy, but abstraction should not replace action as the main focus of collaboration.

When therapists use a limited repertoire of techniques

As therapists seek ways of encouraging clients to deepen their conviction in their newly acquired rational attitudes (promoting emotional insight), they usually experiment with a wide range of multimodal techniques to facilitate this process. They are not afraid of going back to the drawing board to devise new techniques when their present ones have produced little, if any, change in the client. However, some therapists have a limited number of techniques they employ and believe that as they are tried-and-tested they will be effective with all clients, e.g. 'Jump in at the deep end straightaway. This means stay in the uncomfortable situation until your anxiety abates. Then you'll prove to yourself that you can stand it'. If the task is unsuccessful because the client would not stay in the situation or refuses to undertake it, such therapists will usually claim that the client is being 'resistant' rather than conclude that the technique is inappropriate for the client.

One of the chief characteristics of effective REBT therapists is their ability to be creatively persistent in seeking solutions to the clients' problems. This involves risk-taking: a particular technique may provide a therapeutic breakthrough or turn out to be a damp squib. If the latter is the case, the therapist refrains from blaming the client or making excuses. By role modelling the use of trial and error, the therapist hopes that the client will adopt it for present and future emotional problem-solving. In the above example, if implosion (flooding) techniques are ineffective, the therapist can suggest a range of 'challenging, but not overwhelming' assignments that are sufficiently stimulating to promote constructive change but not so daunting as possibly to inhibit clients from carrying them out (Dryden 1985). Therapists ought to remember that what worked for a previous client may not work for the present one.

When therapists are resistant in the ending phase

In this stage of therapy, therapists consider that their clients have made significant progress towards resolving their problems by using REBT skills. They now agree to work towards termination by decreasing session frequency or setting a fixed date for the end of therapy. Therapists encourage their clients to review the course of therapy, what they learnt from it and how they will tackle future problems as self-therapists. Termination issues are addressed. Therapist roadblocks in this phase will now be discussed.

When therapists terminate their clients abruptly

When therapists believe that their client can now stand alone as a competent and confident self-therapist, they begin to signal to their client that the end of therapy is approaching, e.g. 'Now that you're managing your problems, I think two or three more sessions are sufficient to deal with some remaining issues. Would you agree?' This allows both parties time to express their feelings about and review their therapeutic relationship and, sometimes for the client, to discuss any difficulties in disengaging from it. Some therapists, out of boredom, lack of planning, sheer bloody-mindedness or a mistaken belief that 'this is the hard-headed way to do it', suddenly announce that the present session is the last one. If the client protests about this abrupt termination, the therapist views it as a sign of continuing disturbance and suggests that the client 'find out what you're telling yourself about termination'. The client may believe rightly that he or she has been unceremoniously thrown out of therapy.

While REBT therapists do not turn termination into an elongated affair, they are mindful that care and consideration need to be used in deciding the date of the final session. Boredom is not a factor in this process and reflects the therapist's impatience 'to get this client and his problems out of therapy as soon as possible as I can't take much more of it'. Spontaneously ending therapy because 'it feels the right thing to do' is no substitute for premeditation based on the facts of the client's progress and not the therapist's feelings about it. Sheer bloody-mindedness often occurs because the therapist believes that as the client has given her a tough time in therapy, 'I'm bloody well not giving him any fond farewells'. While REBT is a hard-headed approach to tackling clients' problems, it is not carried out in the absence of respect for the client. Therefore the therapist's approach to termination is both misguided and concrete-headed.

If breaking the therapeutic relationship does become a major problem for the client, 'then the client is not ready to terminate, for this is an indication that the client relies on the therapist to fulfil some perceived need' (Wessler and Wessler 1980: 182). It is far better for the therapist to explore this perceived need than boot clients out of therapy and tell them to sort it out on their own.

When therapists urge their clients to remain in therapy longer than is necessary

REBT therapists do not usually attempt to keep clients in therapy once they have proved their mettle as a self-therapist. To do so might be counterproductive as clients begin to doubt their hard-won abilities as the therapist 'still doesn't believe I'm ready to go it alone'. Their doubts would be misplaced, because the real problem lies with the therapist's reluctance to let them go:

Supervisor: In listening to your tapes, your client seems very confident, bright and capable of striking out on her own. She says several times that she is ready to leave, yet you urge her to stay longer in therapy Why is that?

Therapist: Well, she is all those things you have suggested but sometimes a little too confident for her own good. I think there are pitfalls ahead that she hasn't seen yet.

Supervisor: That may be true but isn't it up to her to locate those pitfalls? If she does get caught up in them, why can't she use her obvious REBT skills to get out of them?

Therapist: Surely there's nothing wrong with trying to make her as ready as possible before she leaves therapy?

Supervisor: It seems to me she is ready now. The real test of her degree of change is when she leaves therapy and not

	while she remains within it. She can't stay in therapy for the rest of her life.
Therapist:	Well, of course not. I'm not suggesting that at all. You're being very persistent with this issue, which usually means you've got a hypothesis to present to me.
Supervisor:	Correct. I wouldn't want to disappoint you. How would you feel if she left therapy now?
Therapist:	A little peeved, I suppose. Only because, as I've said, there's still more work to be done.
Supervisor:	How would you describe the other clients on your case load? Are some of them, for instance, making the great progress that she is?
Therapist:	No, she stands head and shoulders above the rest of them. The other clients are a mixture of those making limited progress, resisters, non-attenders, personality disorders, that sort of thing. But what's the point you're going to make?
Supervisor:	That you're keeping her in therapy for your own needs and not because she truly requires further therapy. While she continues to make excellent progress, this proves what a competent and worthwhile therapist you are. Your other clients don't give you this glow of success and that's why you have to hang on to her.
Therapist:	*(rather irritably)* Well, I don't see what's wrong with feeling this glow.
Supervisor:	Because she is being detained in therapy to keep your glow burning. You have made your clinical competence dependent on her continuing success. What's best for her has been subordinated to your needs. That won't do.
Therapist:	*(sighs)* Okay, you're right. That's what I'm doing. I know it's not very therapeutic.
Supervisor:	So what's the next step then?
Therapist:	Release her from therapy as I'm detaining her, as you call it. She is ready to leave, as you shrewdly pointed out.
Supervisor:	But before you do that . . .?
Therapist:	Stop making my competence as a therapist conditional upon client success or failure. That doesn't mean that I won't try my therapeutic best with all my clients.
Supervisor:	*(mock surprise)* I should hope not! Another issue to consider is that you define therapeutic success narrowly, which helps to fuel your irrational belief.
Therapist:	What do you mean by that?

> *Supervisor:* Well, when you said that some of your clients were making limited success, you didn't seem impressed at all. Success is success whether or not it's limited, dull or boring. Not all, even most, clients will make spectacular progress as she has done. Overcoming resistance and encouraging non-attenders to attend are successful endeavours. Do you get my drift?
>
> *Therapist:* I do. I always try to latch on to the high-flyers in therapy. That's the only kind of success I really identify with.
>
> *Supervisor:* Which brings self-esteem problems for you and captivity for the client. So what will I hear in your next tape with her?
>
> *Therapist:* The final session and a non-disturbance-producing goodbye from me.
>
> *Supervisor:* Well done. And let me give you a non-disturbance-producing goodbye as supervision ends.

In this extract from supervision, important points to consider are the following:

1   The client's confidence about her ability to be an independent problem-solver and the therapist's decision to delay termination alerts the supervisor to the possibility that the therapist is harbouring irrational ideas. Something is amiss when the therapist implies that his client has to attain an almost unnatural state of readiness before leaving therapy.

2   The supervisor asks how the therapist would react if his client left therapy now and what the other clients on his case load are like in order to gather further data to support his hypothesis that the therapist needs continual evidence of the client's progress in therapy in order to accept himself as a competent clinician.

3   The therapist confirms the supervisor's hypothesis. The supervisor asks the therapist to suggest ways of undisturbing himself about his competency needs. This is an example of 'letting the therapist's brain take the strain' of problem-solving (clients are not the only ones to suffer 'brain strain' in REBT).

4   The supervisor points out that the therapist's narrow definition of therapeutic success is part of his irrational belief. Success can be measured on a continuum from spectacular at one end to dull and boring at the other end. Success is whatever degree of progress is being made by the client at any particular moment in therapy.

5   Just to ensure that the therapist will be acting in a more constructive way towards his client, the supervisor asks him how he will conduct the

next session with her. The therapist's reply that it will be 'the final one' is a none too soon liberation for the client and the start of one for the therapist.

When therapists think that the elegant solution is the only solution

The REBT therapist's preferred client goals for change are often more ambitious than the client's. The ideal REBT goal is for clients to remove or minimise their musturbatory thinking and strive to accept themselves unconditionally as fallible human beings (the elegant solution to emotional problem-solving). Some clients will not be interested in achieving these ends and will want to leave therapy as soon as their problems recede. Some REBT therapists usually panic at this suggestion because, in their eyes, they are short-changing the clients if they leave too soon as they have not done 'correct' REBT with them yet. The client, however, has reached a plateau of change and does not want to be prodded, pushed or persuaded to ascend to the peak of 'what could be'. Because the therapist is rigidly interpreting the preferred REBT practice, he is more likely to view himself as a failure if the client does not pursue the elegant solution; hence his pleas with her to stay in therapy:

Therapist: You need further help with your anxiety.

Client: No, I don't. I feel less anxious now. I'm better.

Therapist: But it's a deceptive kind of improvement. Those ideas that produce your anxiety are still lurking around. Remember those 'musts'.

Client: Must I? Look, you've helped me to be less anxious about failing and I thank you for that. That's all I wanted when I came here. Why can't you accept that with good grace?

Therapist: Because you haven't properly learnt REBT yet. You're only feeling better at this stage, but not getting better because you haven't completely got rid of those demands about failure. Your self-acceptance is still conditional. These issues are still to be resolved.

Client: I've done all the resolving I want to and I don't like being told when I can go. You're exasperating.

Therapist: All I'm asking you is to please stay in therapy so you can see how REBT will bring about a fundamental change in your attitude. There would be less human disturbance generally if people got rid of their 'musts'.

Client: No!

Therapists can change their rigidity to flexibility if they remember that the elegant solution is a choice to be offered to clients and not imposed upon them. It is not a sign of therapist failure if some clients choose not to pursue this solution, but a salutary reminder to presumptuous therapists that REBT is not the panacea for all psychological ills, and that people can still be happy even if they hold on to some of their 'musts'. That the degree of change is to the client's satisfaction, though maybe not containing much depth to it, should be the source of the therapist's congratulations rather than his despair over her lack of ideological purity in tackling her problems. Even if the client was tempted to stay longer in therapy, the therapist's behaviour is not much of an encouragement for her to do so or the best advertisement for the rational approach he wants to teach her.

In this and the other chapters, we have used our considerable clinical experience as therapists and supervisors to identify and deal with a variety of resistances that afflict clients and therapists. We hope that the guidance offered in this book will assist therapists in enhancing their therapy practice and deepening their understanding of rational emotive behaviour therapy. The two usually go hand in hand.

References

Bard, J. A. (1980). *Rational-Emotive Therapy in Practice*. Champaign, IL: Research Press.

Beck, A. T. (1976). *Cognitive Therapy and the Emotional Disorders*. New York: International Universities Press.

Bordin, E. S. (1979). 'The generalizability of the psychoanalytic concept of the working alliance.' *Psychotherapy: Theory, Research and Practice*, 16: 252–60.

Burns, D. D. (1980). *Feeling Good: The New Mood Therapy*. New York: William Morrow.

Clark, D. M. (1986). 'A cognitive approach to panic.' *Behaviour Research and Therapy*, 24: 461–70.

Dryden, W. (1985). 'Challenging but not overwhelming: A compromise in negotiating homework assignments.' *British Journal of Cognitive Psychotherapy*, 3(1): 77–80.

Dryden, W. (1991). *A Dialogue with Albert Ellis: Against Dogma*. Buckingham: Open University Press.

Dryden, W. (2001). *Reason to Change: A Rational Emotive Behaviour Therapy (REBT) Workbook*. Hove, East Sussex: Brunner-Routledge.

Dryden, W. (2006). *Counselling in a Nutshell*. London: Sage.

Dryden, W. (2009a). *Rational Emotive Behaviour Therapy: Distinctive Features*. Hove, East Susssex: Routledge.

Dryden, W. (2009b). *Skills in Rational Emotive Behaviour Counselling and Psychotherapy*. London: Sage.

Dryden, W. (2009c). *How to Think and Intervene Like an REBT therapist*. Hove, East Sussex: Routledge.

Dryden, W. (2011). *Counselling in a Nutshell*, 2nd edn. London: Sage.

Dryden, W. and Branch, R. (2008). *Fundamentals of Rational Emotive Behaviour Therapy: A Training Manual*. Chichester: John Wiley.

Dryden, W. and Ellis, A. (1997). 'Dilemmas in giving warmth or love to clients (interview).' In W. Dryden (ed.) *Therapists' Dilemmas*, revised edn. London: Sage.

Dryden, W. and Neenan, M. (1995). *A Dictionary of Rational Emotive Behaviour Therapy*. London: Whurr.

Dryden, W. and Neenan, M. (2004a). *Rational Emotive Behavioural Counselling in Action*, 3rd edn. London: Sage.

Dryden, W. and Neenan, M. (2004b). *The Rational Emotive Behavioural Approach to Therapeutic Change*. London: Sage.

Dryden, W. and Neenan, M. (2006). *Rational Emotive Behaviour Therapy: 100 Key Points and Techniques*. Hove, East Sussex: Routledge.

Dryden, W. and Yankura, J. (1993). *Counselling Individuals: A Rational-Emotive Handbook*, 2nd edn. London: Whurr.

Ellis, A. (1958). 'Rational psychotherapy.' *Journal of General Psychology*, 59: 35–49.

Ellis, A. (1963). 'Toward a more precise definition of "emotional" and "intellectual" insight.' *Psychological Reports*, 13: 125–6.

Ellis, A. (1972). 'Helping people to get better rather than merely feel better.' *Rational Living*, 7(2): 2–9.

Ellis, A. (1979). 'The issue of force and energy in behavior change.' *Journal of Contemporary Psychotherapy*, 10: 83–97.

Ellis, A. (1980). 'Rational-emotive therapy and cognitive behavior therapy: Similarities and differences.' *Cognitive Therapy and Research*, 4: 325–40.

Ellis, A. (1983a). 'The philosophic implications and dangers of some popular behavior therapy techniques.' In M. Rosenbaum, C. M. Franks and Y. Jaffe (eds) *Perspectives on Behavior Therapy in the Eighties*. New York: Springer.

Ellis, A. (1983b). *The Case Against Religiosity*. New York: Institute for Rational-Emotive Therapy.

Ellis, A. (1985). *Overcoming Resistance: RET with Difficult Clients*. New York: Springer.

Ellis, A. (1991). 'The revised ABC's of rational-emotive therapy (RET).' *Journal of Rational-Emotive and Cognitive-Behavior Therapy*, 9(3): 139–72.

Ellis, A. (1994). *Reason and Emotion in Psychotherapy*, revised and updated edn. Secaucus, NJ: Carol.

Ellis, A. (2002). *Overcoming Resistance: A Rational Emotive Behavior Therapy Integrated Approach*. New York: Springer.

Ellis, A. and Dryden, W. (1997). *The Practice of Rational Emotive Behavior Therapy*, 2nd edn. New York: Springer.

Golden, W. L. and Dryden, W. (1986). 'Cognitive-behavioural therapies: Commonalities, divergences and future developments.' In W. Dryden and W. L. Golden (eds) *Cognitive-Behavioural Approaches to Psychotherapy*. London: Harper & Row.

Grieger, R. and Boyd, J. (1980). *Rational-Emotive Therapy: A Skills-Based Approach*. New York: Van Nostrand Reinhold.

Hauck, P. (1966). 'The neurotic agreement in psychotherapy.' *Rational Living*, 1(1): 31–4.

Hauck, P. (1980). *Brief Counseling with RET*. Philadelphia, PA: Westminster Press.

Horney, K. (1950). *Neurosis and Human Growth*. New York: Norton.

Kwee, M. G. T. and Lazarus, A. A. (1986). 'Multimodal therapy: The cognitive-behavioural tradition and beyond.' In W. Dryden and W. L. Golden (eds) *Cognitive-Behavioural Approaches to Psychotherapy*. London: Harper & Row.

Lazarus, A. A. and Lazarus, C. N. (1991). *Multimodal Life History Inventory*. Champaign, IL: Research Press.

Maslow, A. (1968). *Toward a Psychology of Being*, 2nd edn. Princeton, NJ: Van Nostrand.

Walen, S. R., DiGiuseppe, R. and Dryden, W. (1992). *A Practitioner's Guide to Rational-Emotive Therapy*, 2nd edn. New York: Oxford University Press.

Wessler, R. A. and Wessler, R. L. (1980). *The Principles and Practice of Rational-Emotive Therapy*. San Francisco, CA: Jossey-Bass.

Index